P9-CMY-718

UNIVERSITY of PENNSYLVANIA
PRESS

IN NECESSARIIS VNITAS

IN DVBIIS LIBERTAS

IN OMNIBVS CARITAS

in necessary things unity

in doubtful things liberty

in all things charity

the broadening CHURCH

a study of theological issues in the presbyterian church since 1869

LEFFERTS A. LOETSCHER

UNIVERSITY OF PENNSYLVANIA PRESS 1957
PHILADELPHIA

UNIVERSITY OF PENNSYLVANIA PRESS

Published in Great Britain, India, and Pakistan
by the Oxford University Press
London, Bombay, Karachi

Manufactured in the United States of America

Library of Congress Catalog Card Number: 54-7110

to my father
Frederick William Loetscher
whose classrooms first awakened
the author's interest in history

note by the publisher

Lefferts A. Loetscher was born in Dubuque, Iowa, in 1904. He was educated at the Lawrenceville School (graduated 1921), Princeton University (A.B., 1925), Princeton Theological Seminary (Th.B., 1928; Th.M., 1929), and the University of Pennsylvania (M.A., 1932; Ph.D., 1943). In 1940 the University of Dubuque conferred upon him the degree of Doctor of Divinity. After serving pastorates, he came in 1941 to the faculty of Princeton Theological Seminary where he is now Associate Professor of Church History. He has served on a number of committees of the General Assembly, is a Director of the Presbyterian Historical Society, a member of the General Assembly's Committee on the Book of Common Worship, and a Corporator of the Presbyterian Ministers' Fund. In addition to articles and reviews, he is the author of A Brief History of the Presbyterians *(pamphlet) and is Editor-in-chief of two volumes shortly to appear supplementing the* Schaff-Herzog Encyclopedia of Religious Knowledge.

preface

Social and intellectual changes have been rapid and far-reaching in the United States since the Civil War. What has been the effect of these changes on the religious thought of the American Churches? Rather than resort to sweeping generalizations in a broad area where foundations in documented monographs are lacking, the present work undertakes an inductive study of theological issues in one of the major denominations, the Presbyterian Church in the United States of America. This Church was in the thick of the struggle most of the time, and much that transpired in it—with appropriate changes of places and names—finds broad parallels in many another leading American Church. Its story is a kind of theological barometer of the times.

The terms "Presbyterian Church" and "Presbyterian," except where more fully defined, will here be used to designate the "Presbyterian Church in the United States of America" and its members, respectively. The abbreviated designations are merely for the sake of simplicity, and imply no slight on any other of the ecclesiastical bodies in America which share the right to the name "Presbyterian."

The author is indebted to a number of librarians and libraries: to Dr. Kenneth S. Gapp, librarian of Princeton Theological Seminary, and to his staff; to Professor William W. Rockwell, librarian emeritus of Union Theological Seminary in New York, for numerous courtesies and kindnesses, as well as to Dr. Lucy W. Markley, former librarian, and to Professor Robert F. Beach, librarian of Union Seminary, and to the staff; to Dr. John F. Lyons, librarian emeritus of McCormick Theological Seminary, Chicago, for many professional and personal courtesies, as well as to Dr. Frank D. McCloy, Jr., dean and librarian of Western Theological Seminary; to Dr. Charles A. Anderson, manager, to his predecessor, the late Dr. Thomas C. Pears, Jr., and to Mr. Guy S. Klett, research historian, of the Presbyterian Historical Society, Philadelphia. The author also received appreciated help from the Library of Princeton University, the New York Public Library, and the Library of Westminster Theological Seminary.

The author is grateful for the opportunity of discussing issues treated in the present study with very many of those, of all shades of opinion, who were leaders in the events dealt with, some of whom are now deceased. While the present work has been based throughout on contemporary documents, the kind interest and frankness of these participants in the events supplied many nuances and insights.

The author is particularly indebted to the following for permission to publish quotations from important manuscripts: to President John A. Mackay of Princeton Theological Seminary for permission to quote from the seminary's official records; to the Presbyterian Board of Foreign Missions for permission to quote from its files; to Dr. William W. Rockwell, custodian of the Briggs Transcript, and to Miss Olive M. Briggs, for permission to quote from the Briggs Transcript; to Miss S. Madeline Hodge for permission to quote from the papers of the Hodge family; to Dr. Clarence E. Macartney for permission to quote from his private papers; to Mrs. Robert E. Speer for permission to quote from the papers of the late Dr. Robert E. Speer; to Dean Tertius van Dyke for permission to quote from the papers of Dr. Henry J. Van Dyke and of Dr. Henry van Dyke. Other manuscript collections used by the author are listed on page 157.

The author is grateful to President John A. Mackay and to the Board of Trustees of Princeton Theological Seminary for sabbatical leave used toward the preparation of the present volume.

The key to abbreviations used in the notes will be found on page 157.

contents

tables

about the notes

The notes will be found on pages 157-80. In the note section, at the upper right-hand corner of each recto page and the upper left-hand corner of each verso page, will be found boldface numbers indicating the pages of the text to which the notes on these two pages refer.

1.

the wedding day

"I got here safely and found young Doctor Hodge all ready and delighted to see me. . . . We had an excellent day yesterday. . . . There was no jar and seemed to be no diversity in organizing the Assembly. . . . Everything indicates that we are to have a peaceful, happy and useful session." [1] Thus the distinguished New School pastor, Dr. George L. Prentiss, described the wedding day of Old School and New School Presbyterians—the first regular General Assembly of the Presbyterian Church after reunion, meeting in Philadelphia in May 1870.

But the honeymoon atmosphere which was so conspicuous in the reunited General Assembly of 1870 had not always prevailed within the Presbyterian Church in the U.S.A. With its chief strength in the more cosmopolitan middle colonies, the Presbyterian Church in colonial days, in the diversity of its constituency, had foreshadowed the later American melting pot. In particular two groups have constituted the poles around which the theological history of the Church has revolved. Scotch-Irish and Scottish elements have formed the nucleus of the one group. This Scotch-Irish wing has been the churchly or Presbyterian "high church" party which has stressed the more "objective" aspects of religion such as precise theological formulation, the professional and distinct character of the ministry, and orderly and authoritarian church government. New England, English, and Welsh elements have constituted the nucleus of the other great tradition in American Presbyterian history. In distinction from the Scotch-Irish more "churchly" wing, this New England element has contributed values of a more "sectarian" type, laying less emphasis upon elaborated, fixed theology and on authoritarian church government and more emphasis on spontaneity, vital impulse, and adaptability. It has been the good fortune and the hardship of the Presbyterian Church to have had—like even the earliest Calvinism—these two elements in dialectical tension within itself from the beginning. During most of the history of the Church these elements have been in rather fine balance—or compromise—which has given to the Church a characteristic moderation and has kept it in a kind of median position within American Protestantism. Twice the tension became so acute as to dismember the ecclesiastical body—in the Old Side-New

Side schism of 1741-58 and in the Old School-New School schism of 1837-69. But the ecclesiastical and dialectical incompleteness of either part alone has on each occasion prepared the way for speedy reunion.

The Presbyterian Church traces its origin in America to congregations founded by New England Puritans on Long Island in the 1640's. An increasing stream of immigration of Scotch-Irish in the latter part of the century further enlarged the constituency. The first presbytery, organized in Philadelphia in 1706, reflected the Church's diversified character with Scotland, Ireland, and New England all represented in its slim ministerial membership of seven. Continued growth made it possible in 1716 to erect the presbytery into a synod having its own constituent presbyteries. The two generic types maintained proportionate growth in the expanding body.[2] Failure to define the relative powers of Synod and presbyteries at this time left problems which were to harass the Church from the eighteenth century to the twentieth.[3]

When orthodoxy seemed threatened in the colonies in the early eighteenth century by rationalistic tendencies from abroad, some of the more churchly Scotch-Irish group demanded that all ministers and ministerial candidates of the Synod be required to subscribe the Westminster Confession of Faith, even though the Westminster Assembly had not drafted this detailed outline of theology with the intention that it be subscribed. The New England group in the synod vigorously opposed theological restraint of this sort, and division was averted only by enacting in 1729 a compromise measure known as the Adopting Act. The Adopting Act required all ministers to accept the Westminster Confession and the Larger and Shorter Catechisms, but not categorically and verbally. Rather, a minister must declare his "agreement in and approbation of" these standards "as being in all the essential and necessary articles, good forms of sound words and systems of Christian doctrine." Any minister who did not accept any particular part of the Confession or Catechisms might state his scruple concerning that part, and the ordaining body should then decide whether or not his scruple involved "essential and necessary articles of faith." [4] Thus, though the theology of the Church was now formally tied to the Westminster Standards, the door was thrown open for a continually expanding breadth of interpretation, a breadth which could be authoritatively defined only by the judicatories of the Church themselves. Now that there was to be subscription, the Adopting Act became a kind of Magna Charta in the Church's theological history, but unfortunately the ambiguity of its crucial phrase "essential and necessary articles" would rise to vex the Church again and again.

Calvinism at its best is a rather fine balance between reason and feeling, between what is definable human knowledge and what is ineffable divine mystery, between formal and experiential elements. In the so-called Protestant "scholasticism" of the seventeenth century the rational and formal elements of Calvinism—the more objective side of its tradition—were overemphasized at the expense of the more subjective part of the heritage—its almost mystical emphasis on the witness and working of God's Spirit in the human heart, together with the unfathomable superrational mystery of God's ultimate being. Among Presbyterians on the American frontier in the eighteenth century this distortion had become still more serious, until for many religion had become dangerously external, a neat and explainable, but rather irrelevant, package of ideas. This type of defection was of course particularly serious in the Scotch-Irish "churchly" party. What proved to be for American Presbyterians an important corrective of this situation was the religious revival known as the Great Awakening. Coming as a highly subjective and vital movement in a Church which had exaggerated its formal and objective heritage, the revival inevitably produced an explosion. Revivalists, or "New Side" men, under the new vital impulse, denounced fellow ministers of the "Old Side" as graceless and unconverted, and became itinerants, invading settled parishes and defying those conceptions of order and government which had been essential to Presbyterianism from the beginning.[5] The inevitable rupture occurred in 1741,[6] continuing until 1758. The terms of reunion in 1758 admirably combined the best elements of both traditions. Old Side churchliness triumphed in the insistence on orderliness: in the case of official action deemed essential by the Church, "every member shall actively concur . . . or passively submit . . . or . . . peaceably withdraw." There was to be no more ecclesiastical anarchy of the sort that had been so rife preceding the division of 1741. Irresponsible accusation of fellow ministers and irruption into the congregations of others were now defined as censurable offenses. On the other hand, the terms of reunion conserved some of the most important emphases of New Side revivalism: presbyteries were to examine ministerial candidates on, among other things, their "experimental acquaintance with religion." While the controversial term "revival" was studiously avoided, the basis of reunion described a work of God's grace in restrained and carefully guarded terms that condemned the wilder excesses of revivalism, but carefully conserved the essential spiritual and moral objectives of the more sober sort of revivalism.[7] A "least common denominator" type of reunion might have sacrificed, in the interests of external harmony, the essential principles of both parties. Fortunately reunion was achieved on a basis that preserved the best elements of both groups and brought each nearer to the common Calvinistic heritage, eliminating, or passing over in silence, the more extreme divergences of each. A truer Calvinistic tension of "objective" and "subjective," of form and spirit, was now restored to the reunited Church.

The years following the reunion of 1758 were years of rapid Presbyterian growth. The Church had a diversified constituency, a good organization, and an educated ministry. Because of its numerous Scotch-Irish members in frontier communities it was peculiarly well suited to push into the new West. During the Revolutionary War, Presbyterians won added prestige through their ardent attachment to the cause of independence. By the end of the eighteenth century the Presbyterian Church was perhaps in a stronger position in comparison with the other American Churches than at any time before or since.

Reflecting the new spirit of postwar nationalism, Presbyterians, like various other denominations in those years, organized on a more adequate national basis. To effect this, the Presbyterian Synod transformed itself into a General Assembly with constituent synods. Of particular significance was the new subscription formula for ordination. Five questions were now asked of the candidate, of which the first two were the theological crux. "Do you believe the Scriptures of the Old and New Testament, to be the word of God, the only infallible rule of faith and practice?" "Do you sincerely receive and adopt, the confession of faith of this church, as containing the system of doctrine taught in the holy Scriptures?" [8] These questions have continued unchanged to the present day. The first question, involving the Bible as an "infallible rule," later gave rise to acute difficulties when there was controversy concerning critical study of the Bible in the latter part of the nineteenth century. In the second question, increasing theological leeway came to be secured through the words "system of doctrine" by interpreting this phrase in the spirit of the words "essential and necessary articles" as used in the old Adopting Act of 1729. That is, it came to be prevailingly understood that a minister is obliged to accept only those articles in the Westminster Confession which are "essential and necessary" to the Calvinistic system of doctrine. And this conception in turn came to be construed increasingly broadly in many quarters during the nineteenth and twentieth centuries.

The conservative reaction in American life and culture which followed the Declaration of Independence and the Revolutionary War, and which found political expression in the United States Constitution, had its ecclesiastical counterpart in a strengthening of conservative sentiment within the Presbyterian Church.[9] This, together with immigration from Ireland, further strengthened those churchly traditions which had borne the name "Old Side" and presently were to be called "Old School."

Following the Revolution, and more especially after the turn of the century, America seemed to be on wheels—rolling westward. State after state was admitted to the Union in rapid succession. Presbyterians and Congregationalists, meeting on the frontier, coöperated in a "Plan of Union" adopted in 1801, whereby a congregation of the one denomination might call a pastor of the other.[10] Partly to meet the needs of the growing home missions field, a spate of benevolent societies came into being, a veritable "benevolent empire," rising from the ruins of the crumbling Puritan theocracies, led and supported largely though not exclusively by Congregationalists and Presbyterians. This fresh contact with New England Congregationalism, and entrance of some erstwhile Congregationalists into the Presbyterian membership and ministry reinvigorated the New England heritage within the Presbyterian Church. Thus circumstances were making for the renewal of dissension between the two historic types of Presbyterianism, discord which reached its climax in the disruption of the Church in 1837.

This Presbyterian struggle was part of a larger effort by the more churchly authoritarian elements in American Protestantism to push back the advancing wave of a democratic, unchurchly, and emotional sectarianism which was threatening to overwhelm them. Powerful elements within all three of the more "churchly" Protestant traditions in America—Angelican, Calvinistic, and Lutheran—reacted in alarm against "freedom's ferment." Bishop John Henry Hobart and others in the Episcopal Church revived High Church traditions over against the prevailing Low Church, or more Puritan, wing of their communion. Schaff and Nevin among the German Reformed repudiated the subjectivism of the "anxious bench" in the name of historic Calvinism, while in the so-called "crisis in American Lutheran theology," historic and confessional Lutheranism successfully repudiated the puritanizing tendencies of S. S. Schmucker's "American Lutheranism." Among Congregationalists, too, more organic views of the Church found expression a little later in Horace Bushnell. The rejection by Old School Presbyterians of New School "errors" was a part of the same churchly revolt against advancing sectarian—and democratic—forces.

The immediate causes of the Presbyterian disruption of 1837 were principally three—differing views on church government, on theology, and on slavery. In church government, New School Presbyterians inclined toward congregationalizing, more decentralized theories and practices.

Theologically, the New School men were much influenced by the "New England" school of theology stemming from Jonathan Edwards. Edwards, in opposing Arminianism with its more optimistic views of human nature, had emphasized not only the immediacy of God's presence and sovereignty, but also the role of man's feelings and will—that is, right "affections." More and more Edwards' followers inclined to restate Calvinism in terms of what can be experienced by man, rather than in terms of the nature of God himself. Thus virtue came to be defined as disinterested benevolence, and sin as self-love. All sin came to be regarded as voluntary acts of the will, and Adam's sin was no longer thought to convey actual guilt to his posterity, but only an inclination to sinful acts. This view was often designated "mediate" as distinct from "immediate" imputation of Adam's sin. Edwardeans spoke of fallen man as having the "natural ability" but not the "moral ability"—that is, not the inclination—to do God's will. Opponents charged that some Edwardeans optimistically regarded the present universe as the best possible, and sin as an incident in the realization of the greatest good. Following Edwards, the New England Theology inclined toward philosophic idealism, whereas Old School Presbyterians, following John Witherspoon and the Princeton lead, inclined toward philosophic realism. The difference was significant, for the dogmatic and literalistic Scottish "common-sense" type of realism was much less inclined to speculation and innovation than was idealism. Then, too, idealism led more directly to the "liberal" theology of the late nineteenth century which was also grounded in philosophic idealism. It has been suggested that the entrance of this Scottish common-sense realism into the South, borne partly by Presbyterian churches and colleges, contributed to the swing of the South away from free thought toward cultural and social conservatism.[11] Whatever the cause, this rightward movement of the South had far-reaching importance for the Presbyterian divisions of 1837 and 1861, and for reunion discussions in the 1860's.

It is now generally recognized that the slavery issue—though deliberately deëmphasized by many at the time—constituted a third important cause of the Presbyterian Old School-New School disruption of 1837.[12]

About the middle of the nineteenth century, in response to the social and cultural movements of the age which were making for toleration and integration, centripetal forces began to overtake the centrifugal in Anglo-Saxon Presbyterianism in both the Old World and the New. American Presbyterians, watching with special interest negotiations begun in 1863 for union between the United Presbyterian and Free Churches in Scotland, drew differing conclusions, depending on the differing inclinations of the viewers.[13]

During the three decades of separation increasingly powerful forces in American life were urging Old School and New School Presbyterians toward reunion. Rapid westward expansion emphasized the need of coöperation among scattered Presbyterian groups. The fire of Civil War fused the American states into a compact modern nation, and centralizing forces grew apace in American political, economic, and ecclesiastical life.

In another way, too, the Civil War hastened the reunion of Old and New School Presbyterians. With the outbreak of hostilities the Old School Church lost its large Southern constituency which comprised some of its socially and theologically most conservative elements. Indirectly this resulted in reducing the difference between the Old School and the New School Churches in the North.

After the war, some elements in the Old School Church—among whom Cyrus H. McCormick of Chicago and the men of Princeton Seminary were prominent—eagerly hoped that reunion might be with the Southern Presbyterians rather than with the New School, since it could not be with both.[14] As the pattern unfolded it became increasingly clear that in general those who favored reunion with the Southern Presbyterians were those who supported President Andrew Johnson's milder policies toward the

South, while former abolitionists and those who favored the radical reconstruction policies of Congress greatly preferred reunion with the New School, and desired harsh ecclesiastical measures against former members who had supported slavery and the Confederacy. As a critical correspondent from Illinois told Dr. Charles Hodge: "This mad furor in favor of reunion [with the New School] is, I believe, an outgrowth of abolition fanaticism." [15]

The wave that swept radical reconstructionists into control of Congress carried parallel policies into control of the Old School Church. The Church took rigorous measures against former members in the South and against those in the border states who protested this ecclesiastical action. A proposal to invite the Southern Church to discuss reunion at the same time that reunion was being discussed with the New School Church was voted down.[16] A clerical correspondent was quite correct when he told Cyrus McCormick, "The North is intensely opposed to any reactionary movement." [17] Nor did Southern Presbyterians desire union with the North at this time. The editor of the Richmond *Central Presbyterian* told a trusted friend in the North: "The very idea of a reunion [between Northern and Southern Presbyterians] is almost universally abhorred." [18] Then, soon after the Old School-New School reunion, the objection was offered that the reunited Northern Church was "doctrinally doubtful." [19] In determining which groups of Presbyterians would unite and which remain separate, it was evident that sociological and secular factors were outweighing theological and ecclesiastical.

With various circumstances urging, reunion between Old School and New School proceeded apace. In 1862, the year after the withdrawal of its Southern constituency, the Old School Assembly proposed exchange of commissioners with the New School Assembly and four years later proposed that the two Assemblies appoint committees to consider reunion. In 1867 both Assemblies sent down to their presbyteries for study a proposed plan of reunion. Dr. Hodge, leading Old School theologian, doubted whether the proposed terms sufficiently guarded distinctive Calvinism, but was powerfully answered by Professor Henry Boynton Smith of Union Seminary, leading New School theologian who defended the soundness of the Calvinism of the New School men in no uncertain terms. "The Scotch bag-pipe," Dr. Smith added, "doubtless discourses most excellent music, and we like to hear it; but do not care to be restricted to it, especially when it is out of sorts." Dr. Smith defined the issue thus: "whether we can have an American Presbyterian Church, or whether we are to be given over to perpetual conflicts, and provincial assemblies." [20] A union Presbyterian convention in Philadelphia in this same year, 1867, impressed very many, including Dr. Hodge, with its enthusiasm and spirit of unity. After some misunderstanding as to the exact terms of reunion that were being voted on, the two Assemblies submitted to their respective presbyteries a basis of union popularly described as the Westminster Standards "pure and simple," without qualifying or interpretive clauses of any kind. Special meetings of the two Assemblies in November 1869 were informed that of the Old School's 144 presbyteries 126 had voted affirmatively on the proposed reunion, 3 negatively, with the others not replying; and that all of the New School's 113 presbyteries had voted affirmatively. Reunion was at last an accomplished fact.

Once again in 1869, as in 1758, the Presbyterian Church was restoring unity not by resolving its differences, but by ignoring and absorbing them. Men who had been denounced as "heretics" in 1837 and who had professed no change of theological viewpoint in the interim were welcomed in 1869 as honored brethren. The result was, of course, that the theological base of the Church (especially of the former Old School branch of the Church) was broadened and the meaning of its subscription formula further relaxed. The gentlemen's agreement of 1869 to tolerate divergent types of Calvinism meant that clear-cut definitions of Calvinism would not be enforceable in the reunited Church, and that it would be increasingly difficult to protect historic Calvinism against variations that might undermine its essential character. But already the Western world was facing quite new issues, which would bring new problems to the theologians.

1869- Gentleman's agreement to tolerate divergent types of Calvinism. This made it difficult to protect historic Calvinism.

The Presbyterian Church, with its heritage from Geneva and the commercial classes, and with its strategic centers in the great cities of the East (except of New England) and of the growing West, fully embodied the vitality of expanding industrialized America in the post-Civil War years. Reflecting the spirit of the times, the Church was becoming increasingly responsive to everything that made for effectiveness of action, and correspondingly allergic to any theoretical considerations that might hamper its vigorous activism. The first regular General Assembly of the reunited Church met in May 1870 in an atmosphere of true connubial bliss.[21] Would the honeymoon last?

2.

shadows of coming events

It was well that Old School and New School Presbyterians were safely reunited in 1869, before the divisive effect of the powerful cultural and theological movements of the late nineteenth century was fully felt. Even while Presbyterians were reuniting in early post-bellum years, a new cultural and theological atmosphere was forming in the United States.

As the Civil War came to an end, the conquest of the newest frontiers was hastening to completion. Every area of American life and thought tingled with the optimism and self-confidence that grew out of the subjugation of a continent. Political democracy, too, continued to cause a steady attrition of historic Calvinism.[1] Men could not forever bow as wretched sinners on Sunday and swell with self-confidence the other six days of the week. Meanwhile a new "frontier" was emerging behind the frontier—the American polyglot industrial metropolis. In the megalopolis, with its uprooted and discontented proletariat, its wealthy and sophisticated upper classes, social and cultural changes were felt with particular force.

Optimism resulting from the conquest of the continent begins to influence the Churches

Science was revolutionizing life in two ways: in its applied form, as technology, it was creating new means of industrial production and so was literally reconstructing American society; in its theoretical form science was creating both a new method of intellectual activity and a new world view. Of course some of these forces had long been operative; but it was not until the decades after the Civil War that their full impact began to be felt in America. As wealth and sophistication increased, life became more smug and, in a shallow sense at least, more complete. Men, conscious of fewer unsatisfied desires, saw less of mystery and depth in life. Not until the twentieth century would the sense of awe and profundity come back into its own, when men would see technology offering menace as well as promise, and find science raising more mysteries than it solved.

Evolution was a concept that organized around itself some of the most characteristic ideas and moods of the late nineteenth century. When raised above its original physical and biological locale to the level of a universal principle, evolution substituted change for fixity as the law of all things. Where the theory was consistently universalized, all absolutes—including religious and ethical absolutes—were smashed at a stroke. Of course the most radical implications of evolution were not immediately drawn, nor were they everywhere accepted, but the disquieting and unsettling effects of the new doctrine were soon felt even in the most conservative circles. Evolution's challenge to the creation narrative of Genesis was direct and immediate. The stimulus it gave to naturalistic developmental views of the Bible was soon apparent. Its implications for the traditional doctrines of the fall and sin and redemption were unmistakable. Was the Person of Christ to be excepted from naturalistic processes of development? What should be the foundations for Christian ethics? Most ultimate of all was the threat of evolution to reduce the concepts of reality and truth themselves to sheer relativity. By the end of the nineteenth century these results of the Enlightenment were beginning to be reached in America. The Enlightenment had emancipated reason, had attacked historic Christian absolutes, and had set up some "self-evident" absolutes of its own. But now critical reason was tearing down even the pseudo-absolutes of the Enlightenment. The ultimate stage of metaphysical disintegration was being reached.

The suddenness with which the cyclone of social and cultural change swept down upon America in the closing decades of the nineteenth century created near-panic in the minds of many,[2] and offers at least part of the psychological explanation of the later fundamentalist movement. It seemed that evil hands had hacked the cables and the elevator was hurtling downward with sickening effect. Happily for the Churches, the full impact of the most extreme views was not felt at once, nor did scientific facts necessitate the most radical philosophic inferences that some drew from them.

At first thought, one is surprised to find so little explicit discussion of evolution among Presbyterians. True, Hodge was against it, McCosh was for it, a few other Presbyterian leaders cast their audible vote, sometimes a Presbyterian editor would tilt a Quixotic lance at the windmill, and Presbyterian ministers' meetings in various parts of the country would brighten an occasional "blue Monday" by toying with it; but there was among Presbyterians amazingly little agonizing discussion of evolution in its far-reaching philosophical and theological implications, whether one turns to General Assembly minutes or to Presbyterian periodicals. The issue hardly had its day in the sun of popular Presbyterian attention until the Bryan flurry of the 1920's threatened to stampede the General Assembly into obscurantist action.[3] While on the surface Presbyterians seemed relatively silent regarding evolution, the larger truth of course is that theories of development—as Presbyterian theologians of whatever viewpoint realized—were conditioning the climate and in part defining the problems of all theological discussion.

Other studies, too, were pointing in a similar direction. The comparative study of religion was challenging the uniqueness of Christianity. And if men sought in the inner recesses of spiritual experience a refuge from a law-bound universe, by the end of the century psychology was laying even this inner sanctum under scientific chains.

In the effort to interpret, or reinterpret, theology in relation to these cultural forces that were coming to the fore in the later nineteenth century, leaders of American religious thought were deeply indebted to European—especially to German—theologians. After the War of 1812 a few Americans, led by such figures as Edward Everett, George Ticknor, and George Bancroft, began going to Germany for graduate study. Theological students soon followed, concentrating especially on what were thought to be the theologically more "neutral" studies of philology and philosophy, but through these coming into contact with thought forms prevailing in Germany, notably with German idealistic philosophy and with Biblical criticism. After the Civil War the number of Americans studying in Germany increased greatly.[4] A young American, Charles A. Briggs, studying in Germany shortly after the Civil War, became greatly enamored of German theological scholarship.[5] By students returning from Germany idealistic philosophy, Biblical criticism, and later the Ritschlian theology were greatly stimulated in America.

What is loosely called the "liberal theology" is best defined as an attempt to mediate between historic orthodoxy and the radically altered scientific and cultural outlook. The key theological idea suggested by the cultural outlook was perhaps the doctrine of God's immanence, which found humanity in God and deity in man and was congenial to optimistic developmental views. Extreme emphasis on immanence inevitably gave entirely different meaning to such historic Christian doctrines as those of revelation, sin, redemption, the Person of Christ. Because the "liberal theology" was an attitude and a method of adapting traditional views to the new situation rather than an accepted system of ideas, its adherents—and there were scarcely any, including revivalists, who were not in some degree responsive to its ideals—differed widely among themselves in the degree and the manner of adapting the old ideas. But they were deeply convinced that the expression of Christian truth must adjust itself to the times or die. Their opponents, the so-called "conservatives" on the other hand—who were usually less completely "static" than exuberant liberals supposed, just as "liberals" were often less "radical" than they were painted—charged that liberals in defending and adapting Christianity were betraying it. "Liberal theology," in recognizing the need of applying critical science to the materials of Christianity, often failed to draw at the proper place the line between what Christian traditions could properly be sacrificed and what must be guarded at all costs if essential Christianity was to be retained; and "conservatives," while recognizing that the very continuance of Christianity in the world depends on preserving inviolable the Holy of Holies of its faith, often erred in failing to differentiate what was ephemeral from what was abiding in the Christian heritage.

While Presbyterians were facing these theological issues in the late nineteenth century, Congregationalists also were dealing with them, though Presbyterian discussions centered on questions of Biblical criticism, while Congregationalists were more concerned with speculative problems. The theology of Jonathan Edwards and his followers, with its increasing emphasis on man's powers and initiative, and Horace Bushnell's thought, with its powerful injection of romanticism, had helped to prepare the way for Congregationalists to pass from the old Calvinism to the newer theology. In 1883, about half a decade before Presbyterians formally considered creed revision, the Congregationalists adopted a new creed, irenic and general in tone. It was at Andover—founded in 1808 to be a bastion of Congregational orthodoxy—that the newer liberalism was most effectively pioneered among Congregationalists. The *Andover Review,* founded in 1884, was the principal organ of the new views. Its short and controversial ten-year career was a major event in American religious journalism. Controversy spread to the Congregationalists' American Board when some candidates seeking foreign missionary service under it were found to hold the Andover doctrine of "future probation." But the sharp controversy came to an end in 1892-93 with the toleration of the new views in both seminary and board.[6] While Presbyterians were involved in somewhat similar controversies during the 1880's and 1890's, unlike the Congregationalists they did not grant toleration to the disputed views until a third of a century later.

It is thus evident that the Presbyterian Church, so recently reunited, must almost immediately face troubled times of theological change. Could her newly regained unity survive such a strain? The first decade after reunion, 1869-79, was a time of exploring the situation.

A small but convinced minority in the Old School Presbyterian Church had opposed reunion, and while most of these tried to put a good face on the matter, some of them were less than happy.[7] In the New School Church a smaller minority had been more mildly opposed to reunion, not because of reluctance to tolerate Old School differences from themselves, but because they feared that their own theological liberty might be imperiled. These and other like-minded New School men went along heartily with reunion, but kept their eyes and ears open.

A number of heresy trials during the first decade after reunion threatened the Church's new harmony and almost seemed to justify the apprehensions with which a few New School men had viewed reunion.

In February 1873, Dr. Francis L. Patton, brilliant young professor of theology at the Presbyterian Seminary of the Northwest in Chicago (later McCormick Seminary), began work as editor of the *Interior,* a Presbyterian weekly which Cyrus H. McCormick had bought less than two weeks before. The next month editorials began warning against theological perils. "Broad Churchism is the land which lies between strict orthodoxy and open infidelity." Progress in theology, the editor wrote, can be only progress in the interpretation of the Bible, which is unlikely. "And it gives us no more uneasiness to believe that Christian theology has come to maturity than it does to know that we shall never be any taller." An editorial lamented: "Few will incur the odium of taking steps for the removal of a minister who preaches heresy." [8]

Professor David Swing, a former New School man, was pastor of the Fourth Presbyterian Church in Chicago. After the Chicago fire in 1871, he, in company with two others, had raised funds in the East for the suffering churches. After the fire he preached for a time in a theater where, by his popular style and sympathetic approach to intellectual problems, he attracted many previously unchurched. Perhaps the *Interior* editorial just quoted had Professor Swing in mind, because six days before the editorial was published Dr. Patton had written to a friend in Brooklyn: "Swing is said to be heterodox & between you & me I sometimes doubt if there is any soundness in him. . . . I have been greatly troubled, but it seems to be wisest to say nothing at least not just now." [9]

This restraint was soon overcome, and the issue was precipitated publicly when Dr. Patton in an editorial criticized a published sermon of Professor Swing. There followed a series of exchanges in the *Interior* between editor and pastor, during the course of which Professor Swing declared the theory of inspiration advocated by the *Interior* too defective and too timid to be considered the undisputed theory of the great Presbyterian Church. Young men, even Presbyterians, he warned, "will soon demand a theory of inspiration very different from the indefinite admiration of the past." The discussion in the *Interior* reached a climax when Dr. Patton accused his respondent of basic departures from the faith. This carried the matter beyond mere debate and in response to a resolution of Chicago Presbytery, Dr. Patton on April 13, 1874, presented formal charges of heresy against Professor Swing, with detailed specifications.[10]

The two charges accused the defendant of violating the sixth ordination vow—"Rev. David Swing . . . has not been zealous and faithful in maintaining the truths of the gospel"—and the second ordination vow—"Rev. David Swing . . . does not sincerely receive and adopt the Confession of Faith of this Church as containing the system of doctrine taught in the Holy Scriptures." In his formal plea of "not guilty" Dr. Swing emphasized the historical and relative character of all creeds. "A creed is only the highest wisdom of a particular time and place. Hence, as in States, there is always a quiet slipping away from old laws without any waiting for a formal repeal." [11]

The negative form of the charges, and the fact that Dr. Swing, as a man of irenic and poetic temperament, had not categorically denied doctrines of the Church, made the prosecutor's task a most difficult one. To assert, for example, as did one "specification," that Professor Swing's ambiguous references to fundamental doctrines "admit easily of construction in accordance with the theology of the Unitarian denomination" [12] was a very different thing from proving that he taught Unitarianism. To convict him of heresy because of alleged omissions and ambiguities before a presbytery that was more sympathetic toward him than toward his prosecutor proved impossible, and on May 20 the presbytery, by a vote of more than three to one, acquitted the defendant of both charges. Dr. Patton at once announced that he would appeal the case, and five days later Professor Swing informed the presbytery that he would withdraw from the Presbyterian Church in order that a prosecutor might no longer have power "to arraign me, from time to time, on some dead dogma, or over the middle of a sentence, or over some Sabellian or Mohammedan word." Professor Swing also placed his withdrawal on the larger ground of helping the Presbyterian Church toward revision of its theology. The withdrawal, said he, was partly "to secure to the Synod and to the Assembly that peace which alone can lead to a calm review and restatement of doctrine" "without the stormy passions that gather around an 'accuser' and an 'accused.' " [13]

The Swing case added serious temporary strain to Presbyterian relations in the Chicago area in general and in the Seminary of the Northwest in particular. Northern Illinois had been settled predominantly from New England and New York, with the result that the New School type of Presbyterians—some of them recently come out of Congregationalism—predominated in the Chicago area.[14] The "progressive" background of the region of course contributed greatly to the acquittal of Dr. Swing.

This New England and New School atmosphere in Chicago was to prove of great significance for the Presbyterian seminary located there, and through it for the entire theological history of the Presbyterian Church. In 1829 a theological department was added to the Hanover Academy in Hanover, Indiana. Eleven years later this theological department moved to New Albany, Indiana, where, after drafting plans to move to Chicago, it closed its doors amid the national financial panic of 1857.[15] Meanwhile Cyrus H. McCormick, hearing of the desire of the seminary at New Albany to move, thought that if it could be located in Chicago it might be just the instrument for strengthening Old School Presbyterianism in the "Northwest" and for checking the rapid rise of antislavery sentiment in the region. Fearing that if the seminary were controlled by local synods it must become responsive to the growing political radicalism of the area, Mr. McCormick offered $100,000 to endow four professorships if the General Assembly (Old School) would take control of the seminary and locate it in Chicago. The offer was accepted.

Following this refounding of the seminary in Chicago in 1859, the Civil

War caused a rapid growth in antisecession and antislavery sentiment in the Old School Church and in the Northwest. Though his desire to see the Old School Church unite with the Southern Presbyterians rather than with the New School Church was not fulfilled, Mr. McCormick labored valiantly to maintain Old School theology and to exclude from the seminary sympathy for the Congressional program of radical reconstruction. Political radicalism for a time controlled the institution, but the Chicago fire of 1871 so seriously weakened other sources of financial support that the seminary had to turn to the bountiful Mr. McCormick. Mr. McCormick then brought to the chair of theology the conservative and brilliant young Dr. Patton. In order that former New School men in the area whose sympathy and support were so vital to the seminary's future might be brought into closer relations with the seminary, arrangements were made for appointing a leader of the former New School Church, Dr. Robert W. Patterson, to the faculty.[16]

Such was the precarious equilibrium within the seminary and the area as a whole when Dr. Patton, barely two years after his arrival, opened the Swing case. The unity of Church, presbytery, and seminary survived the shock. Next to the defendant, it was probably the prosecutor himself who suffered most, for he was conscious of much odium.[17] But his overwhelming election as a commissioner to the General Assembly of 1878 and his election as moderator of that Assembly were construed as evidencing the intention of his critics to let bygones be bygones.[18] The Swing trial was quite inconclusive in view of the negative form of the charges, the poetic and elusive style of the defendant, and the failure to secure a decision from the General Assembly; but it was significant that a man who openly declared that his faith and the Church's were quite different from that of the Westminster Confession at important points was acquitted by the overwhelming vote of an important presbytery. New forces were moving in the Church.

Close upon the heels of the Swing case in Chicago followed the McCune case in another Presbyterian theological center of the Midwest, Cincinnati, home of Lane Seminary. Lane Seminary, founded in 1829, had received in its early years permanent scars from the famous antislavery exodus of Theodore Dwight Weld and fellow students, and from the heresy trial of its New School president, Lyman Beecher. Presbyterian reunion threatened it with further difficulties, because as a New School seminary it had been the only seminary of its Church west of the Alleghenies; but the reunion brought it and the Old School seminaries at Allegheny (Pittsburgh) and Chicago into the same Church and thus into more direct competition.

After the reunion, Lane, with its New School traditions, found itself in a region in which former Old School men greatly predominated. Would the seminary adjust its New School heritage and win the full confidence and support of its Old School environment? This problem was the exact

> Lane Seminary was New School in the midst of Old School country.

opposite to that of the Presbyterian Seminary of the Northwest in Chicago, which was an Old School institution suddenly finding itself amid a predominantly New School potential constituency. This precarious position of Lane Seminary, combined with its longstanding numerical and financial weakness, made it extremely sensitive to theological and ecclesiastical pressures. In its history some of the Church's most troubling theological problems are strikingly revealed. Dr. Edward Morris, who had come to the Lane faculty in 1867 at the age of forty-two, was the very embodiment of this sensitivity, and as such as well as for other reasons was one of the most interesting figures in the denomination. Though moderator of the reunited General Assembly in 1875, he was a particular target of former Old School men, especially after his transfer to the chair of systematic theology at Lane in 1874.[19] It was these personal and institutional factors which gave to the McCune case an importance that it otherwise would not have had. There had been in this city strong reunion sentiment among leaders of both Presbyterian "Schools" [20] and immediately following reunion many Presbyterians inclined to emphasize coöperation among all Protestants, surrounded as they were in Cincinnati by a large number of Roman Catholics and unchurched people.[21]

> McCune urged that denominational divisions be transcended on a biblical basis.

> A non-denominal church was founded, with McCune as pastor

Since shortly before the reunion[22] the Rev. William C. McCune, a member of the Old School Presbytery of Cincinnati, had been urging that denominational divisions be transcended on a Biblical basis, somewhat after the ideal of earlier "Christian Church" and "Disciples" movements. In November 1875, people of various denominations organized, in Linwood, a suburb of Cincinnati, an undenominational church which called Mr. McCune as pastor and invited ministers of various denominations to constitute a council to give formal Christian recognition to the new church. The council installed Mr. McCune as pastor, and Dr. E. D. Morris, moderator of that year's Presbyterian General Assembly, preached the installation sermon.[23] In his zeal for church union, Mr. McCune appears to have tried to transcend the distinction between visible and invisible Church in Reformed theology, a distinction which sometimes led to complacent acceptance of disunity by ascribing unity solely to the invisible Church. He denounced existing denominationalism as sinful and, in the area of practical church administration, he repudiated infant baptism, entered upon extra-presbyterial service without presbytery's permission, and urged revision of the Presbyterian Church's standards in the interests of church union.[24]

> Became so much anti-denominational that he went downright beserk on the subject.

The *status quo* found an eager champion in Thomas H. Skinner, an Old School man who had come soon after the reunion to the Second Church of Cincinnati, a former New School congregation and the wealthiest pastorate in the presbytery.[25] Dr. Skinner had no sympathy with any effort at church union that sacrificed Presbyterian particularities, and he saw in Mr. McCune's modest undenominational church and ideology an aggressive effort to supplant Presbyterianism with a nondescript "liberalism and broad-churchism." When Dr. Morris urged him to participate in the council of neighboring ministers, he replied with a sharp rebuke. In his installation sermon Dr. Morris was reported to have said: "It may be that the best contribution which we in this preparatory age can make to the grand Millenial Unity that is surely coming will be found in such fellowship as this; in the dropping off of differences wherever we find it practicable." The moderator's presence and sentiments were the object of conservative attack from far beyond Cincinnati.[26]

In March 1877, Cincinnati Presbytery entered upon a formal ecclesiastical trial of Mr. McCune.[27] "Never before in all our history," warned Dr. Skinner, "has there been such a disposition to put 'Union before Truth' as there is to-day." But presbytery acquitted the defendant, and Dr. Skinner carried formal "complaint" to the higher courts of the Church.[28] Dr. Morris, because he was implicated in the affair by his installation sermon, used all his influence to have the matter dropped,[29] but without success, for the Assembly of 1878, after electing Dr. Patton moderator, pronounced judgment, by a vote of more than four to one, that Cincinnati Presbytery "erred in not sustaining these charges, and in not reprimanding Mr. McCune for his unsound statements, and his disloyal action in the premises." [30] Dr. Morris now found his own theological soundness under suspicion among conservative leaders, and became increasingly concerned to vindicate his orthodoxy, an ambition which was decisively to affect Lane Seminary's later history.

Throughout this postreunion decade a small minority of former Old School men still had grave misgivings. "Almost the only thing saved out of the wreck [i.e., of reunion] (as at times it seems to me)," wrote one such, "is that we have sound O. S. men on the whole in our theol. chairs. I fear that even that may be carried down in the general sweep." [31] With Charles Hodge teaching theology at Princeton, soon to be assisted, then succeeded, by his son, A. A. Hodge, W. G. T. Shedd at Union, Patton at the Seminary of the Northwest, and Kellogg soon to go to Western, to mention only a few, there was certainly no reason for Old School men to feel that their traditions were vanishing from the land.

If there were during this first decade after reunion some men in the Old School tradition who were apprehensive that the old order was changing, there were at the same time some representatives of the New School heritage who thought they sensed a powerful reactionary movement in the Church. Writing later concerning the first two decades after reunion, Dr. Briggs interpreted them as a time of increasing conservative aggressiveness. "Several trials for heresy . . . were held . . . which were not regarded as sufficiently important to rally the parties in battle array." They were, however, "regarded by the New School as breaches of faith on the part of the Old School. . . . The liberal party became more and more discouraged

. . . and the conservative party became constantly more ambitious as it captured one after another of the strong pulpits of the New School party, and secured the control of all the Presbyterian newspapers, with the single exception of the *New York Evangelist*." [32] Just how correct Dr. Briggs was in identifying so exactly the new theological alignment with the former Old School-New School alignment may fairly be questioned when it is recalled that Dr. Briggs himself and two of those prosecuted for heresy were of Old School background, while one of the most ardent prosecutors was at least of New School descent. But, of course, as the present study maintains throughout, broad continuities can be discerned, if the identity is not pressed too closely, between earlier New School positions and the later "liberalism."

The new theological issues rapidly coming to the fore meant that the equilibrium achieved in the reunion of 1869 could not be statically retained, but must continually be rewon by new discussions and new working arrangements. Would the centripetal forces which had achieved reunion in 1869 prove to be stronger than the divisive effects of the new theological problems in the immediately ensuing decades?

The answer from the first postreunion decade was a resounding affirmative. Reunion was "working." The Church was facing new problems—especially those of organization and expansion—with new confidence and effectiveness. In spite of a few "heresy" trials, some fears of radicalism, or of intolerance, it was the "honeymoon" spirit which prevailed.

3.

biblical criticism

Eighteenth-century rationalism gave the first really powerful impulse to the higher criticism of the Bible, as it did to so many other modern sciences. The philosopher Spinoza, in the seventeenth century, had insisted that the Bible should be critically studied. A French physician, Jean Astruc, in 1753, declared that the Book of Genesis was a composite production. Eichhorn, claiming to work independently of Astruc, pointed out two distinct documents in Genesis and part of Exodus, the one source calling the Deity "Jehovah" (which therefore came to be designated as the "J" document), the other calling him "Elohim" ("E"). The two were woven together, he said, by a later compiler. Other scholars announced discoveries of additional documents in the first five books of the Bible, most generally recognized of which were a Deuteronomic source ("D") and a Priestly ("P"). It was said that the Deuteronomic document had been drafted only shortly before it was brought from the temple and read publicly to the people in the reign of Josiah (cf. II Kings 22:8; 23:2). Efforts to explain Israel's religious history in terms of natural development led to the view of a series of scholars climaxing in the work of Wellhausen (1878) that the Priestly portions of the Pentateuch were even later than Deuteronomy, and were not completed until after the Exile. These new conceptions of the Old Testament—particularly in the form so brilliantly set forth by Wellhausen—rejecting as they did the time-honored tradition of the Mosaic authorship of the Pentateuch, and challenging the credibility of these Biblical books and reconstructing much of the history of Israel's religion, created a tremendous stir throughout Western Christendom as soon as their import was perceived.

The New Testament was subjected to the same critical treatment. Reimarus, in his *Wolfenbüttel Fragments,* published posthumously between 1774 and 1778, entirely rejected supernaturalism and in a thoroughgoing way applied critical methods to the study of the life of Christ. Such scholars as Semler, Strauss, Ferdinand Baur, and others carried the studies further. The conclusions which some scholars reached concerning the dates, trustworthiness, and similar questions in regard to New Testament books were quite revolutionary.

This higher criticism of the Bible also created a new discipline, Biblical theology, which attempted to study each Biblical writer or portion in the light of its historical setting and its individual viewpoint and teaching, with full recognition of diversities within the Bible. The new Biblical theology, with its strong aversion to forcing later preconceptions or a priori harmonies on the Biblical writers, was a challenge to the reigning systematic theology, which it accused of employing a priori methods in the interests of speculation and artificial harmony.

Forced by Biblical criticism to reëxamine its relation to the Bible, Protestantism began to restudy its own historical roots. The Protestant reformers of the sixteenth century, in repudiating the conception of faith as assent to theological propositions guaranteed by the authority of the Church, and in emphasizing the vital conception of faith as personal encounter with God and trust in him, were forced by the necessities of controversy to appeal to authority for their views. In basing their case on the ultimate authority of the Bible, it was not their intention to sacrifice or overshadow the vital conception of faith as personal trust in God which they were championing. But in the act of running to the Bible for arguments to clinch the truth of their theological statements, the Protestants sometimes compromised their basic conviction that Christianity was primarily a personal saving relationship to God by faith, which could never be exhaustively stated in propositional form. The peril increased when, following the spontaneity and insight of the early days of the Reformation, Protestant thought and life began to become more formalized and institutionalized. Prolonged controversies between Protestants and Roman Catholics, Calvinists and Lutherans, diverted Protestant attention more and more from the vital first principles of the Reformation to analysis, definition, and amplification of statements about Christianity.

Meanwhile in the Netherlands, a chief commercial and financial center of Europe, the early seventeenth century saw a mild rationalism take theological form as the Arminian or Remonstrant movement. The answer of the strictest Calvinism to these liberalizing tendencies was a tightening of the doctrine of predestination and further commitment to rational, syllogistic amplification. This theological method depended on a very literal use of Scripture, which now came to be regarded as absolutely inerrant. This Calvinistic scholasticism, as it has been called, found creedal embodiment in the Helvetic Consensus of 1675, which even declared that the Hebrew vowel points in the Old Testament were divinely inspired.[1]

Francis Turretine of Geneva gave memorable formulation to this type of scholastic Calvinism, with his formal summaries of "the state of the question," his sharp analysis, division, and subdivision. Turretine gave large place to human reason as it serves theology in natural theology, in judgment, and in philosophy. But reason is always subordinate to revelation. "The necessity of the word [of revelation] is proved by the goodness of God" and "by right reason." "The Scripture proves itself." Scripture has both external and internal distinguishing marks, of which the internal are the more prominent. Turretine taught inerrancy: "It is asked . . . whether in writing they [i.e., "the sacred writers"] were so moved and inspired by the Holy Spirit . . . that they were free from all error ["*ab omni errore immunes*"] and their writings are truly authentic and divine? Opponents deny; we affirm." Turretine also asserted the substantial correctness of the present text of Scripture. Needless to say, the theology represented by the Helvetic Consensus and by Turretine was uncompromisingly opposed to the embryonic critical studies of their day. Nor is it strange that the heirs of these views in nineteenth-century American Presbyterianism also found themselves inevitably arrayed against all negative conclusions of the by then fully weaned Biblical criticism.[2]

America was slow to develop truly scientific Biblical scholarship. Moses Stuart of Andover and Edward Robinson of Union Seminary were pioneers in the field. But even as late as the 1880's Andover Seminary, which was a very important link between the "New England Theology" and the new "liberalism," continued to be more interested in speculative than in critical problems. It is true, the appearance of the Revised Version of the New Testament in 1881 and of the Old Testament in 1885 helped a little to pave the way for a changed outlook by reminding Americans that there were numerous variant texts and that the "Authorized" Version was far from being identical with the original Biblical manuscripts. But this was quite different from the problems created by the higher criticism. The Presbyterians, in spite of the conservative traditions which were so strong in parts of their Church, were among the first of the evangelical bodies in the land to give full and public discussion to the new Biblical questions.

The Presbyterian Church's two major theological traditions might be expected to have quite different attitudes toward the issues of higher criticism.

One of these traditions found its fullest and most influential expression in Princeton Seminary. Through the years quite a number of Princeton Seminary graduates taught in other Presbyterian seminaries and, after 1872, several Presbyterian seminaries used Charles Hodge's exhaustive *Systematic Theology* as a textbook. In a day of alarming change and subjectivism in religion, the so-called "Princeton Theology" seemed to offer an almost mathematical demonstration of an unchanged and unchangeable religious outlook. The implications of this theology were uncompromisingly hostile to the negative conclusions of the higher criticism. The struggles whereby the Church first accepted and later rejected the Princeton attitude toward the Bible comprise a principal theme of the present book.

A startling confidence in the competence of human reasoning powers was a chief characteristic of the Princeton Theology. Acceptance of the traditional psychology which placed reason in control of the other mental activities contributed obviously to this end.[3] Extensive dependence on the Calvinistic scholasticism of seventeenth-century Holland and Switzerland, such as found expression in the Helvetic Consensus and in Turretine, encouraged the deductive method in deriving doctrines from other doctrines. The earlier forms of the philosophy of Scottish realism, which underlay the Princeton Theology, although encouraging an inductive and empirical rather than a deductive and a priori method, did rehabilitate "common-sense" reason along with sensory experience.

Particularly influential on the Princeton ideal of demonstrating Christianity was the example of the antideistical writers of the eighteenth century. The "Plan" of the seminary provided that "every student . . . must have read and digested the principal arguments and writings relative to what has been called the deistical controversy.—Thus he will be qualified to become a defender of the Christian faith." [4] Although nineteenth-century revivalism and romanticism were currently challenging and altering the conception of man as primarily a "reasoning" being, and although the power of deism as a self-conscious religious movement was collapsing in

America by the time the seminary was founded in 1812, the Princeton Theology seems to have taken as its methodological ideal the use of reason after the fashion of the eighteenth-century antideistical apologists. In many ways this orientation was unfortunate, for most of the representative Princeton men had a depth of piety and of spiritual experience[5] which had little counterpart in their eighteenth-century models. The result was that the Princeton Theology, in spite of its many widely recognized merits, did not fully do justice to itself. It was forced by its method virtually to separate theology from Christian experience. Christian experience, which actually meant so much to the Princeton men, hardly broke into their eighteenth-century pattern of "evidences"; and the "evidences," while pointing toward intellectual conviction, could never produce true Christian experience. The philosophy of Kant with its epistemological dualism was of course abhorrent to the Princeton men.[6]

Archibald Alexander, the seminary's first professor (1812-51), who placed his indelible stamp on the Princeton Theology, was a great admirer of Turretine, the Swiss Calvinistic scholastic.[7] He also closely reproduced the familiar antideistical external "evidences" of miracle and fulfilled prophecy, but went beyond his models to stress the greater importance of internal evidence—that is, the inherent excellences of the gospel. A suggestion of romanticism appeared in the argument from "the adaptation of the truth to the constitution of the human mind." Other internal qualities of the gospel were adduced which the author admitted "may be perceived, and will have their effect, but cannot be embodied and presented, with their full force, in the form of argument." [8] The Calvinistic doctrine of the witness of the Holy Spirit was another salutary counterpoise to an orthodox rationalism: "When the serious mind falls into doubt respecting divine truths, the remedy is not always reasoning and argument, but divine illumination. . . . This may appear to some to savour of enthusiasm. Be it so. It is, however, an enthusiasm essential to the very nature of our holy religion." [9] But logically, at least, these extra-rational elements remained external additions to the system, rather than becoming organic parts of it. The preceding century's one-sided emphasis on reason was virtually maintained: "No doctrine can be a proper object of our faith which it is not more reasonable to receive, than to reject," but it may, of course, transcend the comprehension of reason, because, it is acknowledged, God "must be to us, in some respect, incomprehensible." "There is no just cause for apprehending, that we shall be misled by the proper exercise of reason, on any subject, which may be proposed for our consideration." Scripture itself should be interpreted by reason.[10]

It was by similar use of reason that the Princeton Theology sought to make its Biblical base objectively and unshakably secure. Dr. Alexander sought to ground the Biblical canon, or list of inspired Biblical books, on the authority of Christ himself. He was simply following general Protestantism in denying that the canon is fixed by church authority, but he deviated from many Protestants in rejecting internal evidence (the intrinsic merits of the Biblical books) as the test of canonicity.[11] Instead, said he, we accept as the proper books of the Old Testament those which Christ accepted and endorsed as divine, the list of which has been preserved by separate Jewish and Christian traditions and is attested also by the Jewish historian Josephus.[12] The New Testament canon, said Dr. Alexander, is more difficult to determine. "It is an inquiry respecting the real authors of the books of the New Testament: whether they were written by the persons whose names they bear; or by others under their names." "All that was requisite [i.e., to establish the canonicity of an early Christian writing] was to be certain, that the book was indeed written by the apostle, whose name it bore." [13] In reducing the authority of early Church Fathers to mere historical documentation, in eliminating the subjective factor of "internal evidence," in omitting the witness of the Spirit, and building the canon entirely on the historical claim of Christ's endorsement or of apostolic authorship, the Princeton position escaped both ecclesiasticism and subjectivism, but made itself peculiarly vulnerable to the attacks of higher criticism later in the century. And the vulnerability was only reduced without being removed when later Princeton writers broadened the base of New Testament canonicity from apostolic authorship to apostolic sanction.

Regarding inspiration, Dr. Alexander said that the truth of the gospel can be established on merely the trustworthiness of the gospel records apart from their inspiration,[14] but their trustworthiness then requires us to accept also their inspiration, because they claim to be inspired.[15] Inspiration, among other things, is superintendence by God over the Biblical writers, which does not impair or overshadow their spontaneity, but keeps them from error.[16] Dr. Alexander refused to admit error in any part of Scripture, for to do so would be to admit the impossibility of distinguishing definitely between what parts of Scripture are inspired and what parts are not inspired.[17]

In Dr. Alexander is to be found, in germ, the entire Princeton Theology. Later writers were principally concerned with sharpening definitions—and in doing this they tended progressively to narrow the theology—and with relating its basic principles to the problems of their day.

It remained for Dr. Alexander's more famous pupil, Dr. Charles Hodge, to give classic expression to the Princeton Theology. His masterly three-volume *Systematic Theology* (1871-72), along with the systematic theologies of Augustus H. Strong (1886), the Baptist, and William G. T. Shedd (1888-94), the Presbyterian, constituted a late-autumn harvest of American Calvinism. A Scottish former student said, "Hodge's 'Systematic Theology' is the modern masterpiece of English dogmatic." [18]

Dr. Hodge accepted and elaborated his predecessor's emphasis on the power and function of reason.[19] His treatment of the canon and inspiration of Scripture was also similar to that of Dr. Alexander. But he went beyond his predecessor to distinguish inspiration sharply from revelation,[20] with the result that revelation is regarded as consciously received from outside, whereas inspiration, operating without the recipient's being aware of it, is continuous and plenary without impairing the spontaneity of his writing. Inspiration "is not confined to moral and religious truths, but extends to the statements of facts, whether scientific, historical, or geographical. . . . It extends to everything which any sacred writer asserts to be true." [21] Many of the discrepancies alleged in Scripture "may fairly be ascribed to errors of transcribers." Here and in an earlier reference to "so many errors of transcription in the text of Scripture," [22] Dr. Hodge intimated a distinction between the existing text of Scripture and the original text or autographs, which was to be much more emphasized by his son.

Thus assured of an inspired and inerrant Bible, Dr. Hodge sought to use it inductively as the source of his theology. "The Bible is to the theologian what nature is to the man of science." "The theologian must be guided by the same rules in the collection of facts, as govern the man of science." [23] But the very fair question has often been raised whether theology, which deals primarily with the personal relationship of man and God, can possibly be—or should even aspire to be—an "objective" science. Dr. Hodge—and very few modern students would agree with him at this point—considered this objective theological method "perfectly consistent, on the one hand, with the admission of intuitive truths, both intellectual and moral, due to our constitution as rational and moral beings, and, on the other hand, with the controlling power over our beliefs exercised by the inward teachings of the Spirit, or, in other words, by our religious experience." [24] Be that as it may, it is clear that the Princeton Theology not only tried to guarantee an inerrant Bible, but presupposed it as the foundation of its theological method and structure. It is clear that the differences between this theological method, thus formulated, and the negative conclusions of the higher criticism were irreconcilable.

Dr. Archibald Alexander Hodge—whose name reflects his father's devotion to the seminary's first professor—was chosen to assist and succeed his father as the one best suited "to perpetuate the traditional character of Princeton Seminary." [25] Like his predecessors, he considered the intellect supreme over the affections and will and eschewed the subjective perils of the current emphasis on the "Christian consciousness." Canonicity for him depended on authorship.[26] The Scriptures, which on other grounds are found to be trustworthy, claim to be inspired. This emphatic claim must be accepted or their trustworthiness must be denied entirely.[27] Dr. A. A. Hodge—responding to the growing emphasis on man's powers—emphasized more than did his predecessors that the Princeton conception of inspiration in no way denied the fully human, as well as divine, origin of the Scriptures. The younger Hodge also advanced upon his predecessors by explicitly confining these high claims of inspiration to "the original autographs" of Scripture, the lost first manuscripts,[28] thus by a scholastic refinement removing the evidence beyond refutation, and the guarded treasure beyond use. More clearly, too, than his predecessors he seems to have sensed what has in more recent years become such an acute metaphysical problem, the problem of possible "point of contact" between the infinite and the finite, eternity and time. He faced it, head on, with a paradox: "God is infinite, yet his word, the Bible, is finite." [29] But could the infinite become finite and at the same time remain clothed with the original attributes of infinity undiminished, an infinity which any finite observer should be able to discern in it at any moment?

Dr. A. A. Hodge devoted his inaugural address at Princeton Seminary in 1877 to a defense of systematic theology, partly against the claims of the newer "Biblical theology." He objected to the tendency of some to make only the historical events of Scripture (cf. the later emphasis on "salvation history"), rather than their doctrinal interpretation, the object of Christian faith. Skepticism concerning the methods and conclusions of metaphysics he repudiated: "Whether this policy of preserving the truth by means of its disintegration be urged upon us by subtle enemies or by silly friends, we intend to refuse it utterly." [30]

Dr. Francis L. Patton, who came to the faculty of Princeton Seminary in 1881, fully shared the seminary's high estimate of reason: "I have no confidence in the philosophy that first throws the intellect into bankruptcy, and then pensions us on an allowance of faith." [31] His defense of Scripture and of systematic theology followed the same pattern.[32] He was sharp in his criticism of the current demand for progress in theology.[33]

The Princeton men never claimed originality for the pattern of their theology. In fact, Dr. Charles Hodge at his semicentennial announced: "I am not afraid to say that a new idea never originated in this Seminary." [34] They taught Calvinism of the Westminster type, modified by the Calvinistic scholasticism of the seventeenth century and by eighteenth-century anti-deistical apologetics.

There was another and quite distinct theological tradition in the Presbyterian Church in the U.S.A., that of the New School. What were the implications of New School Presbyterianism for Biblical scholarship, as these implications came to expression in leading representatives of the New School tradition?

New School Presbyterians acquired a Biblical scholar and geographer of the first magnitude in Dr. Edward Robinson, professor at Andover and later at Union Seminary. Dr. Robinson intimated an inclination toward the documentary hypothesis in his edition of Calmet's *Dictionary of the Holy Bible* (1835), but though he had a critical cast of mind, "his habit of doubting appears never to have been let loose against the teachings of Scripture." [35]

It was Dr. Henry Boynton Smith, more than any other, who set the New School theological pattern on the eve of the debates about the Bible. Reared a Unitarian, at a time when American Unitarianism was young and aggressive, he became, after a youthful conversion, a convinced and life-long Trinitarian. Later, when studying philosophy and theology in Germany, he was shocked at the state of religion, and had no sympathy for the radicalism of Strauss's *Life of Jesus*. He made the personal acquaintance of such scholars as Tholuck, Neander, and Hengstenberg, and was both broadened and strengthened by his three years abroad. "I have not the conviction," he wrote to a friend, "that study here has had any other effect than that of making my views more deeply grounded, and of developing them more clearly. If I thought that my heart were losing ground, that I were losing my simple reverence for the Scriptures, and my simple faith in experimental religion . . . I would come right home." [36] He considered the German idealistic philosophy which "threatens to absorb religion in philosophy" "more blasting to piety, and fatal to simple experimental religion than all the biblical criticism of the Rationalists." [37] Though not a popular preacher, Professor Smith was a gifted teacher who encouraged great freedom of classroom inquiry and drew students to Union Seminary.[38]

Dr. Smith was essentially a mediating theologian who modified the New England theology in which he had been reared by generous admixture of earlier Calvinistic and contemporary European strains.[39] It was therefore in accord with his deepest principles that he became the chief architect of Presbyterian reunion.

In view of these elements in Professor Smith's theology, one notes with surprise his rigorous adherence to traditional views of the Bible. He considered "the whole of historical Christianity" at stake in the Biblical criticism controversy recently stirred up in England by the *Essays and Reviews* and by Bishop Colenso.[40] Smith's views on the Bible, while far less precise and elaborated, have a striking resemblance to the pattern of the Princeton Theology.

For Dr. Smith, as for the Old School leaders, the canon of Biblical books is based on "the testimony of Christ and the Apostles," with the Church Fathers serving only as witnesses to this testimony.[41] The Church receives as its Old Testament those books which Christ and his apostles received,[42] and as its New Testament those books "which have apostolic authority." [43] The Biblical revelation is authenticated by miracles, prophecy, and inspiration.[44] The divine character and inspiration of the Bible is evidenced by its wonderful style, its efficacy among men, its own claims to inspiration, the testimony of Christ and his apostles, and "the witness of the Spirit in our hearts." [45]

Dr. Smith's view of inspiration itself is very high. Like the Princeton men, he distinguishes between inspiration and revelation, regarding all parts of Scripture as inspired, even where no revelation is being conveyed. While the Princeton men spoke of inspiration as a divine "superintendence," he spoke of it as a "divine influence," with almost identical significance. This divine influence permits expression of the human authors' individualities. Dr. Smith clearly taught inerrancy: the object of inspiration is "the communication of truth in an infallible manner, so that, when rightly interpreted, no error is conveyed"; "interpreted, as all works must be, by its real spirit, it [i.e., the Bible] gives us truth without error." He described this as "plenary" inspiration.[46] Dr. Smith's views on inspiration left his most sympathetic interpreters of the next generation nonplused and wondering enigmatically "whether he would have continued to hold the position of the Synodical Sermon, if he had lived in our generation." [47]

At the time of reunion and until his death in 1877, Dr. Smith was the unchallenged Nestor of New School men. The fact that his own views on the Bible were so conservative is clear evidence that attitudes toward the new Biblical questions were not determined automatically by the former Old School-New School line of cleavage. This is further illustrated by the fact that Dr. Smith's successor in the chair of theology at Union Seminary until his retirement in 1890 was Dr. William G. T. Shedd, who openly repudiated the negative conclusions of Biblical criticism. While it is true that Dr. Shedd's individual membership had been in the Old School Church, and his theology was less typical of the seminary than that of his predecessor, his presence and influence are further refutation of any oversimplified attempt to extend the Old School-New School line of cleavage directly into the new Biblical questions. But, of course, the New School tradition, with its greater readiness for change, its greater emphasis on emotion and experience rather than on rational demonstration, was inherently more inclined to adjust its Biblical views than was its more rigid Old School counterpart.

It is interesting that the most conspicuous champion of Biblical criticism in the Presbyterian Church was Dr. Charles A. Briggs, who had been in the Old School Church. Five years after graduating from Union Seminary he wrote to Professor Smith from Germany, where he was studying: "I am connected with the Old School & would prefer that side to the other—but I feel more sympathy with the *mediating* theology—which it seems to me you advocate than with the extreme views of either School." [48]

Charles A. Briggs in favor of biblical criticism

While regretting the Germans' lack of reverence and coldness toward the Bible, Briggs was very favorably impressed with their Biblical methods and their Biblical theology.[49] In 1870 he wrote a notable article on Biblical theology,[50] and in 1876 in his inaugural address as professor of Hebrew and the cognate languages at Union Seminary, he urged that critical study of the Scriptures be not fettered by traditional or dogmatic views. "Are the laws of the Pentateuch any less divine if it should be proved that they are the product of the experience of God's people from Moses to

Josiah?"[51] There was some criticism of this address, but Dr. William Adams, president of the seminary, stood by him, and praise was expressed by such advanced Old Testament scholars as Professors Toy and Robertson Smith.[52] As yet, however, Dr. Briggs's genuine zeal for the new methods of Biblical study did not create any great stir or impression in the Presbyterian Church.

It was the case of W. Robertson Smith in the Free Church of Scotland which brought the issue of Biblical criticism vividly to the attention of American Presbyterians. In 1875 there appeared in the *Encyclopaedia Britannica* an article, "Bible," together with other articles by William Robertson Smith, professor in the Scottish Free Church College of Aberdeen. The article took an advanced position on Biblical criticism, which caused increasing tension in General Assemblies of the Free Church from 1876 to 1880.

Professor Smith averred a high view of inspiration, and insisted that the great Protestant reformers grounded the doctrine of inspiration not on the authorship or literary structure of the Bible, but on the witness of the Holy Spirit. In 1880 the General Assembly of the Free Church took action ending heresy charges against the young professor, and at the same time refused to dismiss him from his chair. Shortly after the close of this Assembly, a new volume of the *Encyclopaedia Britannica* appeared with an article by Professor Smith on "Hebrew Language and Literature" in which he committed himself even more clearly to Wellhausen's positions. The redoubled furor which now swept the Scottish Free Church resulted in the expulsion of Professor Smith from his chair by the Assembly of 1881, though astute leaders sought to minimize the curb on critical scholarship by avoiding, in this case, any formal ecclesiastical prosecution for heresy.[53]

American Presbyterian theological scholars—not to mention others—closely followed these long-drawn-out proceedings, most of them sharply hostile to Professor Smith, but a few, like Dr. Briggs, while not fully sharing Professor Smith's advanced critical position, fervently hopeful that the Scottish Church would not refuse to tolerate such views. During the course of these proceedings, Dr. Briggs was receiving inside information from some of Professor Smith's prominent Scottish sympathizers.[54]

Echoes of the Biblical issue had been heard in the American Presbyterian General Assemblies of 1878 and 1879,[55] and in 1880 the Assembly, with obvious allusion to Robertson Smith, declared: "At a period when acknowledged religious teachers, holding high positions in Christian Institutions in Europe, are disseminating doctrines which are calculated to undermine the authority of the Holy Scriptures, we deem it appropriate, that this General Assembly of the Presbyterian Church urge upon the Professors in our Seminaries, to see to it that they do, by no means, even indirectly, give countenance to these fundamental errors."[56] And President

James McCosh, though one of the early clergymen in America to accept evolution, was apprehensive of Biblical criticism.[57]

The Robertson Smith case was the immediate occasion of bringing Biblical criticism before the American Presbyterian Church, principally by forcing the subject upon the attention of the *Presbyterian Review*, a recently founded theological journal.

4.

a theological journal

The *Presbyterian Review*, founded jointly by former Old School and New School interests, was a true expression of the continuing "honeymoon" spirit of the reunion. An earlier joint theological journal had been diverted from its original purpose,[1] but prospects were promising for the new venture. American religious journals, which came into their own in the early nineteenth century, about doubled in number in the two decades after the Civil War.[2] Presbyterians, who had previously maintained two, and at times more, learned reviews, might well be expected, amid continuing reunion good will, to give hearty support to one.

It was Dr. Charles A. Briggs of Union Seminary, still in his thirties, who supplied the leadership. His efforts to secure Scottish coöperation to conduct the projected journal on an international basis proved, after bright initial prospects, unsuccessful and seemed undesirable to some of the American Presbyterians for both theological and national reasons.[3] When, within the American scene, an East-West rivalry was threatened by rumors of a theological and scientific journal at Lake Forest, Illinois, a counter-proposal from the East seemed to envisage a kind of Eastern "imperialism" of culture which should exploit a "colonial" West, after the economic fashion of those years: "There are good reasons for thinking that a better thing can be done for the Church & for theological learning at the East than at the West. . . . Whether a scheme can be devised that will make the responsible control sufficiently simple, & keep it at the East while utilizing the interest & service of the West, is one of the problems to be carefully studied." [4] Arrangements were soon completed along these lines. Western, Northwest, Auburn, and Lane seminaries, after giving their approval, were editorially represented on the project by associate editors; [5] while Drs. Briggs and A. A. Hodge were chosen as the two managing editors by the faculties of Union and Princeton seminaries, respectively. The first number of the *Presbyterian Review*, appearing in January 1880, contained a broad and irenic statement of purpose.[6]

Both the old school and the New School feared that the other would take over the new journal.

But any theological enterprise in the Presbyterian Church at this time inevitably found itself under suspicion from men at opposite extremes. Thus, Dr. Aiken, the acting Princeton coeditor, warned that some in the Church feared that New York interests might use the review as "a local and institutional organ. . . . The Church was *two* not very long ago."[7] If some in the Church viewed the infant *Presbyterian Review* as a dark conspiracy of former New School interests, Dr. Morris of Lane Seminary, still smarting from the wounds he had received in the McCune case the year before, was even more fearful that sinister Old School interests would use the review to strangle "a broad and liberal Presbyterianism as represented in the New School body." [8] In spite of genuine good will between the coeditors in the early days of the project,[9] the divisive higher criticism and other theological issues which were sweeping into the land kept threatening the editorial coalition. But the coeditors finally agreed to run eight articles on issues raised by higher criticism, the series to alternate between the affirmative and the negative.[10] Thus was launched a series which, with the possible exception of Dr. Briggs's inaugural of 1876, first brought home to the Presbyterian Church—and to some other areas of evangelical America also—the higher criticism.[11]

Magazine agreed to present higher criticism pro and con.

The first article in this *Presbyterian Review* series of eight was by Drs. A. A. Hodge and B. B. Warfield on "Inspiration," published in April 1881. It is of prime importance because the theory it expresses was soon embodied in official action of the Presbyterian Church and because in this article Princeton doctrine on the subject reaches its culmination in a statement that is clear, fully rounded, and accepts the ultimate implications of its own position, yet with moderation of tone and language. Dr. Briggs showed great interest in the article in advance, venturing to advise: "If you could . . . keep in mind the difficulties that face those whose attention is given mainly to the original text and critical study of the various passages, you will do a great, a *very great* service to the Church; here & in Great Britain." [12] Did this suggestion lead the authors—to a far greater degree than Dr. Hodge had previously gone[13]—to their famous and unprecedented emphasis on the original Bible manuscripts, as distinguished from the existing text?[14] If so, it certainly was far removed from the solution Dr. Briggs would have desired. Dr. Hodge was quite frank in announcing that his article would stress inerrancy: "The real question on which I must assume the affirmative is, What was the *extent* of that divine superintendence which secured this general infallibility? Did it prevent *all* errors in their communicating to us what they intended to affirm? . . . To this I have been brought up & this I must affirm." [15]

Dr. Hodge was sole author of the first part of the article which developed the doctrine of inspiration positively, though a few minor emendations were suggested by his collaborator; and Dr. Warfield was author of the latter part which undertook to refute the charge of errors in Scripture.[16]

The part of the article written by Dr. Hodge early acknowledges that the doctrine of inspiration is not essential to Christianity. "Nor should we even allow it to be believed that the truth of Christianity depends upon any doctrine of Inspiration whatever." [17] Though Dr. Hodge and the Princeton tradition thus openly admitted that their high doctrine of inspiration did not have priority in their system of theology, either in time or in importance, they built their entire theological system on the assumption that it was true, and then had to defend it to the hilt to save their theological system. Although they acknowledged that those who held to Christian revelation while rejecting all doctrines of inspiration were still in possession of essential Christianity, the Princeton men were unwilling to make common cause with these against naturalists who denied all revelation. This refusal of the Princeton men and others like-minded to adopt the more comprehensive ecclesiastical strategy which was implied in their own theology at this point largely determined the course, for the next half century, of the theological history of the Presbyterian Church, and of much of American Protestantism.

The article—particularly Dr. Warfield's portion of it—teaches inerrancy more stringently than Princeton men had previously done. Dr. Hodge says that "all the affirmations of Scripture of all kinds whether of spiritual doctrine or duty, or of physical or historical fact, or of psychological or philosophical principle, are without any error, when the *ipsissima verba* of the original autographs are ascertained and interpreted in their natural and intended sense." [18] Dr. Warfield, in words that have been the object of much comment, said, "A proved error in Scripture contradicts not only our doctrine, but the Scripture claims and, therefore, its inspiration in making those claims." [19] Dr. Hodge had previously limited inerrance to the "original autograph" manuscripts of the Bible,[20] but, under pressures from both textual criticism and literary and historical criticism, the joint article gives unprecedented emphasis to this idea.[21] Dr. Warfield even throws the burden of proof on the negative, and says that the doctrine of Scripture inerrancy can be overthrown only by proving that error existed in the original (and now lost) autographs.[22] It is not suggested how this could be done. The implications of the doctrine impose very severe a priori restrictions on a truly scientific use of the method of higher criticism, for Dr. Hodge writes: "Every supposed conclusion of critical investigation which denies the apostolical origin of a New Testament book, or the truth of any part of Christ's testimony in relation to the Old Testament and its contents, or which is inconsistent with the absolute truthfulness of any affirmation of any book so authenticated, must be inconsistent with the true doctrine of Inspiration." Dr. Warfield holds the same view.[23] The most important comments on the Hodge-Warfield article did not appear until more than a decade later, when it was evident to all that its theory of Scripture was regnant in the Presbyterian Church.[24]

The second article of the *Presbyterian Review* series on Biblical questions, published in July 1881, was by Dr. Briggs on ". . . The Right, Duty, and Limits of Biblical Criticism." Somewhat inconsistently, Dr. Briggs seems to accept most of the a priori limitations imposed on Biblical criticism by the Hodge-Warfield article when he quotes from that article, "'Any theories of the origin or authorship of any book of either Testament which ascribes [ascribe] to them a purely naturalistic genesis, or dates or authors inconsistent with either their own natural claims or the assertions of other Scripture, are plainly inconsistent with the doctrine of Inspiration taught by the Church,'" and comments approvingly, "We entirely agree with this statement, and propose to show the right of criticism within these limits."

Briggs very much against scholastic theology.

But the chief burden of Dr. Briggs's article is an all-out attack on "scholastic theology" as the deluded foe of evangelical Biblical criticism. He charges that by deductive processes this Calvinistic scholasticism goes beyond both Scripture and creed in its zeal for system-building and that it opposes true criticism, which confidently appeals from such scholasticism to Biblical theology. Seventeenth-century scholasticism, he continues, actually destroyed the vital power of Protestantism's Biblical principle. "It is furthermore our conviction that upon a reaction from the scholastic theology . . . and a revival of the evangelical life and unfettered thought of the Reformation and the Puritans of the first half of the 17th century depends a revival of true evangelical religion." In connection with this main theme, Dr. Briggs rejects the view that canonicity is to be established prior to inspiration or made dependent on authorship or Jewish Rabbinical tradition. Instead, he interprets the Reformation as basing canonicity on the witness of the Spirit. He rejects emphasis on the autograph Bible manuscripts, for they are lost beyond recovery. Distinguishing between "plenary" and "verbal" inspiration, he accepts the former, but rejects the latter.[25]

Dr. Hodge's younger brother, Dr. Caspar Wistar Hodge, professor of New Testament at Princeton Seminary, took an unfavorable view of Dr. Briggs's article. He scouted the idea that only Biblical theology, and not systematic theology, had proper critical foundation or concern for Biblical teaching. He regretted the minimizing of the Bible's witness to itself and thought the conception of inspired contents apart from inspired words dubious. Dr. Briggs's efforts to enlist the Westminster divines on the side of the critical use of the Bible was weakened by Dr. C. W. Hodge's shrewd comment: "The very characteristic of their [i.e., the "Westminster Theologians' "] writing and preaching was extreme textual literalness, showing that the words & forms of expression were to them authoritative."

What was "worst of all," in Dr. Briggs's article, according to Dr. C. W. Hodge, was the author's idea that "the Canon is determined subjectively by the Christian feeling of the Church, & not by history, and that it is illogical to prove first canonicity, & then Inspiration." If this be accepted, "you have given away the whole historical side of the argument for the Apostolic origin of the Books and of Christianity itself." "I also think the article vague and unsatisfactory and am confirmed in my opinion that the author is more learned than clear headed, and does not think himself out in his principles." In the light of changes that soon occurred in American theological thought, Dr. C. W. Hodge's prognostication was strikingly discerning: "What results these principles would lead him [i.e., Dr. Briggs] to, no one can say. Probably nothing bad in his case, but nothing would be too much for others." A repetition of the Robertson Smith heresy prosecution should be avoided: "The Scottish aspect of the question is most unfortunate, for it looks like arbitrary suppression of truth. That state of things need not be imported here." Coming from one who published no theological writings, the letter contains about the best brief analysis which these years produced of the points at issue in the Presbyterian Biblical controversy.[26] A former student of Dr. Briggs on the faculty of the Seminary of the Northwest, Edward L. Curtis, told Dr. Briggs that in that area of the Church Dr. Briggs was "looked upon with some suspicion."[27]

On the other hand, there were some in the Church who were in sympathy with the views expressed in Dr. Briggs's article. Professor Henry Preserved Smith of Lane Seminary at this stage of his career inclined toward making an objective historical presentation of controversial Old Testament problems, but he assured Dr. Briggs, "You shall have my hearty support on anything you may say on the side of freedom," a promise he later fulfilled at great cost. Significant was Professor Smith's testimony concerning New School conservatism on Biblical questions: "The former New School men so far as I know them were (and are) more conservative on questions of [Biblical] Introduction than on any others." Having in mind no doubt the precarious position of Lane as a small former New School seminary in a prevailingly Old School environment, he observed that "many of our friends here would deprecate having any suspicion cast on the teaching at Lane."[28]

It was Dr. Briggs's hope that the Presbyterian Church, rejecting unbelieving or "rationalistic" Biblical criticism, might accept a moderate Biblical criticism on a soundly evangelical basis, and thus avoid the extremes of reactionary conservatism and radical skepticism. At this stage he bent his best energies toward preventing the very thing that later happened in the Presbyterian Church and in much of American Protestantism—a sterile dichotomy between "fundamentalists" and "liberals" over a theory of the Bible which did not involve the essentials of Christianity. Planning boldly, Dr. Briggs thought that if the leaders of opposing viewpoints in the Church could be brought close together in the *Presbyterian Review* and there forge a working unity, they could lead the Church peaceably through its time of trouble. The strategy was as risky as it was statesmanlike. If they could not resolve their differences, proximity would make explosion all the more likely—and deadly. Thus he wrote to his coeditor: "Is it not far better for you & me to have this trouble in private & to strive for adjustment even at the exercise of patience & forbearance, than to have these antagonisms made into strugglg [*sic*] parties in our church?" [29] But relations were not improved when a few months later an anonymous article in the *New York Evangelist,* the authorship of which Dr. Briggs later acknowledged, commented rather sharply on Dr. Patton's inaugural address at Princeton Seminary.[30]

The *Presbyterian Review* series of articles on Biblical issues moved on schedule in spite of editorial complications. The third article, by Professor William Henry Green on "Prof. Robertson Smith on the Pentateuch," appeared in January 1882. With scholarship and analytic keenness he attacked the radical reconstruction of Israelitish history as proposed by Wellhausen and as represented in a recent book by Robertson Smith.[31]

The fourth article in the *Presbyterian Review* series—that by Henry Preserved Smith on "The Critical Theories of Julius Wellhausen"—was of special interest both because it was in connection with its preparation that the author's views on higher criticism began to crystallize, and because his Old Testament views became, a decade later, an object of denomination-wide concern. The article appeared in April 1882. Only a year before it was published Professor Smith had "never paid much attention to Wellhausen" and, at that time, was still inclined to affirm the Mosaic authorship of the Pentateuch.[32] But by the time he had got well into the preparation of the article, his tone had changed: "I am sure I shall be critical enough . . . about the orthodoxy I have more doubt." [33]

Professor Smith possessed much less creative imagination and ecclesiastical leadership than Dr. Briggs, but in analysis he was more painstaking, objective, and relentlessly logical. The general literature and history of Israel are too fragmentary, he declares in his article, to make it possible to apply adequately to Pentateuchal study the principle that an author's work is likely to reflect his historical situation. Accepting it as axiomatic that an author's work will be influenced by the ethical and religious conceptions of his time, Professor Smith says that "it is now universally acknowledged that there is progress in revelation." This view, combined with the author's statement that we must regard "as unsettled all questions touching the age or authorship of these different parts" of the Pentateuch, left the door open for the reconstruction of Old Testament history. Very discerningly the author calls attention to Wellhausen's too exclusively literary method. He also rejects certain specific conclusions of Wellhausen, but the article leaves the author's position in relation to many of Wellhausen's basic conceptions quite unrevealed, and conveys the impression that he is favorable toward Wellhausen's work as a whole.[34] His final word is an exhortation to open-mindedness and self-examination. Although Professor Smith had not fully expressed himself,[35] his article carried the discussion in the *Presbyterian Review* to new ground.

With the mounting interest in the higher criticism, the General Assembly of 1882 commented on "the introduction and prevalence of German mysticism and 'higher criticism,' and of philosophic speculation and so-called scientific evolution" and warned "all who give instruction in our Theological Seminaries, against inculcating any views, or adopting any methods, which may tend to unsettle faith in the doctrine of the divine origin and plenary inspiration of the Scriptures, held by our Church, or in our Presbyterian systems of doctrine."[36] Professor Smith's article soon became the object of adverse comment in a number of church newspapers.[37] Dr. Morris, ever attentive, had heard rumors of an intended attack on Professor Smith and on Lane Seminary, but as it entered upon its autumn work the seminary was uninjured and facing a promising year.[38] Dr. J. G. Monfort, editor of the *Herald and Presbyter* of Cincinnati, a former Old School man and one of the shrewdest leaders of the Church, warned Dr. Briggs that "the feeling is that you & our Professor Smith have conceded too much. . . . This feeling is strong in both O[ld] S[chool] and N[ew] S[chool] circles."[39] The reference to the opposition of former New School men to the negative conclusions of the higher criticism is particularly significant. The summer of 1882 was a warm one, theologically speaking, but by autumn the atmosphere was becoming more comfortable.[40] The widespread controversy which seemed imminent in the wake of Professor H. P. Smith's article was postponed for nearly a decade.

Even during these discussions at least ecclesiastical differences between Old School and New School were receding farther and farther into the background. Until 1882 the moderators of the General Assembly were chosen alternately from former Old School and New School men. But in 1882 Dr. Herrick Johnson of Chicago, formerly of the New School, succeeded a New School man as moderator. This broke the alternation and was widely hailed as one more symbol of unity. When Dr. Edwin F. Hatfield was elected moderator the next year, making the third former New School man in succession, the editor of the *Presbyterian*, a former Old School man, was asked, "How will it be received among the former Old School?" His jovial reply was, "There will be no complaint anywhere this side of six."[41] The old issues had given place to new, and the lines of division were not identical.

The fifth and sixth articles of the *Presbyterian Review* series took a median position and provoked but little comment. Though supposedly representing opposite "sides," they were moderate and mediating.[42]

The seventh article of the series—the last for Dr. Briggs's "side"—was by Dr. Briggs himself. In the article, Dr. Briggs concedes that the Pentateuch is a compilation of four principal documents, but would date them in and very soon after the time of Moses. He admits difficulties in the silence or near silence about these codes in the centuries immediately following, and sees special congruities between the codes and the later periods at which radical criticism supposed them to have originated, but finds these difficulties more than counterbalanced by linguistic factors, by reflections of earlier life in the codes, by the fact that the codes were in part ideal and predictive, by difficulties of securing reception for any supposed "new" codes, as well as by other considerations.[43] The fact that Dr. Briggs's grasp of the problem is so much more vivid and convincing than his solution of it in this article suggests that his thinking on the subject was in a state of unstable equilibrium. That the position as he presents it here could hardly be a permanent one is confirmed by the views of such opposite critics as Professors William Henry Green and Warfield on the one hand and Professor W. Robertson Smith on the other.[44]

The eighth and last article of the *Review* series was by Dr. Patton, who had recently succeeded Dr. Hodge as the Princeton coeditor. In concluding the series, Dr. Patton observed that all contributors to it, though differing among themselves, had repudiated naturalism and the views of Wellhausen.[45] Undoubtedly because he shared the Princeton Theology's fear lest subjectivism lose the objective foundations of Christianity, Dr. Patton decried emphasizing the witness of the Holy Spirit in such a way as to belittle the intellectual defenses of Chrisitanity or as to be indifferent to the conclusions of Biblical criticism. And, he added, our subjective experience of the witness of the Spirit cannot be used to persuade others of the truth of Christianity.[46] The doctrine of inspiration is important to Dr. Patton as a guarantee of the objective trustworthiness of the gospel message. But—it might be objected—is the doctrine of verbal inspiration actually necessary to guarantee the objective trustworthiness of the gospel message, and is it competent to ensure its subjective appropriation by the hearer? More typically and more broadly, the Princeton Theology was accustomed to argue from the trustworthiness of Scripture to its inspiration. To argue back again from its inspiration to its trustworthiness was to move in a circle.

Dr. Patton had a strict view of the limitations that the Westminster Confession placed on Biblical criticism. "He [the Biblical critic] is free to investigate, but he is not free to teach contrary to the Confession of Faith."

He defined as contra-confessional "any opinion inconsistent with the inerrancy of Scripture" and "belief in the non-Mosaic authorship of the Pentateuch." [47]

Contrary to the growing ecclesiastical practice of his day, Dr. Patton disfavored attempts by the General Assembly to settle great theological questions by pronouncements, saying that such important decisions should be reached by the more deliberate processes of "a concrete case"—that is, of a heresy prosecution.[48] Dr. R. W. Patterson of Chicago, who had debated with Dr. Patton in the Swing trial, thought the article "more moderate" than he "expected," and commented, "I am glad of what he says about Assembly deliverances," though apparently ignoring Dr. Patton's allusion to heresy proceedings.[49]

The closing articles of the *Presbyterian Review* series did not arouse controversy. It is true, the General Assembly of 1883, in answer to overtures from five presbyteries, issued a deliverance against "the rationalistic treatment of the Holy Scriptures by Protestant teachers in Europe, whose works are introduced into our country, and whose evil influence is felt in our Church. . . . The denial of the authenticity or truthfulness of the Holy Scriptures is a denial of their inspiration." Presbyteries were reminded that "it is incumbent upon them to see to it that the appropriate constitutional action be taken, if at any time it should become manifest, that any minister of our Church was promulgating theories of dangerous tendency, or contraConfessional doctrine, concerning the Holy Scriptures." [50] The weekly *Presbyterian* was sufficiently satisfied by the Assembly's action to discontinue the series of articles which it had been running for some months attacking Pentateuchal criticism.[51]

During these years Dr. Briggs, who was the recognized leader of Presbyterians favoring larger theological freedom,[52] was also busy as an author. His *Biblical Study: Its Principles, Methods and History*, which appeared in 1883, was a reworking of material previously presented in articles and addresses. Here he again denounces Protestant scholasticism and contrasts with it the spirit and principles of the Westminster divines.[53] He finds pseudonymous writings in the Old Testament—certainly Ecclesiastes, perhaps also Deuteronomy and Daniel—but this does not affect the "authenticity" of the Bible, which does not depend on its human authorship, but on its divine source. He makes the disturbing suggestion that the Bible contains myth and legend without indicating to what areas of Biblical history he considers these literary types limited.[54] Professor A. B. Bruce of the University of Glasgow construed the book as a "polemic with the *Rabbis* of Princeton." Though it received some sharp criticism it provoked no general controversy.[55]

American Presbyterianism, published by Dr. Briggs in 1885, was a very able rewriting of the denomination's colonial history in the light of the assumption that the Old Side-Old School tradition, which at the time of his writing found its most vigorous embodiment in the Princeton Theology, was not the simon-pure orthodoxy that it considered itself, but was rather an orthodoxy corrupted by increasing admixtures of scholasticism. By adding this penetrating historical study to his numerous Biblical studies, Dr. Briggs was coming to be regarded by an increasing number in the Church as a "dangerous" man. But many welcomed the volume. Dr. John DeWitt of Lane, later to be professor of church history at Princeton Seminary, told him, "You have put beyond future controversy the catholic character of American Presbyterianism." [56]

Messianic Prophecy, also by Dr. Briggs, appearing in 1886, clearly takes the position that the latter portion of the book of Isaiah was written during the exile by a "great unknown." [57] The tone in which the author rejects the traditional view of Isaiah's authorship of the entire book is quiet and unobtrusive. Concerning the book of Daniel he says, "We should not be disturbed if its stories were fiction, composed with the design to point the lesson of fidelity to God, or if the predictions were pseudepigraphic . . . indeed we have an example of such fiction in Esther, and of such a pseudepigraph in Ecclesiastes." But Dr. Briggs himself rejects this view and holds that "the predictions were delivered by the Daniel of the exile."[58] The book was a further step in identifying Dr. Briggs's name with critical views of the Bible.

The *Presbyterian Review* during the years 1883-88 was under the coeditorship of Drs. Briggs and Patton. In addition to the underlying differences of viewpoint and strategy of the coeditors, the journal faced difficulties of an economic sort. Efforts to broaden the review's base by including associate editors from the British Isles and Canada met with some nationalistic objections in America.[59] In May 1888, word came that Dr. Patton had resigned as coeditor and that the Princeton Seminary faculty had elected Dr. Warfield as his successor.[60]

Dr. Warfield, when professor at Western Seminary, had opposed the founding of the *Presbyterian Review* "and to the bitter end begged that no such compromise measure should be taken. But," he added, "once founded and the Old School Seminaries once involved & I esteem it my duty to do what little I can to forward the Old School interest in the Review." [61] Having made his decision, Dr. Warfield loyally supported the Review.[62] When he entered upon his duties as coeditor, the quarterly's future was already highly problematical.[63]

The initiative in the founding of the *Review* had been Dr. Briggs's and his successive Princeton colleagues had quite willingly allowed him the editorial lead. But Dr. Warfield, it was evident from the outset, had quite a different view of the matter and was determined to share responsibilities at least equally. This fact, together with accumulated tensions, and the new issue of revision of the Confession, made an explosion inevitable. Nor was it long in coming. Dr. Briggs's letters, as was their custom, poured in a steady stream of information and suggestions with little or no time wasted on pleasantries. The number of suggestions that Dr. Warfield could absorb was quite limited. In November 1888, it was a book review that divided them; the next March it was church and state and the new English creed. But the *coup de grâce* was supplied by disagreement as to procedures for discussing the issue of creed revision, which had been broached by the General Assembly of 1889. When on June 4 Dr. Warfield offered to the Princeton Seminary faculty his resignation as coeditor the faculty declined to accept it, but did accept it when offered again in October, and elected Dr. Aiken to succeed him.[64] But on October 4 the Union Seminary faculty recommended a discontinuance of the *Review*. The Presbyterian Review Association accordingly voted that publication of the *Review* cease with the issue of October 1889, and on motion of Dr. Aiken of Princeton unanimously expressed hearty appreciation of Dr. Briggs's labors. Dr. Morris saw in the collapse of the joint undertaking the threat of rival party organs in the near future with peril to the Church's peace.[65]

Many events had contributed to the final breaking of this important bond of theological unity in the Church, but the immediate occasion was the attempt to revise the Church's principal theological standard, the Westminster Confession of Faith.

5.

revision attempted

Man's dignity and confidence were rising to new heights in the late nineteenth-century world in which the Westminster Confession of Faith found itself. The Renaissance, and after it the Enlightenment, had turned attention away from the next life to the present life, away from God's sovereignty to man's worth and capacity. Economic life was rapidly expanding in most Western nations; industry and imperialism were growing apace. America, with its self-made industrial barons and its rapidly receding frontier, was particularly loud in its emphasis on human initiative.

In such an age and particularly in such a land, the Presbyterian Church could not avoid another look at its Calvinistic heritage, and especially at the formulation of that heritage in the Church's principal doctrinal standard, the Westminster Confession of Faith.

It was religious rather than philosophical or speculative considerations which led early Calvinism to emphasize God's sovereignty. "I was lost in sin," the early Calvinist said in effect, "so completely lost that I did not even desire God's help. But later when I did desire divine help I did so only because God himself first planted that desire in my heart, and so all glory and honor belong to him, and I have no grounds for boasting or pride." But this deeply religious conviction led straight to acute philosophical and speculative problems concerning the relation of the divine to the human will. As the years passed, John Calvin, with his severely logical mind, could not escape increasing involvement in the metaphysics of predestination, and this was even truer of some of his followers. And if the redeemed must credit God with taking all the initiative in their redemption, what must be said about the lack of divine initiative toward the unredeemed? Inevitably, increasing speculation forced into prominence a parallel negative doctrine of reprobation, which even Calvin called "an awful [*horribile*] decree." Often stark "double predestination" with its doctrine of "reprobation" was softened to "preterition," God's negative "passing by" the unredeemed instead of his positively reprobating or predestinating them to perdition.

The Westminster Confession of Faith was written in the 1640's after Calvinism had been challenged by Arminianism. Arminianism, appearing in the Netherlands in the early seventeenth century as one of the harbingers of the Enlightenment, stressed man's free will and spiritual ability. Calvinism's answer to this challenge was to emphasize still more God's sovereignty and such related doctrines as predestination and man's spiritual inability. The Anglican party in the Church of England, under William Laud's leadership, leaned strongly toward Arminianism and this helped to keep to the fore among the Puritan authors of the Westminster Confession an anti-Arminian emphasis. The sixteenth-century Calvinistic creeds, such as the Belgic Confession (1561) and the Heidelberg Catechism (1563), on the other hand, were written before the Arminian issue arose and are much more moderate in their emphasis on the divine sovereignty. It is not surprising, therefore, that while the Anglo-Saxon Presbyterian Churches found difficulties in their Westminster Confession in the later nineteenth century, the Continental Reformed Churches did not find comparable difficulties in their earlier sixteenth-century creeds. Then, too, the Westminster Confession, coming in the second century of the Reformation, shared some of Calvinistic scholasticism's elaboration in analysis and definition. It was, by the same token, the fullest, most "scientific," and exhaustive of all the Calvinistic creeds. The Confession's Chapter III, "Of God's Eternal Decree," and part of its Chapter X, "Of Effectual Calling"—

Optomism of 19th Century conflicted with the pessimism of W.C. concerning man's ability and [illegible] Inevitably to revision.

Calvin had beed dominated by his view of Predestination and Reprobation.

Anti-Armenian emphasis was not found in European Reformed creeds, but it dominated the W.C., 19th C. Europeans, therefore, had less difficulty with their creeds.

especially the phrase "elect infants," with its intimation that some infants might be nonelect—were the chief objects of criticism in the late nineteenth century.

In nineteenth-century America even strict Calvinists like Dr. Charles Hodge inclined toward mollifying rather than accentuating aspects of their heritage. Dr. Hodge's personal temperament, in typically American fashion, was prevailingly optimistic. Reflecting this more optimistic mood was Dr. Hodge's departure from the older Calvinism in his positive expectation that all dying in infancy would be saved, and that the great majority of the human race would be saved.[1] Even these more optimistic speculations could be inserted, it was felt, without drastic overhauling of the framework of the Calvinistic theology. A more serious challenge to the Calvinistic scheme of things had been posed by New School Presbyterianism, which borrowed from the New England Theology various "improvements" on historic Calvinism looking in the direction of greater emphasis on man's responsibility in the face of God's sovereignty. It was natural, therefore, that the New School heritage contributed much to the American Presbyterian revision movement.[2]

The British Presbyterian Churches led the way in seeking to make adjustments in the Westminster Confession.[3] The desire for revision among the various Presbyterian bodies was stimulated and extended by The Alliance of Reformed Churches throughout the World Holding the Presbyterian System, which from 1877 to 1884 was considering the drafting of a consensus creed.[4] Meanwhile, the Presbyterians' ecclesiastical kinsmen, the American Congregationalists, drafted a new creed in 1883.[5]

With creedal revision "in the air" the issue could not be avoided by Presbyterians in America. Hardly was the reunion of Old School and New School consummated in 1869 before some began to desire creedal revision.[6] A series of articles in the *New York Evangelist* in the closing months of 1887 commented on the Westminster Confession, pro and con.[7] An overture on revision to the General Assembly of 1888 from the Presbytery of Nassau on Long Island was, in the rush of business, "referred to the next Assembly."[8] Between General Assemblies, Nassau Presbytery circularized the other presbyteries of the Church, citing the example of Scottish and English Presbyterians. Matters came to a head when fourteen or fifteen presbyteries in addition to the Presbytery of Nassau overtured the 1889 Assembly, asking for revision of the Westminster Confession of Faith. The General Assembly voted by an overwhelming majority to submit two questions to the presbyteries of the Church: "1. Do you desire a revision of the Confession of Faith? 2. If so, in what respects, and to what extent?"[9]

The unexpected action of the General Assembly in thus raising the issue of confessional revision threw the Presbyterian Church into sudden and widespread controversy. Some favored revision, some opposed it, while still others favored the writing of a new and simpler consensus creed.

Many at once thought that they saw in the revision controversy larger and deeper issues than those expressly defined. Some of the best minds of the Church felt that the latent and inevitable conflict between seventeenth-century orthodoxy and the spirit of nineteenth-century science and criticism had now suddenly been forced into the light, and had for the first time become the subject of widespread controversy within the Presbyterian Church. Some on both sides of the debate felt that powerful forces of theological change gathering beneath the surface had now broken forth in an earthquake which would prove to be no mere passing tremor, but would alter the entire theological landscape. Some saw, or hoped they saw, a new and more inclusive conception of the Church taking shape.

Thus Dr. Briggs, who soon took his stand as a leader for a new creed, saw great confusion in contemporary British and American Christianity resulting from the fact that many were dissatisfied with the old theology and the old methods of church work and worship, but had not yet acquired confidence in the new theology and the new methods. Outworn denominational issues were now giving place to the more important contest between conservatives and progressives, cutting across denominational lines. He wanted denominational fences broken down entirely,[10] and saw in the action of the General Assembly in submitting creedal revision to the consideration of the Church the possible beginnings of the needed theological reconstruction. "The General Assembly started the flame . . . and now the whole church is ablaze. . . . We are in the beginnings of a theological reformation that can no more be resisted than the flow of a great river." [11]

Professor Philip Schaff, the distinguished church historian, announced that "the General Assembly of 1889" had "opened a new chapter in the history of American theology." "The old Calvinism," said he, "is fast dying out." "We need a theology and a confession that will . . . prepare the way for the great work of the future—the reunion of Christendom in the Creed of Christ." [12] Other Presbyterians, too, were stressing the possibilities that revision held for church union, without naming any denominations in particular.[13]

Dr. Francis L. Patton, by this time president of the College of New Jersey, and a stanch opponent of revision, thought that the conception of the Church itself was the real point at issue. "The real question in the minds of some of our leading men is whether the denominations have not outlived their usefulness." He saw creedal revision as an intended step in the direction of a more inclusive churchmanship. "The Reunion of Christendom, as that phrase is commonly understood, I do not believe in. . . . The way to conserve that which is common to all is for each denomination to be jealous of the doctrine that is peculiar to itself." While he regretted the emergence of the revision controversy, he did not think that its latent dangers would materialize.[14]

While a part of the discussion dealt with the underlying significance of the revision movement, most of it was occupied with immediate issues. Should the Confession be revised or should it not be?

Opponents of revision took the position that the Confession was entirely satisfactory as it stood. Dr. DeWitt challenged critics of the Confession to draft acceptable amendments. When Dr. Henry J. Van Dyke of Brooklyn accepted the challenge, Dr. DeWitt undertook to show the superiority of the original.[15] The revisionists acquired a valued prize in Dr. Van Dyke, a former Old School man who had voted against reunion, and who had once been noted for his theological conservatism.[16] Dr. Van Dyke had been moderator of the General Assembly of 1876.

While opponents of revision were committed to a defense strategy, advocates of revision necessarily pressed the offensive. With great learning Professor Briggs sought to show that American Presbyterianism had not only radically altered the polity and worship set forth in the Westminster Standards, but had very extensively modified the Westminster theology as well. He even charged that Dr. Charles Hodge and Dr. A. A. Hodge, the theologians most revered by Presbyterians opposed to revision, had been the chief offenders in this regard, substituting Dutch and Swiss scholastic theology for the theology of the Westminster Standards.[17] It was a notable effort to turn the tables completely on the champions of orthodoxy.

Dr. Van Dyke proved to be one of the most effective advocates of revision. He listed three principal objections to the Confession as it stood: its doctrine of reprobation; its phrase "elect infants," which, he said, implied that some infants were damned; and the lack of any clear statement in the Confession of God's universal provision and free offer of salvation in Christ.[18] Discussion throughout the Church focused largely on these same three criticisms. Dr. Van Dyke charged that the Confession stressed God's sovereignty but sadly neglected the complementary truth of his "infinite love for all men. . . . The true Calvinist believes both, and insists that they are consistent. . . . The ultimate and dominant reason why I advocate the revision of the Westminster Confession is that it does not state these two truths in their relations and harmony." [19]

Other church leaders, too, voiced their desires for revision. Professor Herrick Johnson of McCormick Seminary felt that the Confession should be amended to state more adequately the doctrinal foundations of the modern missionary movement.[20] Professor John T. Duffield, of the College of New Jersey, said that the Confession's silence on God's love for all men was not accidental, but that after deliberation the Westminster divines voted to remain silent on the matter. This critic also joined the attack on the ambiguous phrase "elect infants." [21]

When the General Assembly convened in May 1890, it was soon discov-

The following table illustrates the geographical distribution of conservative and liberal tendencies within the Church as shown by the votes of the presbyteries on the revision overture during the year 1889-90.

GEOGRAPHICAL ANALYSIS OF PRESBYTERIAL VOTE ON REVISION

AREA	Number of Presbyteries in Area	Presbyteries Voting in Affirmative	Presbyteries Voting in Negative	Presbyteries Not Voting	Percentage of Presbyteries of Area Voting in Affirmative	Percentage of Total Affirmative Vote Supplied by This Area
NEW ENGLAND	1	0	1	0	0%	0%
NEW YORK	25	22	2	1	88%	16%
NEW JERSEY	8	5	3	0	63%	4%
PENNSYLVANIA	21	4	17	0	19%	3%
SOUTH (entire Southeast and also Delaware, Maryland, Kentucky, Missouri, Indian Territory, Texas)	33	12	19	2	36%	9%
EAST CENTRAL (West Virginia, Ohio, Indiana, Illinois, Michigan, Wisconsin)	51	43	8	0	84%	32%
WEST CENTRAL (Minnesota, Iowa, North Dakota, South Dakota, Nebraska, Kansas)	33	25	8	0	76%	19%
ROCKY MOUNTAIN	11	11	0	0	100%	8%
PACIFIC COAST	11	8	3	0	73%	6%
FOREIGN	19	4	7	8	21%	3%
TOTALS	213	134	68	11		

ered that the Church as a whole strongly desired revision. Of the 213 presbyteries in the Church, 134, or almost 63 per cent, had voted in favor of undertaking some kind of revision. Any specific amendments to the Confession which might later be proposed would have to receive a still larger vote, a two-thirds majority of the presbyteries, but this was a very impressive opening response in favor of alteration and made further action on the matter almost mandatory. Of the remaining presbyteries, sixty-eight opposed revision, while eleven, of which seven were on the foreign mission field, failed to vote at all.

The table reveals at a glance that the strength of Presbyterian liberalism—at least with reference to the revision issue—lay in New York and in the Middle West (that is, "New York" and the "East Central" and "West Central" states on the table). It is also apparent that the stronghold of opposition to revision lay in Pennsylvania and the South.

The responses of the presbyteries to revision, when analyzed according to their content by the General Assembly's stated clerk, revealed some interesting facts. More presbyteries criticized the Westminster Confession of Faith in Chapter III, "Of God's Eternal Decree," and in Chapter X, "Of Effectual Calling," than at any other point. Chapter XXV, Section 6, which branded the pope as anti-Christ, was challenged by fifty-five presbyteries. Clearly, the religious bitterness of Reformation days—the American nativist movement to the contrary notwithstanding—had waned.

The presbyteries also had a number of positive suggestions. To mention only a few, ninety-three presbyteries desired a more explicit statement of the "Love of God for the world." Sixty presbyteries wanted recognition in the Confession of Faith of the "Church's duty to evangelize the world," an emphasis which had arisen since the meeting of the Westminster Assembly in the seventeenth century. Twenty-one presbyteries asked for a "brief, popular creed." [22]

The great majority of presbyteries desired revision of some sort, but prevailing sentiment was found to be opposed to any radical alterations. Though 134 presbyteries desired revision of some kind, 69 (later 93) of these expressly declared that they did not desire any revision which would impair the integrity of the system of doctrine taught in the Confession. When to those desiring limited revision are added the 68 opposed to all revision, it is evident that a total of 137 (later 161) presbyteries were opposed to radical revision.[23]

In the light of these facts, what action would the General Assembly of 1890 take? Debate on the floor of the Assembly was protracted. Dr. Adam McClelland of Dubuque Seminary reminded revisionists that if the peace of the Church was to be preserved they must offer as well as demand compromise. But it was Dr. Patton who captured leadership of the movement. Seeing the large majority favoring some revision, rather than allow moderate revisionists to unite with more radical revisionists, he effected a combination of antirevisionists and moderate revisionists to make sure that any revision would be relatively innocuous. He vigorously supported the motion to appoint a Committee on Revision and at the same time to instruct it not to propose "any alterations or amendments that will in any way impair the integrity of the Reformed or Calvinistic system of doctrine taught in the Confession of Faith." [24] One lone antirevisionist spoke against the motion. Die-hard opponents of revision refrained from voting, and the Assembly unanimously adopted the motion to appoint a revision committee and to instruct it not to impair the Reformed system of doctrine.[25] The *Andover Review,* watching intently from the sidelines, was deeply chagrined at what it considered the surrender of the revisionists to the moderates in the interests of peace.[26]

An entirely separate committee was created to explore the possibilities of drafting a new consensus creed in conjunction with other Presbyterian and Reformed Churches. This movement was thus separated from the movement to amend the existing Confession. It attracted but little attention and quietly petered out seven years later.[27] Thus the various forces seeking creedal alteration were divided and weakened.

The General Assembly of 1890 elected a Revision Committee of twenty-five. After an organizing meeting and a later session lasting two weeks, the committee was able to present to the General Assembly of 1891 tentative recommendations for revision of the Confession. This Assembly voted to send copies of the tentative report to all the presbyteries with the request that presbyteries forward criticisms and suggestions to the committee before December 1, 1891, in time to be incorporated in a definitive report to the Assembly of 1892.[28]

After making extensive use of various suggestions received from the presbyteries the committee had its final report ready for the General Assembly of 1892. The committee proposed that overtures amending the Confession of Faith be sent down to the presbyteries, at the same time assuring the Assembly that the proposed amendments were quite safe: "None of them, if adopted, will, in the judgment of the Committee, impair in any way the integrity of the Reformed or Calvinistic system of doctrine taught in the Confession of Faith." In signing this report, twelve of the twenty-four members of the committee took exception to individual overtures. One member took exception to twelve of the twenty-eight overtures.[29] The revision issue was somewhat complicated by the fact that some had misgivings as to whether constitutional procedures were being properly followed. Some church weeklies, too, regretted the haste with which the Assembly adopted the Revision Committee's report.[30]

The revision proposals were now before the Church in their final form. Some revision leaders voiced extreme discontent and even implied that relief was necessary if church fellowship was to continue unbroken. Some of the most conservative, too, were keenly aware of a state of tension. Thus

Dr. Warfield concluded his comments on the Revision Committee's final report with a veiled warning of a possible disruption of the Church: "When the proposed revisions are incorporated into the Confession, shall we still have a Confession which is Calvinistic and can be accepted? . . . The answer to the . . . question will determine whether, if all these revisions were forced upon us, the situation would be tolerable." [31] Not many opponents of revision seem to have regarded the committee's final report so apprehensively.

The General Assembly of 1893 received the answers from the presbyteries of the Church on which depended, for the present at least, the fate of the revision movement. There were 220 presbyteries. To be enacted any amendment to the Confession had to receive the approval of two thirds of these presbyteries, that is, 147. The highest vote received for any revision overture was 115, the lowest 67. Thus no revision took place. Some of the presbyteries threw away their votes—fifteen made no report on any overture, thirteen reported no action on any, and seventeen doubted the constitutionality of all the overtures.[32] This bloc of forty-five unused votes, if cast in the affirmative, would have enacted all but three of the twenty-nine overtures. But even if the presbyteries which challenged the constitutionality of the procedure had voted in the affirmative, no overture would have been adopted thereby.

For the moment the revision movement had failed. But, though no amendments to the Confession were adopted, the controversy was an important milestone in the Church's history. The general lines along which revision might be feasible had been explored. Still more important—and ominous—the inherent conflict was revealed between the forces of theological change so prominent in the latter part of the nineteenth century and the forces opposed to all theological change. This conflict transcended in importance the propositions specifically discussed in the revision controversy and was vaguely sensed rather than sharply defined.

One important factor in defeating the revision movement was the charge of heresy which was formally made against Professor Charles A. Briggs, a leading advocate of revision.

6.

the briggs case

The prosecution of Professor Charles A. Briggs for heresy was the result of theological and personal forces that had long been building up within the Presbyterian Church. Presbyterians had been alarmed by the debate of Biblical questions in the *Presbyterian Review* and by Dr. Briggs's book-length studies of Biblical and denominational questions, as well as by his attitude toward revision of the Westminster Confession. Dr. Briggs later thought, too, that a debate in the journal *Hebraica* (1888-92) between Dr. William Henry Green and Dr. William Rainey Harper, incoming president of the University of Chicago, by identifying higher criticism in America with the more radical views, had prejudiced some against his own more moderate position.[1]

In various ways Dr. Briggs had been inviting personal enmities. His criticism of the recent Revised Version of the Old Testament as too timid had been sharp and his retort to an influential New York critic in the spring of 1889 was characteristic of his less diplomatic moments.[2] Early in June 1889 relations between him and Dr. Warfield as coeditors of the *Presbyterian Review* were becoming mutually unbearable, and before the end of the month Dr. Briggs completed the first draft of a new book entitled *Whither?* On September 14 it came off the press.[3] Although he had been many years collecting materials of this type,[4] and although parts of it had been foreshadowed in some of his previous writings, the tone and time of appearance of *Whither?* clearly mark it as a tract for the times. Citing numerous passages by name from the Princeton theologians Archibald Alexander and the two Hodges as well as from the writings of his colleague, Dr. Shedd, and Dr. Howard Crosby, a leading conservative in New York Presbytery, he sought to show that these and other pillars of orthodoxy had actually departed from the Westminster Confession again and again in the direction of a Calvinistic scholasticism. He belittled traditional dogmatics in comparison with the newer Biblical theology. The tone was so far from objective that many—including some of Dr. Briggs's friends—regretted it.[5] But the book was in such demand that early the next year a third and revised edition was published.[6] What was perhaps most offensive, there was enough theological correctness in the attack to make it hurt.

If the course of events was leading an increasing number of Presbyterians to suspect and fear Dr. Briggs's theological views, it was also leading him to fear for the success of the theological ideals which he held for the Church. The last issue of the *Presbyterian Review* was dated October 1889, and under date of January 1890 a new theological journal, the *Presbyterian and Reformed Review*, under the complete control of Dr. Warfield, had come into being, with an "associate editor" appointed by Dr. Warfield from each of the seminaries represented in the old review.[7] That such impressive support should be organized around so conservative and vigorous a leader boded ill for the broader policies that Dr. Briggs had in view for the Church, especially since nothing came of Dr. Briggs's own intermittent—and this time apparently half-hearted—explorations for a new liberal journal.[8]

It was while church affairs were at this juncture that the Union Seminary directors in November 1890 transferred Dr. Briggs from the chair he had been occupying since 1876 to the newly created chair of Biblical theology. If Dr. Briggs was discouraged about recent ecclesiastical trends, a letter of congratulations over this new appointment from his distinguished friend, Principal Andrew M. Fairbairn of Mansfield College, Oxford, whom he had known since their student days in Berlin,[9] must have been heartening: "Hold the fort. The drift in the Presbyt. Church is not happy. . . . It would not do to leave her [the Church] to the dominion of the Old School in a new access of narrowness. . . . I was alarmed at your tone as to the Church, & am anxious you shd. feel not solitary in your brave fight. So many hang on you that your battle is not simply your own." [10]

On January 20, 1891—exactly one month after Principal Fairbairn had penned his exhortation—Dr. Briggs, wearing the hood of his Edinburgh doctorate of divinity and speaking for an hour and three quarters, delivered his inaugural address.[11] The inaugural echoed from coast to coast, and permanently affected the fortunes of himself, the seminary he loyally served, and the Church he loved.

Dr. Briggs's inaugural was entitled "The Authority of Holy Scripture." In discussing the sources of divine authority, he noted three—the Church, the Reason, and the Bible—without saying whether they were coördinate or not. He selected as examples of those who have found God by each of these methods, respectively, Newman, the Roman Catholic; Martineau, the Unitarian; and Spurgeon, the Protestant. "The average opinion of the Christian world would not assign him [Spurgeon] a higher place in the kingdom of God than Martineau or Newman." [12]

Dr. Briggs then listed six "barriers" to the operation of divine authority in the Bible. *Superstition* in the form of "Bibliolatry" often constitutes such a barrier. So, too, he said, does the doctrine of *verbal inspiration*. "No such claim is found in the Bible itself, or in any of the creeds of Christendom." [13] Too great anxiety for the *authenticity* of the Biblical books can be a barrier to their spiritual effectiveness. Here he was attacking the familiar conception of canonicity held by the Princeton Seminary men as well as by his former teacher, Professor Henry Boynton Smith, whom he greatly revered. "The only authenticity we are concerned about in seeking for the divine authority of the Scriptures is *divine authenticity*." And in words that were often to be quoted against him, he added: "It may be regarded as the certain result of the science of the Higher Criticism that Moses did not write the Pentateuch. . . . Isaiah did not write half of the book that bears his name." [14] He had said this before,[15] but more hesitantly and with important qualifications.

Dr. Briggs then listed the doctrine of the *inerrancy* of the Bible as a fourth barrier to the operation of divine authority in the Bible. "It has been taught in recent years . . . that one proved error destroys the authority of Scripture. I shall venture to affirm that, so far as I can see, there are errors in the Scriptures that no one has been able to explain away; and the theory that they were not in the original text is sheer assumption." This was a called shot at the central teaching of the Hodge-Warfield article on "Inspiration" [16] which was on the verge of being proclaimed the Church's official doctrine. The common conception of miracles as a *violation of the laws of nature* the inaugural also branded as a barrier for scientifically-minded men. Dr. Briggs found a sixth barrier in the conception of prophecy as *minute prediction*, as though prophecy were "a sort of history before the time." "Kuenen has shown," he noted with apparent approval, "that if we insist upon the fulfilment of the details of the predictive prophecy of the Old Testament, many of these predictions have been reversed by history; and the great body of the Messianic prediction has not only never been fulfilled, but cannot now be fulfilled, for the reason that its own time has passed forever." [17]

In discussing the theology of the Bible, Dr. Briggs in his inaugural threw out some further challenges to accepted views. He showed little sympathy for the doctrine of original sin. "Protestant theologians have exaggerated the original righteousness in order to magnify the guilt of our first parents." [18] Particularly disconcerting to some was his rejection of the widely held view that the Christian at death is immediately made perfect. Rather, he said, "progressive sanctification after death, is the doctrine of the Bible and the Church." [19] This was an echo of Professor I. A. Dorner,[20] under whom Dr. Briggs had studied at the University of Berlin, with whom he retained lifelong friendship, and for whom he named his second son.[21] Dr. Briggs's letters written from Berlin as a student as early as 1867 were imbued with an almost evangelistic zeal to expound this and related views on sanctification which he considered more soundly Biblical than those current.[22] Dr. Briggs expressly repudiated universalism, but saw salvation extended to the vast majority of the race.[23] Large areas of Old Testament ethics, he felt, leave much to be desired. "The ancient worthies, Noah and Abraham, Jacob and Judah, David and Solomon, were in a low stage of moral advancement. Doubtless it is true, that we would not receive such men into our families. . . . We might be obliged to send them to prison." [24]

Dr. Briggs in his address made clear that he regarded his attitude as constructive rather than destructive. "I have not departed in any respect from the orthodox teaching of the Christian Church as set forth in its official creeds." He thought the Christian Church about to enter into a greater future: "Let us cut down everything that is dead and harmful, every kind of dead orthodoxy . . . all those dry and brittle fences that constitute denominationalism, and are the barriers of Church Unity . . . the life of God is moving throughout Christendom, and the spring-time of a new age is about to come upon us." [25]

In this startling inaugural address Dr. Briggs did much less than justice to his own theological position. He had previously published the principal ideas contained in it, but with a careful guarding and qualifying of innovations and generalizations which had set these in the context of his own evangelicalism. Some of the language of the address was inexcusably careless, as when he seemed to imply that his three sources of divine authority —the Church, the Reason, and the Bible—were coördinate and even mutually independent. His selection of Martineau, the Unitarian, as an illustration did gross injustice to his own extremely high view of the Person of Christ.

Dr. Briggs had originally intended to speak on Biblical geography, which had been the specialty of Professor Edward Robinson, after whom the chair was named. But the donor of the chair, who was also president of the seminary's Board of Directors, said, "that . . . under the circumstances forced upon us at the time, it was necessary to select a theme that would vindicate the seminary and myself in the matters under debate." [26] The tone in which Dr. Briggs finally cast the inaugural was peculiarly offensive. For more than a year he had been under sharp attack for his part in the controversy over revising the Confession of Faith, and the address smoldered with indignation and contempt for opponents. Even his friends found themselves forced to apologize for the tone of the address,[27] and adversaries felt that they could not ignore such a manifesto without seeming to countenance its more radical implications.[28]

Why did he do it? Even Dr. Briggs's most intimate extant papers do not fully explain his motives—if indeed they were fully rationalized. He considered the attacks on his revision views grossly unjust. He saw opponents of change currently winning the Biblical and theological struggle all along the line in the Presbyterian Church. He saw the three former New

School seminaries which might be expected to lead the van for the newer views all in precarious theological position—Auburn was still on the fence, opponents were already sapping at the foundations of Lane, and efforts were being made within Union itself to divert it to a more rightest position.[29] Added to this was a combination of wishful thinking and personal confidence which for years had caused him to think that his sympathizers were far more numerous in the Church than they were. Perhaps a good hard blow now would hearten wavering progressives and stop reactionary forces in their tracks.[30] Dr. Briggs's motives can only be conjectured, but later evidence makes it certain that he neither foresaw nor intended what actually did happen.[31]

The religious press was almost unanimous in condemning Dr. Briggs's inaugural.[32] A director of Union Seminary regretted it.[33] The Rev. Allen Macy Dulles of Watertown, New York, later to be professor at Auburn Seminary, criticized the address for its lack of certainty. "It is almost inconceivable how a man of such learning as Professor Briggs can consent to appear before the thinking public in such an ambiguous attitude. And must it not be a matter of regret that such vague teaching should characterize one of the most important chairs in the educational world?" [34] Excited discussion of Dr. Briggs and his inaugural was widespread.

But there were not lacking public defenders of Dr. Briggs's inaugural. Professors Herrick Johnson and E. L. Curtis of McCormick Seminary stood by him.[35] Professor Samuel M. Hopkins of Auburn Seminary warned that attacks on Dr. Briggs were also attacks on the views of those who agreed with him, that such attacks threatened disruption of the Church. "Professor Briggs holds to the dynamic rather than the mechanical theory of inspiration. Is that a heresy?" [36] Many friends wrote to Dr. Briggs privately praising his stand, among them Professor Samuel R. Driver of Oxford, to whom the inaugural appeared "as harmless as it was excellent." [37]

The early months of 1891, between the inaugural and the meeting of the General Assembly, were crucial for the seminary as well as for Dr. Briggs. The decade before, Union Seminary had become financially the strongest seminary in the Church, but Princeton Seminary had the largest student body.[38] Union Seminary's future was therefore a matter of wide concern. In this crucial spring of 1891 the seminary was also facing the problem of finding a successor for Dr. Shedd in the important chair of systematic theology.[39]

Dr. Briggs's inaugural and the Church's reaction to it had produced a real crisis within Union Seminary. Would the seminary stand by him? A few of the institution's directors had criticized Dr. Briggs's much milder first inaugural of 1876, and some doubts about his theology still lingered.[40] When the storm broke in 1891, forces which had been seeking to draw the seminary to a more "rightist" position exerted extreme pressure on the

Board of Directors to prevent it from endorsing and following Dr. Briggs.[41] The president of Union Seminary was Dr. Thomas S. Hastings, son of the hymn writer of the same name. Dr. Hastings was a gracious, mild-mannered gentleman who apparently had not himself accepted critical views of the Bible, and some feared whether his leadership in the crisis would be sufficiently aggressive.[42] But as events unfolded he proved to be almost as firm as he was gentle, and won the nearly universal acclaim of the seminary's friends.[43] A number of strong laymen on the Board of Directors together with Dr. Hastings formulated the seminary's policy during this crisis.

If the seminary were to retain the power to decide its own future, it must close ranks before the Assembly of 1891. Some of the directors wished to see Dr. Briggs clarify ambiguities in his inaugural. Under date of May 4, 1891, he released a reprint of his inaugural with an appendix which set some matters in more adequate context,[44] but this did not fully satisfy the Board of Directors and they submitted to him a series of questions, to which he wrote the answers from his sickbed. Two of the "Andover liberals" regretted these concessions,[45] but Dr. Briggs was less radical than some even among his sympathizers realized. A day or two after the board's emissary had secured his answers, and only six days before the General Assembly was to convene, Dr. Briggs was deeply despondent: "There is no agreement among us. In the meanwhile, the conservatives advance in solid (?) mass to their victories." Presbytery's menacing attitude tempted him to flee away to the Congregationalists.[46]

But his pessimism was excessive. Already there was in the mail a letter from one of the more critical directors with word that he and the entire board were reassured by Dr. Briggs's answers to the board's questions,[47] and a few days later the board formally resolved to stand by him on the basis of these answers, but they wanted him to remain silent and leave public relations in their hands.[48] The faculty, too, in a statement signed by all except one professor who was absent in Europe and Professor Shedd, endorsed Dr. Briggs's position, though expressly deprecating the irritating tone of some of his utterances. Students and alumni also rallied behind him.[49] The seminary had closed ranks just in time. Two days after the board's action the General Assembly convened in Detroit.

The General Assembly which gathered in May 1891 found overtures awaiting it from sixty-three presbyteries calling attention to Dr. Briggs's inaugural address and asking that some appropriate action be taken. The Assembly could not avoid the issue and referred the matter to its Standing Committee on Theological Seminaries.[50]

That the Presbyterian Church at this time was overwhelmingly opposed to the newer theological views is shown by the commissioners whom the presbyteries elected after the months of discussion of the revision and Briggs issues. Sentiment among the commissioners was strongly adverse to

The presbyteries were after Briggs' scalp, and they elected commissioners on the G.A. who were sure to get it.

Dr. Briggs, as was manifest in their election of the outstanding American conservative Old Testament scholar, Professor William Henry Green of Princeton Seminary, as moderator. Dr. Patton was appointed chairman of the strategic Committee on Theological Seminaries. The Rev. Dr. Charles H. Parkhurst, famous anti-Tammany reformer and a stanch supporter of Dr. Briggs, commented on the leadership of Princeton Seminary men in this Assembly: "If ninety per cent. of the members were sheep waiting to be led, ten per cent. were bell-wether waiting to lead them, and Princeton was that bell-wether." [51] Dr. Patton's influence in this Assembly was particularly notable.

The G.A. won the right to veto nominations to professorial chairs in the semenaries.

By an agreement made in 1870 just after the reunion of the Old School and New School Presbyterian Churches, Union Seminary had granted to the General Assembly the right to veto professors elected by the seminary's Board of Directors. This was done because the Old School Church, in accordance with the more churchly ideals of that branch, had exercised tight ecclesiastical control over its seminaries, whereas the New School branch, in accordance with its more individualistic ideals, left its seminaries in a more decentralized and autonomous position. It seemed unjust that the General Assembly should rigidly control the former Old School seminaries and have little or no direct jurisdiction over the former New School seminaries. In the interests of equity, therefore, the Assembly surrendered to its Old School seminaries' boards of directors the election of their professors, but retained for itself the right of veto; while the New School seminaries in turn granted to the Assembly what it had not previously had, a veto over the election of their professors. It was this right of veto which the opponents of Dr. Briggs now desired the Assembly to exercise. The situation was complicated in the case of Dr. Briggs by the fact that he had already been on the Union Seminary faculty for many years before he was transferred by the Board of Directors to the newly created chair of Biblical theology. Opponents of Dr. Briggs insisted that the veto power extended to all elections of professors including transfers, whereas the seminary took the position that the Assembly's right of veto did not apply to transfers of professors within the faculty.

Union claimed that this power applied only to new admittals and not to old hands like Briggs who was just being transferred.

The General Assembly's Standing Committee on Theological Seminaries, having achieved unanimity after some difference of opinion within the committee,[52] recommended that the election of Professor Briggs be vetoed and that a committee of fifteen be appointed to confer with the directors of the seminary concerning the seminary's relation to the Assembly. The Assembly's adoption of this report by a vote of 449 to 60 indicates how strong at this time was the Church's opposition to critical views of the Bible.[53]

By order of the Assembly every vote was recorded. The large Synod of Pennsylvania revealed its conservatism, only one vote being cast against the veto by the commissioners from its presbyteries. The elders in the

Assembly voted more conservatively than did the ministers, casting only sixteen of the sixty votes against the veto.[54]

The separation of the Church and the seminary proceeded apace. Two conferences between the General Assembly's Committee of Conference and the seminary's Board of Directors revealed that neither party was prepared to abandon its own interpretation of the veto power.[55] The Board of Directors then memorialized the General Assembly of 1892 to concur with it in annulling the agreement of 1870 which had conferred upon the Assembly the right of veto. This concurrence the General Assembly refused to grant.[56] Thereupon, on October 13, 1892, the Board of Directors by unilateral action annulled the agreement of 1870, claiming constitutional and legal grounds for so doing.[57] The next month four of the directors showed their approval of this action in a very substantial way by contributing $175,000 to the seminary.[58] The General Assembly of 1893 answered the annullment with the following action: "The Assembly disavows all responsibility for the teaching of Union Seminary, and declines to receive any report from its Board until satisfactory relations are established." [59] The Church and the seminary were for practical purposes separated. It is perhaps significant that by the middle of the twentieth century all of the Church's former New School seminaries had either left the denomination entirely or had ceased to exist as separate institutions. The Church's entire program of theological education by mid-twentieth century was built on its former Old School seminaries and on seminaries organized after their ecclesiastical pattern.

The action of Union Seminary in 1892 of annulling its compact with the General Assembly went far toward neutralizing the victory of its critics. From beyond the boundaries of the Presbyterian Church, Union Seminary continued to influence the Presbyterian Church and its history in a potent way, as coming decades were to show.

Opponents of Dr. Briggs had a twofold strategy. Having by executive action secured the veto of his election as professor, they also attempted by judicial process to remove him from the Presbyterian ministry.

In April 1891, some three months after Dr. Briggs had delivered his inaugural address, his Presbytery of New York appointed a committee to study the relation of the address to the Westminster Confession, and in the following October a five-man prosecuting committee presented two formal charges of heresy against him.[60] Then, at a meeting of New York Presbytery on November 4, 1891, Dr. Briggs presented a carefully prepared "Response to the Charges and Specifications." The Response made such a highly favorable impression that supporters of Dr. Briggs were able to secure the immediate dismissal of the case in presbytery by the decisive vote of ninety-four to thirty-nine. The wording of the resolution dismissing the case is based on a desire for inclusive churchmanship. Though expressly declining to endorse Dr. Briggs's views, it desires to leave room for him in the Church. "Without approving of the positions stated in his inaugural address, at the same time desiring earnestly the peace and quiet of the Church," the Presbytery of New York "deems it best to dismiss the case, and hereby does so dismiss it." [61] This type of broader churchmanship which seeks to make room for men holding contrary views was to become increasingly influential in the Presbyterian Church in coming decades. Thus vindicated, for the moment at least, it was Dr. Briggs's desire to withdraw quietly from the Presbyterian ministry, but a group of leading members of his seminary board and faculty gave their "unanimous decision" that he "should continue in Presbyterian Church to the End." [62]

Dr. Briggs's prosecutors, not content to rest in defeat, appealed directly to the General Assembly nine days after presbytery had acted.[63] Dr. Shedd warned that the very nature of the Church itself was the point at issue. He wrote: "This appeal from the action of the Presbytery of New York brings before the General Assembly a question more serious and important in results than any that has ever been presented to it; the question, namely, whether a type of theology utterly antagonistic to the traditional theology of the denomination shall be solemnly condemned by its highest tribunal, or whether it shall be indorsed by it directly in words, or indirectly by inaction and tolerance." [64]

The Assembly of 1892 by an overwhelming majority voted to sustain the appeal of the committee prosecuting Dr. Briggs. Dr. Briggs's strongest support came from his own Synod of New York, which cast thirty-four of the eighty-seven votes against the prosecutors' appeal. The Assembly's final action reversed New York Presbytery's dismissal of the case, and remanded the case to the presbytery for a complete trial on its merits.[65]

This same General Assembly of 1892, meeting at Portland, Oregon, also dealt in a positive way with the Biblical issue underlying the Briggs case by adopting what was often spoken of as the "Portland Deliverance." This pronouncement declared in part: "Our Church holds that the inspired Word, as it came from God, is without error. . . . All who enter office in our Church solemnly profess to receive them [i.e., "the sacred Books"] as the only infallible rule of faith and practice. If they change their belief on this point, Christian honor demands that they should withdraw from our ministry." [66] This was an effort to declare the rigid doctrine of inspiration taught by the Hodge-Warfield article[67] to be official church dogma, under the supposition that it had always been such. After the Assembly adjourned there were not lacking those who denounced this declaration as an unwarranted alteration of the terms of ministerial subscription, and Dr. Briggs complained that it prejudiced his case.[68] Indeed, some felt that the prosecution of Dr. Briggs itself was "*a determined and organized effort to introduce and apply a new test of orthodoxy in the Presbyterian Church, and thus to make a radical revolution in its constitution and practically abrogate its essential law.*"[69]

That such a resolution might be adopted by a divided vote over determined minority opposition would hardly be surprising in 1892, but the apparent unanimity with which the Assembly committed itself to this extreme position can be accounted for only by the ambiguity of this "Portland Deliverance" and by the fact that it was adopted on the closing day when the docket was crowded. The crux of the deliverance lies in the sentence, "Our Church holds that the inspired Word, as it came from God, is without error." As Professor Duffield later pointed out, the phrase, "the inspired Word" might denote (1) our English Bible in the King James, the Revised, or some other version; (2) the present Hebrew and Greek text; (3) the original manuscripts; or (4) "the concept of Dr. Briggs, the inspired Word as it came *from* God, as distinguished from the form in which it came from the sacred penmen." Furthermore, the clause, "as it came from God," might mean "inasmuch as it came from God," or "*in the form in which* it came from God."[70] That is to say, the deliverance is emphatic about inerrancy, but does not make clear exactly what is inerrant —whether it is merely the divine germinal ideas which the writers of Scripture then clothed in purely human and errant language; or the original autographs; or our present Scriptures.

This ambiguity underlay the presentation of the resolution to the Assembly. The chairman of the committee, in reporting it to the Assembly, "sought to pour oil on the boisterous waters by a very irenic exposition of the deliverance." As a result, a leading paper noted with relief that the deliverance was of no particular significance and could honestly be accepted by one holding even the most liberal views.[71] The Portland Deliverance, therefore, along with the Briggs case, became matter for widespread discussion in the Church until the next Assembly in 1893 should take further action on both matters.

Meanwhile, the General Assembly of 1892 having remanded the Briggs case to New York Presbytery, the eyes of many throughout the country turned again toward that presbytery. On November 9, 1892, the prosecuting committee, taking advantage of the Assembly's permission to rearrange the form of its presentation, offered to presbytery amended charges and specifications. There were now eight charges. The first two declared that Dr. Briggs taught that the Reason and the Church, respectively, were fountains of divine authority which may and do enlighten even those who reject the Scriptures. Thirdly, Dr. Briggs was charged with teaching "that errors may have existed in the original text of the Holy Scripture." The fourth charge declared that he taught "that many of the Old Testament predictions have been reversed by history."

Dr. Briggs was charged under the fifth and sixth heads, respectively, with teaching "that Moses is not the author of the Pentateuch, which is contrary to direct statements of Scripture," and "that Isaiah is not the author of half of the book that bears his name." The seventh and eighth charges declared that he taught "that the processes of redemption extend to the world to come in the case of many who die in sin," and "that Sanctification is not complete at death." One or more specifications were offered by the prosecution in support of each charge.[72]

After Dr. Briggs had offered some preliminary objections of a technical sort which led presbytery to modify slightly the form in which the charges were presented,[73] he offered his formal defense on December 5. Along with other arguments he sought to show from the works of Origen, Jerome, Augustine, Luther, Calvin, and later writers that these men "testify that there are errors in Holy Scripture." His defense ended with a long list of "higher critics" in Germany, other countries of Continental Europe, Great Britain, and America. He added: "The number of Professors in the Old Testament department who hold to the traditional theory may be counted on one's fingers." [74] Instead of attempting to deny the views attributed to him in the charges, he sought to show that they were innocuous.

On January 9, 1893, the Presbytery of New York, by a majority vote, decided that each charge and specification was "not sustained." The closest vote on a specification was sixty-one to sixty-seven, while the most decided majority against sustaining a specification was forty-nine to seventy-three. Presbytery therefore formally acquitted Dr. Briggs of all the offenses alleged against him. The presbytery's decision closed with an exhortation to all "in view of the disquietude in the Presbyterian Church" to keep the peace and "to devote their energies to the great and urgent work of the Church which is the proclamation of the Gospel and the edifying of the Body of Christ." The spirit of tolerance and inclusiveness for the sake of the Church's more efficient functioning is apparent in this closing exhortation of the presbytery.[75]

This decision of the New York Presbytery, with its exhortation to peace and work, was drafted by Dr. van Dyke, then on the eve of his literary fame, and Dr. George Alexander, who, though not himself inclined to theological innovation, was to be a leading champion of tolerance and broad church principles in New York Presbytery for more than a third of a century.[76] The month after presbytery's decision these two gentlemen, together with four others, circulated among ministers of the Church *A Plea for Peace and Work*, with 235 signatures. It was in the spirit of New York Presbytery's decision, and amplified its exhortation to cease strife for the sake of the Church's practical work. "We join our voices," the *Plea* declared, "in a plain, straight-forward fraternal expression of the desire for harmony and united devotion to practical work. . . . We do not express any individual opinion in regard to the theory of the inerrancy of the original autographs of Scripture in matters which are not essential to religion, but . . . we protest unitedly and firmly against making assent to it a test of Christian faith or of good standing in the Presbyterian ministry." [77]

Both New York Presbytery's decision and this *Plea* make explicit a motive that was an important factor in the reunion of 1869 and that was to become increasingly prominent in the first half of the twentieth century—the subordination of unresolved theological differences to the necessities of coöperation for the successful prosecution of the Church's work. It implied a shift in emphasis in the Calvinistic doctrine of the Church. Following the dominant patterns of American life, there was an increasing tendency to think of the Church as a kind of business corporation chartered to do the Lord's work. The subordination of questions of truth—though only of those regarded as "unessential"—to efficiency of operation carries a recognizable suggestion of pragmatism. It is interesting that Presbyterians—who did not formally hold the tenets of the pragmatistic philosophy at all—were implying a more pragmatic doctrine of the Church at just about the time that Peirce and James were formulating the philosophy of pragmatism. The philosophy and the ecclesiology were products of the same forces in American life.

This *Plea,* with its pragmatic objectives, meant, too, that a third party was emerging, between the party demanding theological innovation and the party resisting all theological innovation—a third party composed of those who might or who might not incline personally to one or the other of these more extreme positions, but who were resolved to transcend ideological differences in united action. To this party the Church's future, for more than half a century at least, was to belong. In an increasingly confusing, pluralistic culture such a program held promise of maintaining outward unity and efficiently conducting large enterprises.

This conception of the Church did not pass unchallenged. Three months after the appearance of the *Plea* Dr. William Brenton Greene, Jr., professor-elect at Princeton Seminary, wrote in quite opposite vein against what he called "Broad Churchism." He saw three parties in the Church: those who agreed more or less with Dr. Briggs and desired to see the case dismissed; those who did not agree with Dr. Briggs and desired to see the case decided against him; and a third party consisting of those "who, while they do not agree with Dr. Briggs, would still have the appeal [i.e., of Dr. Briggs's prosecutors] dismissed, on the ground that the Presbyterian Church should be broad enough to include him." He argued against this type of "Broad Churchism." "It would mean, as Dr. Briggs has said that he desires and intends, the end of denominationalism. . . . Would this, however, be for the advantage of Christ's cause? . . . The broader a church becomes, the fewer and the less definite must be the truths to which it witnesses." [78]

With the opponents of Dr. Briggs defeated in the New York Presbytery, much pressure was put on the prosecuting committee to refrain from appealing the case, while on the other hand it received some fifteen hundred letters urging it to appeal directly to the General Assembly.[79] Within nine days of its defeat in presbytery, the committee filed an appeal directly to the Assembly.

Agitation in the Church and jockeying for strategic advantage now rose to fever pitch. A younger clergyman of that day has more recently given his recollections of the period: "Indeed, in the days of controversy over Doctor Briggs, I had seen party spirit carried to such lengths that there was not a single trick known in the political game that I did not see churchmen using in their struggle with one another." [80] Dr. Briggs received expressions of unsolicited sympathy and equally unsolicited advice, among them a scolding letter from his former friend, Dr. Morris, notable for its discerning prediction: "Do not do anything that will *break up any further the party of progress*. . . . That party was getting on well, was really gaining the day, when this distracting issue came in. Now it is almost in pieces. . . . The majority of the progressives, at least in this region, are not with you on the errancy doctrine. . . . What I fear is such a triumph of the conservative dogmatic party as will put you & all of us in the positions of the 'underdog in the fight' for a long time to come." [81]

The General Assembly of 1893 met in the New York Avenue Presbyterian Church, Washington, D. C. During the Briggs proceedings every available seat on the floor was occupied, with many standing. The gallery, which extended around three sides, was filled with visitors, including many women.[82] The Briggs case was the absorbing interest of this General Assembly, and many of the commissioners had been elected on the basis of their attitude toward it. The Assembly, by a vote of 410 to 145, decided to entertain the appeal, thus bringing the case before the Assembly for retrial. The recorded vote indicates that the Synod of New York was the only synod to cast a majority of its votes against entertaining the appeal. Pennsylvania voted more conservatively than the Church as a whole, favoring entertainment of the appeal by a vote of seventy-nine to five. Having decided this, the Assembly instructed its Judicial Committee to prepare the case for trial.[83]

The Briggs case was then tried by the Assembly on appeal, four hours and a half being allowed to the appellant, seven hours to the appellee, and two hours to members of the Presbytery of New York, the judicatory of original jurisdiction. The final decision of the Assembly was rendered by a roll-call vote. Each commissioner, in casting his vote, was allowed to speak for three minutes, and more than a hundred did so, some using the luncheon or dinner recess to prepare their brief remarks. Time was rigidly limited, and a number were interrupted by the moderator in the middle of a sentence. During the casting of the votes "an almost painful stillness" prevailed throughout the Assembly, "the spectators in the gallery rising to their feet in their anxiety to catch every response." [84] The decision of the Assembly was against Dr. Briggs, 295 voting to sustain the appeal of the prosecutors as a whole, 84 to sustain it in part, and 116 not to sustain it.

The Assembly then created a committee of fifteen to draft the final decision. After one of its members, as a gesture of courtesy, had interviewed Dr. Briggs without avail,[85] the committee presented its report, which the Assembly adopted as its final decision in the case. "This General Assembly . . . does hereby suspend Charles A. Briggs, the said appellee, from the office of a minister in the Presbyterian Church in the United States of America, until such time as he shall give satisfactory evidence of repentance to the General Assembly of the Presbyterian Church in the United States of America." [86]

The Assembly also adopted an explanatory minute rejecting views attributed to Dr. Briggs, namely, the errancy of Scripture; the doctrine that reason and the Church are, along with Scripture, fountains of divine authority; and the doctrine of progressive sanctification after death. Having thus completed the matter, the Assembly discharged the prosecuting committee with thanks and declared the case terminated. Sixty-two commissioners filed a formal protest against the conviction of Dr. Briggs as involving "acts of doubtful constitutionality"; "as seeming to abridge the liberty of opinion hitherto enjoyed under our Standards"; "as tending . . . to the discouragement of thorough study of the Bible"; and as inflicting an injustice on both Dr. Briggs and the Presbytery of New York.[87]

Closely related to the Biblical questions involved in the Briggs case was the action of this same General Assembly in dealing with the ambiguous and widely discussed Portland Deliverance of 1892 on Biblical inerrancy. As an interpretive statement the Assembly of 1893 adopted the following: "This General Assembly reaffirms the doctrine of the deliverance of the Assembly of 1892 . . . viz., That the original Scriptures of the Old and New Testaments, being immediately inspired of God were without error." The resolution further declared that this "has always been the belief of the Church."[88] Again the next year, the Assembly denied that this was a new definition of dogma.[89] The resolution clarified the Portland Deliverance by expressly predicating inerrancy of the original (and now lost) Biblical manuscripts. The position taken by the Hodge-Warfield article a dozen years before[90] was now unambiguously declared to be the Church's official teaching.

Dr. Herrick Johnson and eighty-six other commissioners of the General Assembly of 1893 made bold to sign a formal protest against the Assembly's pronouncement, even though Dr. Briggs had just been suspended from the ministry for views which among other things involved a repudiation of the doctrine of Biblical inerrancy. Because the original Bible manuscripts are irrevocably lost, the Johnson Protest opposed this attempt to build the faith of the Church on an "imaginary Bible," and branded the doctrine as "an interpretation of our Standards which they never have borne." "It is disparaging the Bible we have, and endangering its authority under the pressure of a prevalent hostile criticism." [91] Soon afterwards, this Assembly, perhaps reflecting the concern of the Johnson Protest for the existing Bible, "unanimously adopted" the resolution, "That the Bible as we now have it, in its various translations and versions, when freed from all errors and mistakes of translators, copyists, and printers, is the very Word of God, and consequently wholly without error." [92] Considering that advocates of the newer views were not entirely unrepresented in the Assembly, it is surprising that such a resolution would be adopted "unanimously." This shows once more the conservatism of the Assembly and explains the overwhelming vote favoring the conviction of Dr. Briggs.

The net result of the Briggs case was undoubtedly the opposite of that desired—it publicized and disseminated the new critical views within the Church and far beyond. A distinguished Scottish observer was amazed that a "great church like yours could . . . commit itself to a definition of the inerrancy of Scripture which must make it a gazing stock and object of wonder to intelligent Christians everywhere." [93] Ecclesiastical liberty was directly threatened, and even before the proceedings against Dr. Briggs were completed, Dr. William Henry Green found evident difficulty in reconciling them with proper liberty, a difficulty which the distinguished scholar, Professor George Foote Moore, at that time still a Presbyterian, emphasized.[94] A venerable New School leader of prereunion days, Dr. Robert W. Patterson, even challenged the form of church government which made possible such procedures.[95] In the Briggs case, as in the controversy between the General Assembly and Union Seminary, the plea for a New School type of theological liberty naturally favored the New School tradition of greater decentralization in church government. But the expanding home and foreign missionary enterprises of the Church during these decades, as well as authoritarian ideals of theology, combined to increase ecclesiastical power more in line with Old School conceptions of church government.

There were intimations of a possibility—presumably rather remote—that Dr. Briggs might enter the Cumberland Presbyterian Church.[96] In 1898 he entered the ministry of the Protestant Episcopal Church.[97]

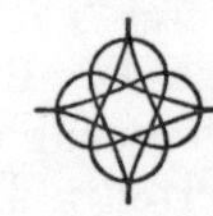

7.

the smith case

The prosecution of Professor Henry Preserved Smith for heresy set in motion events that changed the character and future prospects of Lane Seminary, Cincinnati, in which he served. The seminary's numerical and financial weakness was no index of its importance as the most assertive and influential organized representative—after Union Seminary—of the theological heritage and spirit of the former New School. In 1890, on the eve of the crisis, Lane's faculty of seven included a former moderator and the stated clerk of the General Assembly, two who held German doctorates of philosophy, two scholars who were to acquire international reputation, and a lucid popularizer of a mediating theology—no mean assets even for a much larger institution.

The Smith case was enmeshed in a complex of theological and ecclesiastical rivalries that had been present in Cincinnati Presbytery and Lane Seminary since before the reunion of 1869. As a former New School seminary in a predominantly Old School environment, Lane Seminary had to tread cautiously, especially because it was surrounded by competing Presbyterian seminaries at Danville, Allegheny, and Chicago. Even the former New School men in the area did not incline to embrace the new critical and theological positions.[1]

The Presbytery of Cincinnati, of which Professor Smith was a member, at a meeting early in 1891 considered an overture to the General Assembly against the inaugural address which Dr. Briggs had delivered some two months before. Dr. Smith had promised his friend, "If it comes to an open battle, I will take your side." Though admittedly embarrassed by Dr. Briggs's doctrine of progressive sanctification after death, he set out to fulfill his promise, concentrating on defending Dr. Briggs's rejection of Biblical inerrancy. Having in mind the overture then pending in Cincinnati Presbytery, Dr. Smith read a paper on Biblical inspiration before the Presbyterian Ministerial Association of Cincinnati in March 1891. He dealt courageously with issues raised by Dr. Briggs's inaugural, and joined him in attacking the doctrine of verbal inspiration. This address, together with another by a Lane colleague, Professor L. J. Evans, was published under the title, *Biblical Scholarship and Inspiration*, and gave offense to many.[2]

In spite of Dr. Smith's paper, Cincinnati Presbytery adopted the anti-Briggs overture by a vote of more than three to one.[3] Presbytery later declared its approval of the veto of Dr. Briggs by the Assembly of 1891, and appointed a committee "to have this subject under consideration." Quite correctly Dr. Smith felt threatened with prosecution by the appointment of this committee.[4]

In the face of the gathering storm the Lane faculty was sadly divided. Professors Smith of the Old Testament and Evans of the New Testament were committed by the addresses just mentioned to critical views of the Bible. Young Dr. Arthur Cushman McGiffert, who had studied under Harnack at Marburg, at this date could still say, "I do not deny the inerrancy of the Scriptures," [5] but was thoroughly committed to progressive policies. "Whatever happens," he assured Dr. Briggs, "I will stand by the liberal party. I do not believe in compromise, and do not intend to be compromised." [6] As has already been observed, Dr. Morris for some years had been cooling in his zeal for theological progressivism. He had never accepted for himself the negative conclusions of Biblical criticism, but in earlier years had vehemently asserted the right of others to proclaim them within the Church. By the 1890's, however, he was talking much of a mild, mediating theology, and avoided lending any active assistance to Dr. Smith in his trial. Dr. Morris proved to be the key man in Lane's history at this juncture.[7]

Dr. William H. Roberts, stated clerk of the General Assembly, had been brought to the Lane faculty as part of the policy of securing board and faculty members of more conservative type to win the support of the seminary's strongly "Old School" environment. Before the controversy broke out he was considered "invaluable to us as conciliating more distinctly than any one else could the remains of the old hostile sentiment still quite perceptible in this region." [8] But in the discussions that followed the Briggs inaugural he strongly asserted the inerrancy of the Bible autographs, and was accused of trying "single-handed to make out of Lane a second Princeton," [9] though later still he became a conspicuous leader in movements for church coöperation and union.

Professor Smith was not one to be frightened from his convictions by opposition. Two articles which he contributed to the *New York Evangelist* early in 1892 dealing with the basic problem of the nature of Presbyterian churchmanship aroused further criticism. In the first of these, entitled "How Much is Implied in Ordination Vows?" he propounded the startling view that "doctrinal qualification is required only at ordination. . . . The candidate for ordination is nowhere warned that if his doctrinal views should change, he must acquaint his Presbytery with the fact." [10] In the second of these articles, entitled "The Sin of Schism," Dr. Smith wrote: "There are denominations enough. . . . Schism is a sin, and . . . the sin rests on the exscinding church."[11]

Quite unmoved by the arguments of its dissenting professor, the Presbytery of Cincinnati, two months after Dr. Smith's article was published, drafted a pastoral letter to its churches on the Bible and inspiration, ordering a printing of 10,000 copies.[12] The situation was ominous for Dr. Smith.

Meanwhile, the theory of ministerial subscription to the Church's doctrinal standards advocated by Dr. Smith and others was being widely discussed in the Presbyterian Church. Did the constitutional questions put to ministerial candidates at ordination apply only at the moment of ordination, as Dr. Smith said, or was creedal subscription binding throughout ministerial life? If the "momentary" theory were accepted, the Presbyterian ministry had suddenly ceased, for all practical purposes, to be bound by any doctrinal standards. The Presbyteries of Chester, Pennsylvania, and of Genessee, New York, therefore overtured the General Assembly of 1892, calling attention to these views and asking for an authoritative deliverance.

In reply to these overtures and in order to deal with the problem which Professor Smith and others were raising, the General Assembly of 1892 adopted the so-called Portland Deliverance, which, without naming Dr. Smith or anyone else, declared that the Bible was inerrant; that church officers, in their ordination vows, professed to believe in Biblical inerrancy; and that these vows were binding throughout the period of holding office.[13] The ambiguities and subsequent history of the Portland Deliverance have already been discussed.[14]

With Dr. Smith's views repudiated so directly, even though anonymously, by the General Assembly of 1892, his own Presbytery of Cincinnati, whose prevailing conservatism on Biblical issues has already been noted,[15] made the next move. From the beginning, Dr. Smith considered his case hopeless.[16] In September 1892, presbytery, by a vote of 42 to 16, created a committee to prosecute, and on November 14 the trial started.[17] The accused professor later claimed that the presbytery had done him a serious injustice by delaying eighteen months before prosecuting him, because by that time the action of two unusually important General Assemblies had quite altered the theological atmosphere.[18]

The Presbytery of Cincinnati found Dr. Smith guilty on two of the three charges, and on December 13, 1892, by the close vote of 31 to 26 suspended him from the Presbyterian ministry "until such time as he shall make manifest, to the satisfaction of Presbytery, his renunciation of the errors he has been found to hold, and his solemn purpose no longer to teach or propagate them." [19]

Needless to say, while Church and presbytery were so distraught, policies of Lane Seminary's sharply divided Board of Trustees were quite unpredictable. Rumors that the board would forbid any teaching denying Biblical inerrancy proved unfounded.[20] Instead, the board declined to accept Professor Smith's resignation which he tendered in January 1893 after his suspension by the presbytery, and on the other hand abolished Dr. Roberts' chair on grounds of financial stringency.[21]

The board was trying to evolve a compromise policy which no faculty member except Dr. Morris favored. Dr. Morris, defending the policy in a letter to his old friend, Dr. Briggs, reported that "*every minister* in *the Board* . . . rejects the views of Dr. S[mith]. . . . The . . . laymen in the Board are about equally divided. . . . The *Alumni* in this Presbytery voted three or four to one against S[mith] in the trial. . . . The suggestion that *the Sem. cut loose from the ch.* cannot be carried in the Board: three fourths of the Trustees wd. vote against it." [22] Lane's future course was hanging in the balance, and Dr. Morris chose to tip the balance on the side of caution and continuance in the denomination. What live option did Dr. Morris have? More discerningly than his New York friend, he realized that Cincinnati was not New York, and that this predominantly conservative Presbyterian environment would not at that time support a free-lance progressive institution. He was convinced that Dr. Briggs's inaugural, by precipitating conflict at a time when new ideas were slowly gaining ground in the Church, had wrecked Lane's precarious but succeeding moderatism. A case could be made for Dr. Morris' interpretation. As so often with moderate views in times of intense struggle, his mediating position was rejected by both extremes.

The General Assembly of 1893 rebuked the Lane trustees for having abolished Dr. Roberts' chair, and for having retained Dr. Smith after his suspension by presbytery. The trustees thereupon accepted Dr. Smith's resignation, but with a protest against the Assembly's interference, as lying beyond that judicatory's proper authority.[23] "So Lane has gone by the board for lack of backbone," lamented one of Dr. Smith's sympathizers.[24] All faculty members resigned except Dr. Morris, and the trustees directed him "to keep the keys, and to open the doors if in the coming autumn [of 1893] any should come here seeking instruction." Some twenty-three came, an increase of six over the preceding year. The Assembly of 1894 expressed disapproval of a pamphlet by Dr. Morris, but uttered no word of appreciation for his large part in saving the seminary for the Church.[25] His resignation to the trustees in 1895 was accepted "to take effect when his successor is appointed." [26] The final completion of his seminary labors in 1897 was appropriately signalized by a banquet in his honor.[27] Lane was reorganized and came under the presidency of Dr. Smith's prosecutor. It abandoned its moderately progressive tradition, but did not fully satisfy more pronounced conservatives. In 1932 Lane Seminary merged with Presbyterian Theological Seminary, Chicago (formerly, and again later, McCormick Seminary).[28]

Professor Henry Preserved Smith, after being convicted of heresy by his Presbytery of Cincinnati in December 1892, appealed to the Synod of Ohio, but the synod on October 13, 1893, refused to sustain any of his twelve grounds of appeal,[29] with the result that presbytery's suspension of him remained in force.

Dr. Smith then appealed to the General Assembly of 1894. The whole case in the Assembly really revolved around the second charge, which charged Dr. Smith "with teaching . . . that the Holy Spirit did not so control the inspired writers in their composition of the Holy Scriptures as to make their utterances absolutely truthful, *i.e.*, free from error when interpreted in their natural and intended sense." [30] Basically, therefore, the case involved a single issue, viz., whether it was to be the policy of the Presbyterian Church to suspend from the ministry those who refused to affirm the inerrancy of the lost autograph manuscripts of the Bible.

Dr. Smith insisted that in order to make good its second charge the prosecution would have to prove that the doctrine of the inerrancy of the Biblical autographs was a fundamental doctrine of the Church. "So far as I know, no judicial decision on record has (until that of 1893) declared the doctrine before us to be one of the essential and necessary articles of our faith. . . . The doctrine before us is asserted in no one of the Reformed Confessions." Then, too, Dr. Smith regretted the exaltation of the lost Biblical autographs at the expense of the existing Biblical text. He failed to see how lost autographs could in any way promote Christian living. Insisting that the real issue was the degree of tolerated divergence—"where you will draw the line of ministerial fitness"—Dr. Smith closed his appeal to the Assembly with a plea for comprehensive churchmanship based on the Church's growth and increasing coöperative activity.[31]

Quite another conception of the nature of the Church was, however, in the ascendant among Presbyterians in 1894, and the General Assembly decided the case by not sustaining the appeal. There were 55 voting to sustain it; 47 to sustain it in part; and 396 not to sustain it. The result was that the Cincinnati Presbytery's suspension of Dr. Smith from the Presbyterian ministry remained operative. Once again the Synod of New York showed its more liberal sympathies, casting 22—nearly half—of the Assembly's 55 votes in favor of sustaining the appeal. One notices with surprise that in spite of Dr. Smith's fewer alleged errors, and less polemic tone and manner, the majority of the Assembly against him (396 to 102) was slightly larger than the majority against Dr. Briggs the year before (379 to 116).[32] He had hoped to receive a larger vote than Dr. Briggs as proof of the advance of critical views in the Church during the year.[33] On the contrary, the difference is probably to be explained by the fact that opinion in the Church had become crystallized during the discussions attending the Briggs case and that by the following year the Church felt ready to declare itself even more confidently. Though some church papers were critical of the Assembly's decision in the Smith case,[34] it is quite evident that the Church in 1894 was definitely taking the position that a Presbyterian minister must be able to affirm belief in the inerrancy of the original manuscripts of the Bible. Once again the Hodge-Warfield doctrine of inspiration was officially affirmed. In 1899 Dr. Smith was received into a Congregational Association.[35]

8.

aftermath

The revision controversy, together with the Briggs and Smith cases, was not without peril to the Church's unity, and rumors were heard of the possible organization of "another Presbytery" and even of "another Presbyterian Church." But responsible leaders like President Hastings and Professor Schaff of Union Seminary and Dr. Morris of Lane were against such action.[1] Of course feelings became sharper after the condemnation of Dr. Briggs by the Assembly of 1893, but Dr. Briggs himself, though recognizing the possibility of a division of the Church, did not expect it.[2]

Instead of taking rash, irrevocable action, progressives arranged for a conference at Cleveland, Ohio, in the autumn following Dr. Briggs's suspension by the Assembly.[3] The group adopted an eight-point manifesto complaining that recent Assemblies had been guilty of breaches of Presbyterian law and order, had violated the constitutional rights of ministers, and had imposed extraconstitutional doctrinal requirements upon church officers. Most of the church papers were hostile in tone to the Cleveland group, but several expressed sympathy with its aims. Though less than a hundred were present at the original meeting in Cleveland, supporters of the protest the next year claimed that it had been signed by hundreds of ministers and elders.[4]

More significant was the "Presbyterian League of New York," organized in May 1894. It adopted as its formal statement of purpose "the promotion of constitutional liberty, truth and progress within the Presbyterian Church." It aimed to alter the policy of doctrinal exclusiveness followed by General Assemblies during the Briggs and Smith cases. Among the specific planks in the League's platform was the reversal, "sooner or later, of the burdensome and unjust ecclesiastical action recently taken by courts of the Presbyterian Church"; the securing of a new, shorter creed; a new or amended Book of Discipline; liberty for attempts to "re-state the difficult questions of theology." The League expressed a desire for the visible unity of Christendom, and announced that it was "ready for some ventures in sociology." [5] But a few, living outside of New York City, were impatient for more drastic action.[6]

Those favoring strict interpretation of creedal subscription, on the other hand, having won the contest to date, had nothing to gain and perhaps something to lose by any prolonging of the struggle. Therefore, like victorious majorities nearly everywhere, they advocated peace and quiet, strongly deprecated continued agitation, and regretted the organization of the League. The twenty-fifth anniversary of the reunion of the Old School and New School was the occasion of a veritable love feast, and a little later, a former moderator, ignoring the recent contention over somewhat different issues, was able to write with at least literal correctness, "None of the questions involved in the separation of 1837 have risen to mar the harmony of the reunited Church." [7] This outward calm did not mean that basic differences were forgotten; it simply meant that those who had won the recent contests remained in undisputed control. But liberals, who felt that the future was with them, could not permanently accept such terms of subordination.

The Assemblies of 1895 and 1896 were not without controversial issues inherited from the disagreements of the immediately preceding years. The alienation of Union Seminary which followed the vetoing of Dr. Briggs in 1891 thrust on the attention of the Church three important questions: (1) Was the Church's control over its other seminaries enforceable in the civil courts? (2) What were to be the relations between the Presbyterian Church and Union Seminary in the future? (3) What policy would the Church follow regarding ministerial candidates studying at Union Seminary?

The first of these questions attracted widespread attention. Did the Presbyterian General Assembly have any authority over its seminaries that could be enforced by property suits in civil courts? Actually the various Presbyterian seminaries had been founded according to four quite different plans: (1) Some of the seminaries, like Princeton and Western, had from their origin been placed under the immediate control of the General Assembly. (2) Other seminaries had been placed under the control of a synod or synods. (3) Still others, like Auburn, had from the beginning been under a presbytery or a group of presbyteries. (4) Two seminaries, Union and Lane, while calling themselves by the name "Presbyterian," had been founded entirely outside of ecclesiastical control.[8]

G. A. tightens control over semenaries.

The movement toward tighter control of the seminaries by the Assembly was opposed by some heirs of the New School tradition,[9] but these were "states rights" voices from the prereunion past, and the Church, like the nation in these post-Civil War years, and for much the same reasons, was facing in the direction of increasing centralization. The Assembly of 1894, by a vote of nearly four to one, asked all the Church's seminaries to amend their charters in such a way as to state that all funds and property are held in trust for the Presbyterian Church.[10] Two years later the Assembly was told that five seminaries had already amended their charters or were willing to do so.[11]

A second question raised by events following the veto of Dr. Briggs's election was, What were to be the future relations, if any, between the Presbyterian Church and Union Seminary? Under circumstances already discussed in connection with the Briggs incident, the Union Seminary directors in 1892 abrogated the so-called "Compact of 1870," on the ground that their board had acted *ultra vires* when it had conferred upon the Assembly a veto over election of its professors. Following this action, the Assembly of 1893 disavowed all responsibility for the teaching of Union Seminary and declined to receive any annual report from its board until satisfactory relations should be reëstablished.[12] The Assembly of 1895 instructed a committee "to inquire into, and report to the next General Assembly, as to the rights of the Presbyterian Church in the United States of America, in the property now held by The Union Theological Seminary." [13] The committee reported the next year: "We are compelled to believe and to report that the present administration of the funds is not in accord with the intention of the donors during the period above named [i.e., 1870-92]. Nevertheless, while we are compelled to make this declaration, we deem it inexpedient to recommend the General Assembly at the present time to enter into any contest in the matter of the endowments and property of the seminary." [14] Relations between Assembly and seminary remained in this ambiguous and unsatisfactory condition until clarified by a more thorough analysis in 1915.[15]

A third question raised by events following the Briggs veto was, What policy should the Church follow regarding ministerial candidates studying at Union Seminary? In the long run this proved to be the most engrossing problem of the three. The Assembly of 1893 enjoined the Board of Education "to give [financial] aid to such students only as may be in attendance upon seminaries approved by the Assembly." [16] In 1895 the Assembly ordered the Presbytery of New York "not to receive under its care for licensure, students who are pursuing or purpose to pursue their studies in theological seminaries respecting whose teaching the General Assembly disavows responsibility." [17] But two years later the Assembly, after hearing an analysis of the respective powers of Assembly and presbyteries in relation to ministerial candidates and licensure, reaffirmed an Assembly action of 1806 which acknowledged that presbyteries possessed much broader discretionary powers in these matters. The action of 1806, reaffirmed in 1897, directed presbyteries to inspect the education of candidates "during the course of [both their academic and] their theological studies, choosing for them such schools, seminaries and teachers as they may judge most proper and advantageous, so as eventually to bring them into the ministry well furnished for their work." [18]

A widely discussed theological issue during these years was the McGiffert case. Dr. Arthur Cushman McGiffert, formerly professor at Lane Seminary, where he had been Professor Henry Preserved Smith's most unwavering supporter, had come to the chair of church history at Union Seminary. In 1897 he published *A History of Christianity in the Apostolic Age,* which many felt contained teachings contrary to the Westminster Confession of Faith.[19] An overture from Pittsburgh Presbytery to the General Assembly of 1898 brought the matter officially before the Church. The overture charged that in Dr. McGiffert's book "the New Testament is very irreverently handled, no special supernatural guidance is ascribed to its sacred writers, the genuineness of more than one-half of the books composing it is called in question; discordant and mutually contradictory teachings are declared to be contained in it and its authority as a divine rule of faith and practice is set aside. . . . The said volume by Dr. McGiffert is a flagrant and ominous scandal . . . it is the most daring and thoroughgoing attack on the New Testament that has ever been made by an accredited teacher of the Presbyterian Church in America." [20]

Dr. Sheldon Jackson, who was chairman of the Assembly's Committee on Bills and Overtures, to which the Pittsburgh overture was referred, attempted to make light of the matter, and appeared more concerned over the death of nearly three hundred of the famous reindeer which he had recently introduced into Alaska than over the McGiffert issue.[21] But the question could not be lightly dismissed, and the Assembly, after hearing three conflicting reports, took action calculated to condemn the alleged errors in Dr. McGiffert's recent writing and at the same time to avoid the threat to the Church's welfare thought to lie in formal heresy proceedings. New York Presbytery's great size and financial strength were particularly strong deterrents from the latter procedure, especially following so closely upon the Briggs case. The Assembly's action declared in part: "The General Assembly deplores the renewal of controversy occasioned by the publication of this book at a time when our recent divisions were scarcely healed. It sympathizes with the widespread belief that the utterances of Dr. McGiffert are inconsistent with the teachings of Scripture as interpreted by the Presbyterian Church and by evangelical Christendom. . . . But the Church needs peace. . . . The Assembly, therefore, in the spirit of kindness, no less than in devotion to the truth, counsels Dr. McGiffert to reconsider the questionable views set forth in his book, and if he cannot conform his views to the Standards of our Church, then peaceably to withdraw from the Presbyterian ministry." [22]

The Assembly's action in 1898 was offered in the form of counsel rather than as a mandate. Dr. McGiffert chose not to follow the counsel. The following March he published in the *New World* an article entitled "The Study of Early Church History," which showed that his views had not changed.[23] Dr. Francis Brown, who had supported Dr. McGiffert in the Assembly of 1898, viewed the whole question of doctrinal standards in a broad way in an article, "What is Orthodoxy?" in the *North American Review* for April 1899. Our present "sects," Dr. Brown insisted, have no right to define or enforce orthodoxy. Looking toward the reunion of Christendom, he demanded that orthodoxy be formulated briefly and broadly in terms of universal Christian faith.[24] The Presbyterian weekly, the *New York Evangelist,* likewise favored an inclusive churchmanship.[25]

Quite different opinions, however, prevailed in the Presbyterian Church. The General Assembly of 1899 received overtures from ten presbyteries calling attention again to the views expressed by Dr. McGiffert in his book. A letter from Dr. McGiffert to the Assembly was read in which he said that the Pittsburgh overture of the preceding year had grossly misrepresented his opinions. "So far as my views are concerned, they have been and remain, as I believe, in accord with the faith of the Presbyterian Church and evangelical Christendom in all vital and essential matters, and I, therefore, cannot feel that it is my duty, or even my right . . . to withdraw from the ministry of the Presbyterian Church." The letter closed with some words of appreciation that the previous Assembly had endeavored to act with consideration, and professed the writer's devotion to the Church. The loud applause with which the letter was greeted showed a widespread desire to avoid, if possible, any prolonged controversy.[26]

In dealing with the case the Assembly, on recommendation of its Committee on Bills and Overtures, by a rising vote "unanimously" adopted a declaration that four doctrines were "fundamental doctrines" of the Church, as over against views attributed to Dr. McGiffert—the inerrancy of the Scriptures; the inerrancy of all statements made by Jesus Christ; the belief that the Lord's Supper was instituted by Christ himself; and the doctrine of justification through faith alone. "This Assembly enjoins upon all Sessions and Presbyteries loyally to defend and protect these fundamental doctrines of this Confessional Church." Since the "Portland Deliverance" of 1892, the General Assembly seemed increasingly ready to define the Church's "essential" doctrines by Assembly resolutions, a practice which was to become even more conspicuous during the first quarter of the twentieth century. This same Assembly referred back Dr. McGiffert's case to his Presbytery of New York without instructions.[27]

The Presbytery of New York was forced by this action of the Assembly to take cognizance of Dr. McGiffert's case. The professor appeared before a special committee of the presbytery and stated his beliefs on the four subjects which the Assembly had declared to be "fundamental doctrines." As to Scripture, he said he believed it to be "the only infallible rule of faith and practice" as the Confession teaches, but not inerrant. As to the Assembly's second doctrine, Dr. McGiffert insisted on his belief in the deity of Christ, but did not think that Christ's deity necessarily carried with it "absolute freedom from all liability to error, during his earthly existence." The Lord's Supper was a sacrament of which Dr. McGiffert partook "with the greatest joy and spiritual profit." He believed that Christ ate the last supper with his disciples, but doubted that he himself instituted it as a ceremony to be permanently observed. As to the fourth of the Assembly's "fundamental doctrines," justification through faith alone, Dr. McGiffert said he was unaware that he had ever said or written anything which "in any way modifies or belittles the essential act and exclusive necessity of faith in human salvation." [28]

The Presbytery of New York, after extended discussion and various motions, took a middle course by amending and adopting resolutions offered by Dr. Henry van Dyke and another. Dr. van Dyke, it will be recalled, had previously had an important part in drafting both the presbytery's acquittal of Dr. Briggs and *A Plea for Peace and Work*. The resolutions as adopted condemned parts of Dr. McGiffert's book, but refrained from prosecuting him for heresy. Presbytery's specific criticisms did not exactly coincide with the Assembly's four "fundamental doctrines." Presbytery condemned the author's view that the Lord's Supper was not instituted by Christ; that the Third Gospel and the Book of Acts were not written by Luke; that the authorship of the Fourth Gospel is uncertain and that at least some of the discourses in it attributed to Christ are the composition of the author; that Christ stressed not faith in himself but in his message. But in view of Dr. McGiffert's positive affirmations of faith and in view of the clear defense of Presbyterian doctrine made by the recent General Assembly, presbytery felt that a trial for heresy would do more harm than good to the interests of the Church as a whole.[29]

Not all within New York Presbytery were satisfied by this action. Dr. George W. F. Birch, stated clerk of the presbytery, who had served as chairman of the committee that prosecuted Dr. Briggs some years before, presented himself to the presbytery as a private prosecutor and filed heresy charges against Dr. McGiffert. Four of the five charges followed closely the recent Assembly's statement of four fundamental doctrines, while the fifth charged Dr. McGiffert with violations of his ordination vow, "that is, that he has not been zealous and faithful in maintaining the truths of the Gospel and the purity and peace of the Church." When the Presbytery of New York in February 1900 declined to act on the charges on the ground that presbytery had already decided not to institute judicial process, Dr. Birch appealed to the General Assembly of 1900.[30]

With appeal being made to the Assembly that Dr. McGiffert be convicted on formal charges of heresy, the issue became an even more serious peril to the peace of the Church. Since the Assembly of 1899 had expressly condemned certain views which it had at least implied were contained in Dr. McGiffert's book, the outcome of any prolonged litigation appeared to be a foregone conclusion. In the interests of peace, therefore, Dr. McGiffert quietly requested New York Presbytery to permit him to withdraw from the jurisdiction of the Presbyterian Church and to drop his name from the roll of ministers.[31] Presbytery granted the request. The General Assembly of 1900, meeting the next month, granted the desire of Dr. Birch not to prosecute the appeal further and officially declared the case closed.[32] Those who advocated strict doctrinal conformity and opposed a more inclusive type of Church had won another victory. More than two decades of struggle within the Presbyterian Church saw the Church's Biblicism becoming more literal, and saw every attempt to modify Confessional Calvinism turned back. Could the line still be held after the turn of the century? The ultimate answer to this question depended in part on the theological complexion of the teaching which ministerial students would receive in the Church's seminaries.

9.

the church's seminaries

The relation between the American Churches and their theological seminaries was a reciprocal one: the theology that the seminaries taught at any particular time was soon widely held throughout the Churches; and, contrariwise, changes in the Churches' activity and thought, reflecting changes in American social and cultural life after the Civil War, created demands for changes in the curricula of the seminaries.

Thus President Eliot of Harvard and others, noting such new theological disciplines as Biblical introduction and Biblical theology, comparative religion and missions, psychology, philosophy of religion, social studies, religious education, and variations of practical theology, urged the elective system in ministerial education to make possible concentration of study and preparation for specific aspects of ministerial service. Before the turn of the century a few pioneering seminaries ceased to require Hebrew and were experimenting with the elective principle, a tendency which was carried much further during the first quarter of the twentieth century. Theological education, like secular education, was now threatened with loss of integrating principles.[1]

The Presbyterian Church was a decidedly conservative force in theological education. In accordance with the Church's longstanding traditions, Presbyterian seminaries continued to favor systematic theology and its foundations in Biblical studies over against the newer disciplines. By the middle of the twentieth century, courses in Hebrew and Greek were still required. True, a number of General Assemblies discussed the Church's program of theological education, but very few curricular changes were introduced into Presbyterian seminaries before the twentieth century.[2] This emphasis by Presbyterian seminaries on the historically "given" aspect of Christianity was of course a bulwark against theological innovation in general. Before the end of the first quarter of the twentieth century some Presbyterian seminaries—for example, Auburn, Western, and McCormick —were admitting newer elements into their curricula, but Princeton was still stoutly resisting these tendencies.[3]

Because the seminaries were continually molding the Churches' theological future, a theological history of the Presbyterian Church must take cognizance of the direction in which the theological influence of its various seminaries was being exerted. A representative sampling will suffice.

With Union Seminary withdrawing from the Church after the Assembly's veto of Professor Briggs, and with Lane Seminary undergoing drastic theological overhauling after Professor Smith's suspension,[4] Auburn remained as the only unaltered former New School seminary within the Church. This reduction by two thirds (really by more than two thirds) of New School institutional leadership for theological change delayed for decades the Church's adjustment to the newer theological situation.

In what theological direction did Auburn, the surviving representative of the New School heritage, exert its leadership? For nearly four decades after reunion the Old Testament chair at Auburn was occupied by Professor Willis J. Beecher, who demanded freedom for Old Testament scholars, but largely retained traditional views himself.[5] To the end he knew of "no sufficient reason" for disagreeing with those who held that "the accounts in Genesis are at least virtually of Mosaic origin." He did not exclude "some actual errors of fact in the Bible," but insisted on the basic historic trustworthiness of the Old Testament. The line of theological division, he urged, should be run not between varying views of Old Testament scholarship, but between those who affirm evangelical faith in Christ and those who do not.[6] With such views being taught during transitional years, Auburn escaped the overwhelming attack that was made on the Old Testament chairs of Union and Lane. But the new professor of Semitic languages and religions at Auburn, in his inaugural address in 1909, presupposed the newer view of the Old Testament, as did also Dr. Beecher's successor.[7]

From soon after reunion until 1906, the chair of systematic theology at Auburn was occupied by two men of mildly conservative views. The first of these, Dr. Ransom B. Welch, was described by a colleague as "cautiously progressive." Coming out of a childhood background of Unitarian beliefs, he was a convinced Trinitarian. He had clear views on inspiration and atonement, and held to a fully developed system of theology. He favored revision of the Confession of Faith, but was willing to lend his name as associate editor to the journal which Dr. Warfield founded after breaking with Dr. Briggs.[8] Dr. Welch's successor, Dr. Timothy G. Darling, transferred from another Auburn chair, was a moderate and tolerant Calvinist. He regarded Scripture and not experience as the ultimate basis of theology. He rejected Christocentric in favor of theocentric views, and had little sympathy for the "new theology," which he regarded as merely "a transitory phase of theological thought, inadequate to the solution of the deeper problems of life." But he was tolerant of the views of others and aware of the limitations of his own thinking. But Dr. Darling's successor had a very different theological outlook, in which change rather than fixity was the keynote.[9]

The first president of Auburn Seminary, Dr. Henry M. Booth, advocated "fair consideration" for Biblical criticism. In his inaugural, less than half a year after Dr. Briggs's suspension, he demanded toleration and a place in the Church for those holding varying critical views and warned against identifying scholastic theories with the Bible itself. But, while his policy was broad, his own views of Scripture were high.[10] Much more aggressive in his support of the new critical and theological views was Dr. George B. Stewart (president, 1899-1927; professor, 1898-1932). It was his belief that the seminary should not be satisfied with a "middle of the road" theology, but should throw its full strength on the side of theological progressivism.[11] Dr. James S. Riggs (1885-1925) and Dr. Arthur S. Hoyt (1899-1924), together with President Stewart, were important influences in leading the seminary to acceptance of newer views about the Bible. Dr. Allen Macy Dulles, professor of theism and apologetics (1905-30), stressed the newer, more subjective type of apologetic that sought "to put religion beyond the reach of science," and shifted the relative emphasis on creed and life in favor of the latter.[12] Dr. Dulles, who a decade and a half before had criticized Dr. Briggs's views,[13] was representative of those among the Church's theological leaders, who were still a minority but were becoming increasingly important, who were seeking to adjust to the new cultural forces. A later prominent exponent of theological progressivism at Auburn Seminary was Professor Robert Hastings Nichols.

As late as 1891, amid the Briggs commotion, Professor Samuel M. Hopkins lamented that Auburn was "in a fair way to drift clear over on to

Princeton ground," [14] but during the first decade of the twentieth century this sole surviving New School seminary was committing itself quite unambiguously to the newer Biblical and theological views. Auburn, though not one of the largest seminaries, exerted important influence in the Church toward theological change and adaptation. In 1939 Auburn Seminary became affiliated with Union Seminary and moved to New York City.[15]

With the withdrawal or reconstruction of two of the three former New School seminaries in the 1890's, the theological leadership of the Church was held largely by the former Old School seminaries. In what direction, or directions, did they lead?

The Presbyterian Seminary of the Northwest, located in Chicago, and dominating the rapidly growing Midwestern section of the Church, was to exert large, perhaps decisive, influence on the Church's theological history at a crucial juncture in the twentieth century.

Cyrus H. McCormick's desire to maintain in Chicago a Presbyterian seminary that should be politically and theologically conservative was challenged from the beginning by the strong antislavery sentiments of the region and by the predominantly New School complexion of the Presbyterianism of the "Northwest." Concessions were made by receiving former New School men into the seminary's board and faculty, but Dr. Patton's prosecution of the Rev. David Swing hardly aided *rapprochement*.[16] In 1880, the seminary directors asked all professors except Dr. Patton to resign, and presently Dr. Patton accepted a call to Princeton Seminary.[17]

What would be the theological complexion of the new faculty? Dr. Herrick Johnson, the seminary's incoming teacher of sacred rhetoric and pastoral theology, who favored progressive theological views, worked to secure professors of like mind, but found the completed faculty more conservative than he had hoped. Observers of differing viewpoints agreed that a conservative theological outlook was dominant in the reorganized faculty.[18] For a time Mr. McCormick had seemed ready to see the seminary somewhat liberalized in order that new supporters might share his financial responsibilities, but when this hope dimmed he accepted additional responsibilities himself, thus eclipsing prospects of equal representation of former New School elements.[19]

During the decade of the 1880's following the reorganization of the faculty, there were two defenders of the newer theological tendencies, Dr. Herrick Johnson, moderator of the General Assembly of 1882, a preacher and person of great influence,[20] and Dr. Edward L. Curtis, instructor, later professor, in Old Testament and a friend and former student of Dr. Briggs. Dr. Curtis on the whole was quite moderate and reticent about his progressivism, a fact which some of his friends outside of the seminary regretted, particularly after Dr. Briggs's address sharpened theological alignments throughout the Church.[21]

Influential in holding the Seminary of the Northwest to traditional theological views during the 1880's were Dr. Thomas H. Skinner, professor of systematic theology (1883-90), former heresy prosecutor in Cincinnati and conservative stalwart who had influence with the McCormick family;[22] Dr. D. Marquis, professor of New Testament (1883-1908), who held firmly to verbal inspiration;[23] and Dr. Willis G. Craig, professor of church history (1882-91) and later of systematic theology (1891-1911). By nature a more assertive man than Dr. Marquis, Dr. Craig was at first somewhat reticent theologically,[24] but presently became the leader of forces in the seminary opposed to theological innovation. A man of marked ability,[25] he was moderator of the 1893 General Assembly. In his second inaugural, which occurred in the midst of the Briggs case excitement, Dr. Craig pledged himself to teach the inherited federal theology and "to avoid the pride of opinion and the lust for novelty." He affirmed the "verbal or plenary inspiration" of the Bible autographs, a doctrine which he found in the Westminster Confession, and he defended the Mosaic authorship of the Pentateuch. He took a strict view of confessional subscription, and suggested that those who were dissatisfied with the Confession should secure its revision or withdraw from the Church.[26] Dr. Craig in his continuing resistance to theological innovation at the seminary during the 1890's and after the turn of the century was supported by Dr. Marquis, Dr. W. S. Plumer Bryan, a Chicago pastor who came to the seminary's Board of Directors in 1895, and others.[27] When the new *Presbyterian and Reformed Review* was seeking an associate editor from McCormick Seminary—the name which the former Seminary of the Northwest took in 1886—two theological viewpoints on the faculty were in evidence. Discussions in the Church over revision of the Westminster Confession and over the Briggs case made these differences within the McCormick Seminary faculty further manifest.[28]

In 1891 there came to the McCormick faculty one who—excluding of course those now living—influenced the seminary perhaps more than any other professor in its history, Andrew Constantinides Zenos. Born in Constantinople, educated at Robert College and Princeton Seminary, he was at once recognized by Drs. William Henry Green and A. A. Hodge as a scholar of promise. At first, probably reflecting his training under Dr. Green, he was decidedly cool toward negative conclusions of the higher criticism.[29] But even before he came to McCormick, and increasingly through the years, he held a theory of progress which enabled him to make adjustments to new critical and theological views while still keeping evangelical faith warm and bright. "It behooves the scientific investigator," he said two years before coming to McCormick Seminary, "to watch lest he clog the way to true progress, on the one hand, by a fanatical adherence to the old, after it has been proved wrong; or lead and be led to ruin . . . by readily falling in with every new theory, or even by giving it the presumptive right against the old. . . . That which has been accepted for a long while and proved a source of comfort and a means of guidance has some foundation of truth. . . . True progress must from the nature of the case be the result of slow processes." [30]

If there was here a faint intimation of a pragmatic attitude toward old truth, there was also a deep, almost mystical, realization that true progress and life itself involve both continuity and change. In discussing critical or theological problems Dr. Zenos commonly presented first the demands of change, and then closed on the reassuring note of conservation and continuity. He never flew off into doctrinaire radicalism, but treated theological issues in relation to the needs of personal piety and of practical church life. Though not a research scholar like Dr. Briggs, he was amazingly broad and versatile in his theological learning, and was keenly aware of the cultural forces of his day. Full of the zest of living, overflowing with a contagious optimism so characteristic of the America of his day, he was idealistic, kindly, wise, with a touch of enlightened shrewdness. The result was that through critical transitional decades he commanded increasing respect and confidence as the theological guide of the seminary and of its entire ecclesiastical environment.[31]

Hospitable to change within carefully guarded limits, Dr. Zenos soon moved toward a more thoroughgoing acceptance of critical views of the Bible. Within three years of Dr. Briggs's suspension, he was sanctioning, as evangelical, views of the Bible condemned by the Assembly's "Portland Deliverance" and by its judgment against Dr. Briggs. A decade later still he found more advanced critical views not vitiating Christian faith or fellowship.[32]

Before the outbreak of World War I, theological adjustments at McCormick Seminary were about completed. Dr. Marquis had retired and Dr. Craig had died less than a decade before. Dr. James G. K. McClure, who had become the seminary's first president in 1905, was hospitable to the newer views, as were others who came to the faculty during the second decade of the twentieth century.[33] A distinguished alumnus described the resulting theological position of the seminary and of the Westminster Confession to which it adhered as being, in "a fine middle course . . . with a reasonable liberty . . . with an affirmatory faith, with a sound, inclusive theology." [34] With more than two thirds of the strength of the former New School seminaries removed from organic relation to the Church, it was to be of incalculable importance for the Presbyterian Church's theological history in the troubled 1920's and 1930's that the seminary which dominated the Church's Midwestern area had made its own internal theological adjustments and had already graduated a number of academic generations indoctrinated in the newer theological views before these times of renewed controversy arrived. It was partly due to the quiet but powerful influence of McCormick Seminary over the years that the Church in the 1920's and

1930's finally adopted a quite different theological attitude from that which had prevailed in the 1880's and 1890's.

Another important seminary of the former Old School was Western Seminary, founded in 1827 at Allegheny, Pennsylvania, now part of Pittsburgh. Its location in a chief stronghold of the Church's Scotch-Irish constituency early committed it to the more churchly, authoritarian type of Presbyterianism. In its early years it was sometimes spoken of as "the Princeton of the West," and more than once vigorously orthodox supporters of Princeton Seminary threatened to transfer their support and add it to the existing resources of Western if Princeton's orthodoxy showed signs of flabbiness. Western Seminary showed more reluctance than Princeton to coöperate in the somewhat broad policies of the *Presbyterian Review*. The seminary's influence was very great in the entire Pittsburgh area, which, with Philadelphia, was a chief center of theological conservatism in the Church. If this seminary should modify its position and make adjustments to the newer viewpoints, the rightist forces in the Church would be greatly weakened.

Dr. Samuel H. Kellogg (1877-85), who succeeded Dr. A. A. Hodge as professor of systematic theology at Western, was a foe of theological change and taught the premillennial return of Christ.[35] Dr. Robert Christie, professor of theology (1892-1912) and of apologetics (1912-23), held to the Church's historic theology and used Hodge's *Systematic Theology* as a textbook. But he was not a controversialist and was a man of independence of thought, who helped to pave the way for change of theological outlook.[36] Dr. James H. Snowden, who succeeded to the theology chair (1912-26), moved a little further into fresh paths. Bones, said he, speaking of theology, are useful members of the anatomy, but the higher animals "do not wear them on the outside." He thought of theology as a progressive science. He was ready to accept many of the conclusions of Biblical criticism, such as the plural authorship of Isaiah, the postexilic completion of the Pentateuch, and the postexilic origin of many other Old Testament books. While he did not emphasize "inspiration," he insisted that there was in the Bible a uniquely divine element. He emphatically taught the deity of Christ who was "perfect God and perfect man," and held to the virgin birth, Christ's death as "a vicarious sacrifice," and a resurrection which left Christ's tomb empty, to mention doctrines very much under discussion at the time.[37]

The history of Western Seminary's Biblical chairs is a parallel story of the emergence of a moderate progressivism during the first two decades of the twentieth century. From 1877 to 1900, Old Testament professorships, with some overlapping, had been held by Dr. William H. Jeffers, who boasted of Western Seminary's theological "conservatism,"[38] and by Dr. Robert Dick Wilson, later a champion against critical views of the Old Testament, but at this more moderate stage of his career seriously considering using as a textbook Dr. Briggs's controversial *Messianic Prophecy*.[39]

Their successor, Dr. James A. Kelso (1901-43), who held a Leipsic Ph.D., introduced a more favorable attitude toward Old Testament criticism. During most of this time (1909-43) Dr. Kelso was also president of the seminary.

In the New Testament chair at Western Seminary Dr. B. B. Warfield (1879-87) was succeeded by Dr. Matthew B. Riddle (1887-1911), one of the most notable professors in the seminary's history. Older alumni still fondly recall his picturesque classroom mannerisms and his inspiring qualities as a teacher. He was a member of the American Committee of New Testament revisers, but was particularly proud of his chaplaincy in the Grand Army of the Republic. In his personal views on New Testament questions he seldom deviated far from traditional conclusions, but he inspired his students to openmindedness and fresh, independent investigation of the facts. He thus helped to prepare those who studied under him and the seminary as a whole to adjust to the critical viewpoint.[40] The very moderate progressivism which began to characterize Western Seminary on the eve of World War I contributed in an important way to modifying the Church's right-wing tradition.

San Francisco Seminary, the only Presbyterian seminary on the Pacific Coast, was opened with four students in 1871, soon after the Old School-New School reunion. For nearly a decade faculty members served without salary. One of the principal founders, Dr. William A. Scott, a man of Southern connections and sympathies, sought advice in the East concerning possible faculty members. In 1892 the seminary moved to its present site in San Anselmo. Physical vicissitudes were still experienced, but in the twentieth century the seminary forged ahead, becoming after World War I the third in size of the Church's seminaries.[41]

Dr. William Alexander, the longest in service of the original professors (1871-1906), was a lifelong opponent of theological change. He was against revision of the Confession of Faith, protesting that the example of the Congregationalists and other denominations was no adequate argument for it. "We have long had an element in the Presbyterian Church," he lamented, obviously caricaturing the New School heritage, "which felt it to be their duty to sneeze whenever the Congregationalists take snuff." He urged Dr. Warfield not to make the irenic policy of the new *Presbyterian and Reformed Review* too broad and pacific: "If you should find it necessary to do battle in defence of the truth, just please count me in." [42]

One of San Francisco Seminary's notable figures was Dr. Henry Collin Minton, professor of systematic theology (1892-1902) and moderator of the General Assembly of 1901. At least as much as did typical Princeton theologians, he emphasized the role of reason in Christianity. "There is really no essential difference between religious knowledge and any other kind of knowledge. The conditions of knowledge, the laws of cognition, are not contingent upon the nature of the truth apprehended." [43] The result was a rather rigorous rational orthodoxy much after the Princeton pattern.

The attempt of a professor shortly before World War I to teach the documentary view of the Pentateuch brought adverse discussion in the Synod of California, and his successor deëmphasized critical problems.[44] In the middle 1920's, such a well-known fundamentalist as Dr. Lapsley A. McAfee boasted of the seminary's orthodoxy.[45] As with Princeton Seminary, it was not until well on in the twentieth century that critical views were treated sympathetically. With its enlarged faculty and student body and with its expanding program, San Francisco Seminary today occupies a position of great influence in the Church.

Louisville Presbyterian Theological Seminary is a distinguished example of an institution jointly operated by Northern and Southern Presbyterians. Formed in 1901 as "The Presbyterian Theological Seminary of Kentucky" by the merger of Danville Theological Seminary (Northern, founded 1853) and the Louisville Presbyterian Theological Seminary (Southern, founded 1893) it received its present name in 1928.[46]

Two seminaries—Dubuque Theological Seminary (begun in 1852 and taken under care of the Presbyterian Church in 1864, for a time known as "The German Theological School of the Northwest") and Bloomfield Theological Seminary (founded in 1869, and in 1870 taken under care of the General Assembly of the reunited Church as "The German Theological School, Newark, New Jersey")—in earlier years specialized in training pastors for German-speaking Presbyterians, but for many years have been serving a broader constituency, with some specialization in training ministers for rural and industrial fields, respectively.[47] Two seminaries—the Lincoln University Theological Seminary (chartered in 1854 as the Ashmun Institute) and the Johnson C. Smith Theological Seminary (founded in 1867 as the Biddle Memorial Institute)—have specialized in the training of Negro ministers. The Evangelical (Theological) Seminary of Puerto Rico is the only seminary reporting directly to the General Assembly that is located outside of the continental United States. Two institutions, in addition to others previously mentioned, have ceased within the period 1869-1953 to function as Presbyterian seminaries—Blackburn University and Omaha Theological Seminary.[48] The theological complexion of Princeton, Union, and Lane seminaries is discussed in other chapters.[49] As the Church faced theological issues in the twentieth century, the decisions which it would make would be to an important degree the result of the instruction that had been given and was being given in its theological seminaries.

10.

revision accomplished

The movement in the Presbyterian Church to revise the Westminster Confession of Faith had seemingly been brought to an end in 1893 when no one of the proposed amendments received the necessary vote of two thirds of the presbyteries. But eighteen of the twenty-eight amending overtures had been supported by a majority of the presbyteries, though lacking the constitutional two-thirds majority, and the situation could hardly be expected to rest permanently in this state of unstable equilibrium. The problem, furthermore, had been complicated in 1893 by the fact that some doubted the constitutionality of the method of revision which was being used, and the whole issue was colored by the heated discussion of the Briggs and Smith heresy cases. Meanwhile, the forces which originally prompted the revision effort were growing stronger rather than weaker.[1] Another attempt among Presbyterians to revise the Westminster Confession was therefore to be expected.

The second revision movement came to birth very suddenly in the spring of 1900 just as the McGiffert case was coming to a close. Writing in the middle of May, one denominational editor was able to say of the renewed attempt at revision, "No one predicted it three months ago." [2] But the General Assembly of 1900 received overtures from some thirty-seven or thirty-eight presbyteries requesting revision of the Confession, or a new creed, or both.[3] As there was diversity of opinion among the overturing presbyteries, a Committee of Fifteen was appointed to study the matter, to receive recommendations from all the presbyteries, and to report to the next Assembly.[4]

Among the distinguished laymen appointed to the committee were Benjamin Harrison, former president of the United States, and John M. Harlan, associate justice of the United States Supreme Court. Dr. Benjamin B. Warfield, professor of theology at Princeton Seminary, was also appointed to the committee, but declined. "It is an inexpressible grief to me," he explained, "to see it [i.e., the Church] spending its energies in a vain attempt to lower its testimony to suit the ever changing sentiment of the world about it." [5] The professor of theology at McCormick Seminary, Dr. Willis G. Craig, was likewise opposed to revision. The moderator of the recent Assembly, Dr. Charles A. Dickey, commented in a general way that there was among some in the Church "a determined purpose to resist all endeavor to harmonize the Church unless the Church is willing to accept the harmony of standing still." As one who would give strong leadership to forces of moderate change he therefore appointed to the committee position left vacant by Dr. Warfield's resignation Dr. Henry van Dyke of Princeton University, whose father had been a principal leader of the earlier revision movement.[6]

The Assembly's committee met in August 1900 and drafted four questions to send to all the presbyteries of the Church:

"1. Do you desire a revision of our Confession of Faith? or

"2. Do you desire a supplemental explanatory statement? or

"3. Do you desire to supplement our present Doctrinal Standards with a briefer statement . . . ? or

"4. Do you desire the dismissal of the whole subject . . . ?"[7]

Revision was widely discussed throughout the Church. Dr. Duffield, professor emeritus at Princeton University, who had been a prominent advocate of revision a decade before, again took up his pen in its defense.[8] Dr. Geerhardus Vos, like others on the Princeton Seminary faculty, put himself on record against revision. He thought that one of the gravest symptoms of the revision movement was its lack of serious appeal to Scriptural authority for the confessional changes it advocated.[9] The *Presbyterian*, which like the *New York Observer* was opposed to revision, thought it discerned in the autumn of 1900 a reaction away from the movement.[10] This hope, however, was to prove vain.

One of the most interesting symposia which the controversy brought forth was that held under the auspices of the Presbyterian Union of New York in March 1901. The three speakers were all members of theological seminary faculties: Professor John DeWitt, then of Princeton Seminary; President George B. Stewart, of Auburn Seminary; and Professor Herrick Johnson, of McCormick Seminary.

Dr. DeWitt, speaking against any kind of revision of the Confession of Faith, employed the rather pragmatic argument of "peace and work" which was now, somewhat paradoxically, frequently being used even to preserve truth against change! "In the present crisis of our Church we shall pursue the wisest policy if . . . we shall hold unchanged our present Confession, and shall direct our undistracted forces to the Christian work to which the new century summons us and in respect of which we are happily and profoundly united." The expanding activity of the Church was becoming an increasingly weighty, and sometimes a determining, factor in deciding the Church's policies. Groups in power—whether conservative or liberal or mediating—were making more and more use of it as an argument against disturbing the theological *status quo* or altering existing policies.[11]

As against revision, Dr. DeWitt asserted further that successful creed-making periods are ages of faith, whereas the present is an age of doubt. Some were urging that new doctrines based on new developments in science, philosophy, and theology should now be given creedal statement, but Dr. DeWitt insisted that these recent views were as yet unripe fruit, "and unripe fruit is always disappointing, often painful and sometimes fatal to the organism which attempts its assimilation." [12]

President Stewart, in addressing the Presbyterian Union of New York, advocated the writing of an entirely new, briefer creed. While paying tribute to the great historic influence of the Westminster Confession, he denied that it represented the faith of the Church today. "We are not taken seriously when we affirm that it does." He enumerated some of the things in the Confession most frequently criticized—its doctrine of preterition, its designation of the pope as Antichrist, its reference to "elect infants," its failure to affirm God's universal love, its inadequate treatment of the Holy Spirit, and its silence on the Church's world-wide mission. Furthermore, the philosophy, science, and theological terminology of the seventeenth century are not those of the twentieth. "The God of the Confession is a Sovereign after the notion of sovereignty that obtained in a monarchial country of the seventeenth century. We to-day believe quite as truly in the sovereignty of God, but it is a sovereignty interpreted not in terms of monarchy but of Fatherhood." He envisaged a new Presbyterian creed as a possible contribution to church unity: "While other churches are laboring to bring in a unity in forms of worship, or attitude toward the sacraments, we should labor to bring in a unity in doctrine. This is a unity by far the most important and a unity which we might rightly regard as our mission to believers." [13] This type of plea for creedal revision in the interests of creating a more inclusive Church, voiced so often by Dr. Briggs and others during the first revision controversy, was less frequently heard during the second attempt at revision.

Dr. Herrick Johnson of McCormick Seminary, the other speaker before the Presbyterian Union, advocated revision in two ways, by textual alteration and by supplementary doctrinal statement. Dwelling particularly on the latter, he urged that it could adequately provide the needed confessional treatment of the Holy Spirit, of missions, and of God's universal love. As matters now stand, he charged, "across our Confession could justly be written, 'The Gospel for the elect only.' . . . Go search our Confession for an unequivocal statement of God's love for all men as sinners. You will not find it." The remedy for this and for its other defects lies in a supplemental statement which "will be to the old Confession something like what the Shorter Catechism is to the Larger." [14] It was reported that "the sentiment of the audience seemed about evenly divided" among the diverging views of the three speakers.[15]

The General Assembly of 1901 found that revision was the absorbing issue confronting it. The report of the Committee of Fifteen as amended and adopted analyzed communications received from 202 presbyteries. Of these presbyteries, sixty-three favored some revision of the text of the Confession; while sixty-eight—the two categories are not mutually exclusive—desired some form of supplemental statement. The report interpreted this and other information as showing that the Church "desired some change in its creedal statement," but none that "would in any way impair the integrity of the system of doctrine contained in the Confession of Faith." Radical revision was, therefore, ruled out. Specific points were named at which the presbyteries had expressed desire for revision. The report as adopted recommended that the Assembly appoint a new committee to draft and to present to the next Assembly a brief statement of the Reformed faith and also amendments to the Westminster Confession. The brief statement drawn up "as far as possible in untechnical terms" should be designed for giving information, but was not to become a part of the Church's formal doctrinal Standards.

The new Committee of Twenty-one which was to prepare the amendments was representative of many views in the Church, including in its membership Drs. DeWitt, Stewart, and Johnson, who had expressed their diverging opinions before the New York Presbyterian Union earlier in the year. Dr. van Dyke and Associate Justice John M. Harlan were also members.[16]

The movement for moderate revision, which was rapidly gaining ground, was not entirely without opposition. Professor Geerhardus Vos, for example, had the revision movement in mind when he chose for his address at the opening of Princeton Seminary in the autumn of 1901 the topic "The Scriptural Doctrine of the Love of God." He made the claim that, though orthodoxy in its period of supremacy did not stress God's love exclusively as was now the tendency, it did in those days appreciate more fully "the infinite complexity and richness of the life of God." He found the new extreme emphasis on the love of God at least partly due to new ethical interests: "Where the religious interest is exclusively concentrated upon the will, and entirely exhausts itself in attempts at solving the concrete, practical problems of life, no strong incentive will exist for reflecting upon any other aspect of the nature of God than his love, because all that is required of God is that he shall serve as the norm and warrant for Christian philanthropic effort." He cited the German theologian, Albrecht Ritschl, as an extreme example of the effort to rebuild theology on the basis of God's love and of the restriction of religion to the sphere of the will. The divine love which is stressed in the Bible, he said, "is not God's general benevolence, but His special affection for His people." Pointing to the failure of the French school of Saumur in the seventeenth century to incorporate into Calvinism greater emphasis on God's universal love, Dr. Vos urged the Church to act only with the greatest care and caution in the task of revision "which, wisely or unwisely, she has set herself." [17]

Meanwhile the revision committee appointed by the General Assembly of 1901 set itself heroically to the task of having its report completed for the Assembly of the next year. The committee held five meetings and was in session a total of thirty days. The greater part of its time was devoted, not to drafting amendments for the Westminster Confession, but to preparing the new "Brief Statement of the Reformed Faith." [18] In undertaking to formulate the Brief Statement, the committee was not without suggestions from outside, furnished by most of the professors of theology in Presbyterian seminaries in response to the request of Dr. DeWitt, a member of the committee. Dr. Adam McClelland of Dubuque, for example, though of Old School background, suggested that some of the creeds used by local congregations of the Congregationalists might prove helpful to the committee.[19] Others, too, submitted proposals, but the task of the committee was nevertheless great.

In spite of its heavy schedule the committee was not without its social diversions. When it met in Washington, its members were the guests one evening of a fellow committeeman, Mr. John W. Foster, former secretary of state. "The Army was there in the person of General Miles; the Supreme Court, in Justice Harlan; the Navy, in Admiral Simpson; Science was represented in Graham Bell; . . . and members of Cabinet, the Senate, and House, unnumbered." [20] When the committee met in Philadelphia two months later, it was entertained by Mrs. John Wanamaker, "at her handsome residence on Walnut Street. . . . A number of our more prominent ministers were present." [21]

At the General Assembly of 1902 the committee presented its report. Making use of the discretion granted it, the committee employed three methods of revision—by declaratory statement, by textual modification, and by supplementary statement. A Declaratory Statement explained that "Chapter III, of God's Eternal Decree," was to be interpreted in harmony with the belief that God loves all mankind; and that Chapter X, Section 3, which speaks of "elect infants" "is not to be regarded as teaching that any who die in infancy are lost. We believe that all dying in infancy are included in the election of grace."

The committee proposed three textual modifications. In Chapter XVI, 7, which discusses the good deeds of unregenerate men, the committee recommended slight verbal alterations, especially to change the statement that these deeds are "sinful" to read "they come short of what God requires." The committee suggested omitting from Chapter XXII, 3, the statement that it is sinful to refuse a legal oath, and dropping from Chapter XXV, 6, the accusation that "the Pope of Rome" is "antichrist." The third type of revision, supplemental statement, was used to add two new chapters to the Confession entitled, respectively, "Of the Holy Spirit" and "Of the Love of God and Missions." [22]

The committee also submitted a "Brief Statement of the Reformed Faith" in sixteen short articles. The Brief Statement, because not offered as an amendment to the Confession, was not to be submitted to the presbyteries for approval. This Brief Statement, of which the principal author was Dr. van Dyke,[23] was heartily acclaimed at the time but never as fully used by the Church as its merit might have warranted. A leading theologian has commented on the Brief Statement: "Its tone is religious rather than speculative . . . and, while the sterner truths of Christianity receive their due recognition, they are subordinated to the great unifying purpose of love." A few years later the Assembly rejected a proposal that the Brief Statement be adopted as the creed of the Church, which would of course have constituted a revolutionary simplifying of the Church's theological standards.[24]

The General Assembly of 1902 devoted less than two hours to the revision question. President James D. Moffat of Washington and Jefferson College in arguing for revision followed the growing habit of basing theological arguments on the importance of the Church's work. "We ought to bring this creed business to as speedy an end as possible. It has been before us for twelve years. There is danger that the workers in our Church will grow weary of all these disturbances and theological distinctions. They cannot understand them." The Assembly adopted with only two dissenting votes the committee's report recommending that the proposed amendments be transmitted as overtures to the presbyteries for their rejection or adoption, and that the Assembly adopt at once the "Brief Statement." [25]

A professor in the Southern Presbyterian Church, interpreting this action of the Northern Assembly from a very conservative point of view, acknowledged that the revision overtures now sent down to the presbyteries were "much less radical" than those proposed ten years before. "Over a score of changes in the text of the Confession were then proposed, and some of them were quite important. The present revision proposes only three changes in the text of the Confession." He concluded with the concession, "If they [i.e., the revision overtures] should be enacted, the generic Calvinism of the Standards will yet remain, though perhaps toned down a little here and there." [26]

The revision movement which had appeared so ominous to many in the early 1890's, and whose resurrection in 1900 had been accompanied by renewed fears, was now rapidly coming to completion. The result of nearly fifteen years of struggle was a few verbal alterations in the Confession which even the stanchest conservatives in the Church acknowledged did not seriously alter its basic Calvinism. These results of a decade and a half of discussion reveal how strong conservative influence in the Church was at the turn of the century.

Facing the overtures quite fearlessly, the *Presbyterian*, which two years before had urged that no opponent of revision consent to the movement merely out of courtesy, now advised, in effect, that the Church innoculate itself with the present mild dose in order to be immune against a more serious epidemic of revision in the future.[27]

Dr. Warfield remained in opposition to confessional revision to the end. But it was interesting that his criticisms of the revision overtures were directed against their diction rather than their theology. "There are few accurately conceived or justly expressed sentences in them," he said. "Why should a great Church adopt such a body of loosely expressed sentences as part of its profession of faith?" [28] The voting of the presbyteries shows that the *Presbyterian Journal* undoubtedly expressed the views of great numbers of conservatives when it wrote editorially, "If Professor Warfield's microscope reveals no more flies than those mentioned, then the revision ointment is about as pure as human ingenuity can make it." [29]

When the General Assembly of 1903 officially counted the votes of the presbyteries, it was found that no overture had received the endorsement of less than 215 of the Church's 238 presbyteries. Thus all eleven overtures had been approved by well over the necessary two-thirds majority of the presbyteries. After the Assembly "unanimously by a rising vote" had adopted the overtures, they were declared to be a part of the Church's constitution.[30]

There was a feeling of relief that the matter was settled. After the unanimous vote, the Assembly sang the Doxology and engaged in "praise and prayer."[31] The *Presbyterian Journal* rejoiced that the matter was now merely a "past issue." "No doctrine has been touched, so the church stands just where it did before." The editor was glad that certain ambiguities of the Confession had been removed, and scoffed at fears that this was "but the beginning of a series of agitations." [32]

The Philadelphia *Public Ledger* hastened to pay its editorial tribute to the Church's action. Viewing the spreading belief in divine immanence as well as current tendencies to simplify theology as forces operating against Calvinism, the *Ledger* marveled at the vitality of Presbyterianism which without altering the basic doctrines of its Confession was able "to render it instantly so much more congenial to the modern mind." [33]

This action brought to an end a controversy about revision which with intermissions had lasted nearly a decade and a half. It showed that the Church was ready to make some theological alterations in response to the spirit of the times, but revealed still more that as the twentieth century began, basic theological conservatism controlled the Church's counsels. Viewed in perspective, this revision is seen as an important stage in the Church's very gradual theological change.[34] Quite apart from revision, there were some who thought that by this time the Presbyterian Church had come to "the practical abandonment" of Calvinism.[35] But this view of the matter was not widely asserted.

11.

the emerging issue

With the coming of the twentieth century, critical reason, as developed by the Renaissance and further emphasized by the Enlightenment, came to full fruition. After Josiah Royce, the idealist, there was less interest in philosophical systems. More typical of the new century in America was William James, the pragmatist, who rejected all absolutes and ultimate security, and said that truth is in process of becoming: truth is what works. At the close of World War I, relativism found fuller expression than it had ever before had in American literature, and challenged democracy and other traditional ideals with a new note of deep cynicism. Joseph Wood Krutch and Walter Lippmann discerningly analyzed the new mood. Even the natural sciences, which previously had seemed thoroughly "solid," now took on the relativism of the times and further undermined faith in human reason. The social sciences began to lose confidence in their earlier ideal of "objectivity." Ethics, too, felt the shock of relativism. Meanwhile the psychology of religion invaded the inner shrine of spiritual experience, and attempted a thoroughly naturalistic explanation of what it found there.

American theology met these radical changes in the cultural pattern in three different ways—by a left-wing viewpoint, a right-wing viewpoint, and a viewpoint borrowed from recent theology of the European Continent. Hardly had Biblical criticism won the day in most scholarly circles before a small but growing minority of American theologians veered off sharply to the left, fully accepting relativism in religion. The effort was made to develop an empirical theology on the basis of the natural sciences and the social sciences, a naturalism which abandoned revelation as the foundation of Christian thought, and increasingly departed from historic Christianity. In these and some other circles the philosophy of religion began to supersede theology. Some of the more radical theologians tried to devise a "theism" within the framework of naturalism, while others went on at once to humanism. Ethics among thinkers of this type of course followed the same pattern of relativism. Rejecting the authority of the Bible and of the example of Jesus, ethics, too, sought to be empirical and scientific. This type of theology in America was almost entirely confined to secular universities, and had little if any root in the actual life of the American Churches. Sociologically it was associated with the sophisticated industrial civilization of the great cities. Within most of the Churches themselves—and this was notably true of the Presbyterian Church—advocates of theological change stopped short of radical naturalism, preferring a mediating liberalism which accepted much of the scientific spirit and methodology, but held tenaciously to historic Christianity. No doubt, for some at least, this mediating position was in unstable equilibrium—as opponents at both extremes continually charged—but the "liberal" theological viewpoint became increasingly influential within the Churches. Thus, theological discussions on the popular and ecclesiastical level, which in the late nineteenth century had been confined largely to Biblical questions, now extended over a much wider front to include many other theological issues.

Over against this leftward movement a right-wing movement, dubbed "fundamentalism," sought to defend the "fundamentals" of Christianity against liberalism and ultimately against the outright naturalism which it suspected lurked behind liberalism's compromises. "Fundamentalism," which reached its climax amid the tensions and maladjustments of the decade following World War I, was not entirely new, but was an extension of the late nineteenth-century struggle against the negative conclusions of Biblical criticism and the rising theological "liberalism." American Protestant fundamentalism had its Roman Catholic counterpart in the condemnation of "Modernism" by Pope Pius X in 1907.

The evangelistic tradition and individual evangelists made a notable contribution to the fundamentalist movement, as did Bible institutes and Bible conferences in various parts of the country. In 1895 the Niagara Bible Conference drew up a list of basic doctrines—the inerrancy of the Scriptures, Christ's deity, virgin birth, substitutionary atonement, bodily resurrection, and future physical return to earth. Many date the beginnings of fundamentalism from the publication of *The Fundamentals*, a series of twelve pamphlets which began to appear in 1909. American fundamentalism first organized on a quasi-national basis with the creation in 1919 of the World's Christian Fundamentals Association at a meeting in Philadelphia.[1] Most conservative Presbyterians, while welcoming every movement that promised to aid in the struggle against liberalism, did not identify themselves completely with interdenominational fundamentalism at the double price of abandoning distinctive Calvinism and accepting premillennialism.

Though rightly apprehensive of the deadly error of naturalism in trying to reduce Christianity to the dimensions of natural science, fundamentalism—using the term broadly to include the aggressively conservative party in the various denominations—failed to grapple profoundly or creatively with the issues involved. Against the challenge to revelation fundamentalism continued to offer only Biblical inerrancy; questions concerning the Person of Christ were met with emphasis on his virgin birth; and the threats of a pantheizing or mechanistic world view were answered by stressing physical miracles. It is true, five or six such "fundamentals" lent themselves readily to ecclesiastical use. On their surface they appeared to make concrete the highly abstract and elusive (and crucially important) theological issues of the hour. They could be briefly stated, and, best of all, from the point of view of their sponsors, they promised to classify the theological position of any minister or ministerial candidate by means of a few brief, formal questions. But could the basic issues of contemporary culture and religion be packaged so neatly and handled so externally?

Just before theological controversy in Presbyterian judicatories came to an end in 1936, an important new movement, "neo-orthodoxy," was beginning to appear in American theology. It was born amid suffering and disillusionment in Continental Europe following World War I, and appeared on the American scene during the economic dislocation of the 1930's. It radically challenged the pantheizing tendencies of an optimistic liberalism that had glorified man and forgotten that God is "totally other" than man. While accepting, sometimes even in radical form the results of Biblical criticism, neo-orthodoxy emphasized revelation and redemption as acts of God's initiative and grace. It accepted the prevailing skeptical attitude toward metaphysical speculation and did not undertake to deliver culture as a whole from the relativism and historicism which had engulfed it. But it insisted with all the energy of its powerful dialectic that, by God's grace coming through Christ, man could, at the one point of an actual "divine-human encounter," escape the quagmire of relativism and have true, even if paradoxical, contact with the absolute God. This theology was too sophisticated and too antithetical to long-prevailing American optimism to secure wide acceptance in the United States, but some of its insights and many of its catchwords enjoyed increasing vogue. It was a challenge to naturalism and to naturalistic tendencies, in the name of historic Christianity and somewhat after the pattern of John Calvin, which arrested attention throughout the Protestant world and beyond.

As the Presbyterian Church dealt with these theological issues, the forces that were really decisive in the discussion were not theological, but ecclesiastical; not ideological, but sociological and physical. This was the case at least after the reunion of 1869, and especially after the turn of the twentieth century. Amazing activity in Christian service at home and abroad has been the chief glory of American Christianity and to this activity the Presbyterian Church has contributed its full share. Partly arising from such activities the Church has faced two basic problems which were also troubling statesmen during these years—the problems of power and freedom. To promote and administer its rapidly expanding home and foreign missionary and educational program the Church had to develop the necessary administrative power. This meant steadily increasing centralization. More and more the General Assembly became occupied with promotional and administrative matters. The responsibilities of its official boards and agencies grew apace. New executive agencies, like the Executive Commission which later became the General Council, were created to give firmer and more aggressive leadership to the expanding program. These developments in the Church exactly paralleled the increasing activity and centralization of the federal government during these years.

Could freedom be preserved in the face of growing governmental power? It is too early for a final answer in either church or state, but during the years to be viewed in coming chapters the Presbyterian Church was forced, in order to preserve its unity, to decentralize control over the theological beliefs of its ministers and candidates for the ministry. The problem of power and freedom has thus been solved to date by simultaneously increasing administrative centralization and decreasing theological centralization; increasing physical power while at the same time anxiously seeking to prevent its trespassing on the realm of the spirit. This was also a concession to the pluralistic character of modern culture. Implicit in the reunion of 1869, explicit in the *Plea for Peace and Work* of 1893, and increasingly prominent through at least the first third of the twentieth century was a pragmatic conception of the Church which, in the interests of avoiding divisions that would injure the Church's work, has substituted broad church inclusion of opposing theological views for theological answers to them. To adapt Santayana's figure, the Church's theology has been living in a modest colonial house, more and more overshadowed by the skyscraper of the Church's active work.[2]

There were other forces, too, which were affecting the nature of the Church and its attitude toward theological thought. The interdependence of modern industrial life, accompanied by the pronounced swing from individualism to more organic conceptions, was reflected in the Christian Church's conception of itself. As men were becoming associated in great power blocs—whether as industry, labor, civil government, or in other ways—churchmen felt the need of larger and tighter association for effective religious testimony and work. This was reflected in increasing interest in church coöperation and union, reaching a high point in the formation of the Federal Council of Churches of Christ in America in 1908. The theological effect of emphasis on coöperation and union was of course to minimize theological particularities and differences, and to stress broader theological similarities. Efforts to apply Christian remedies to social ills caused the Churches to think of themselves more organically, and to entertain larger, more "churchly" views of their responsibilities to society as a whole. The cultivation of greater dignity and richer symbolism in worship, with the Presbyterian General Assembly in 1906 approving a Book of Common Worship for voluntary use, reflected as well as stimulated more mystical and organic conceptions of the Church.

These and other "churchly" forces of cohesion and integration were operating within the American Churches to counteract such powerful "sectarian" influences in American Christianity as the great numerical strength of Churches having the congregational form of government, the separation of church and state, the extensive activity and influence of laymen, the importance of the heritage of revivalism, radical democracy, the multiplicity of denominations. The growth of more organic views of the Church made the conception held by many fundamentalists seem unsatisfying and irrelevant—e.g., the idea that the Church was a theological voluntary society formed *ad hoc* by individuals because they agreed in their theological opinions. In the larger organic conception, the Church's theology was felt to be a part of the larger whole of the Church's total common life, and not its sole *raison d'être.* These tendencies toward more organic conceptions of the Church also tended to counteract that other contractual conception often implied in American activism that the Church is primarily a business corporation chartered to do the Lord's work. With the widening acceptance of Biblical criticism, Protestants were even becoming ready to acknowledge a larger role for the Church's authority in theology, ready at least to give increasing weight to the common "consensus" of Christians. Thus along with perilous theological change, the times were bringing a new, or at least a rediscovered, dimension into American Protestantism—some recovery of "the communion of saints," the sense of a common participation in the Christian heritage, and a growing sense of spiritual solidarity. This budding mystical conception of the Church, together with the more external need for teamwork if the Church's work was to be administered efficiently, made church splits and divisions for theological or any other reasons less and less palatable to twentieth-century Americans.

In the more than eight decades since the reunion of 1869, the Presbyterian Church has sought to work out its relation to the newer cultural and theological forces through two long and painful controversies. The first of these, as has already been observed, extended over nearly a decade and a half, from 1889 to 1903, and ended in a very decided, though slightly qualified, conservative victory. The Church officially took its stand for Biblical inerrancy; Dr. Briggs, Dr. Smith, and Dr. McGiffert were driven out of the Presbyterian ministry largely for holding views at variance with this doctrine; and all radical revision of the Church's Confession of Faith was successfully resisted. The sweeping conservative victory was qualified only by the slight changes made in the Confession, which even the most orthodox agreed did not alter its basic Calvinism.

This protracted struggle was followed by nearly two decades of comparative calm, from 1904 to 1922. Then came the second, and, in a sense, more conclusive struggle over the same basic issue of the proper attitude of the Church toward the theological views which were now no longer new. The second controversy also lasted almost a decade and a half, from 1922 to 1936, and issued in quite different results from those attending the earlier struggle. During the second period it was very definitely decided after prolonged discussion that the Church should adopt a more inclusive policy. Heresy prosecutions during this later contest were not even attempted by the most conservative. The Church finally felt its way toward an open recognition of the full right of moderate liberals to be ministers and officials.

The years between controversies, 1904 to 1922, were somewhat quieter, but were none the less important. Exclusive principles of churchmanship triumphed completely in the controversy preceding this interlude. More inclusive principles gained the ascendency in the controversy which followed the interlude. It must therefore be inferred that during these years of comparative peace attitudes of churchmen, unseen and unrealized, were quietly changing.

During these two decades there were developing within the Presbyterian Church the two opposing forces of ecclesiastical inclusiveness on the one hand and a new self-conscious among the more pronounced conservatives on the other hand.

The tendencies toward inclusiveness found expression in the negotiations for reunion with the Cumberland Presbyterian Church. In 1810 some of the leaders of the Kentucky revival, charging that the creed of Presbyterians was fatalistic, and also finding fault with that Church's great emphasis on an educated ministry, organized a separate denomination which soon took the name the Cumberland Presbyterian Church. The Cumberland Church grew rapidly, but continued to feel that the alleged "fatalism" of the Presbyterians necessitated its continued separate existence. Efforts, for example, by the Presbyterian Church a few years after the Old School-New School reunion looking toward union with the Cumberland Church foundered on the same theological rock.[3]

In connection with the attempt of Presbyterians to revise the Westminster Confession of Faith both in the 1890's and at the turn of the century it was sometimes argued that revision would contribute toward church union in general, but the present writer has found no Presbyterian arguments offered at the time of those revision discussions that revision should be undertaken for the purpose of making possible union with the Cumberland Church in particular. But the possibility of union with the Cumberland Church proved to be a happy by-product of revision. Hardly had the Presbyterian General Assembly of 1902 sent down the revision overtures to the presbyteries, before newspapers, presbyteries, and individual leaders in the Cumberland Church were saying that these amendments, if adopted, would remove the stigma of "fatalism" from the Presbyterian Church's theology, and would open the door to reunion.[4] After the success of revision was assured, the Cumberland General Assembly proposed to the Presbyterian Assembly the appointment of committees to confer regarding union, a proposal to which the Presbyterians heartily agreed.[5]

In 1904 the General Assemblies of the two Churches sent down to their presbyteries a proposed plan of union. Some conservatives among the Presbyterians had been looking askance at the negotiations, fearing that union with the Cumberland Church would imply that the Church's creed, as the double result of revision and of the Cumberland merger, would now be construed in a non-Calvinistic, Arminian sense. To prevent such implications the Presbyterian Assembly in submitting to its presbyteries the question of union, recorded its judgment that "the revision of the Confession of Faith effected in 1903 has not impaired the integrity of the system of doctrine contained in the Confession and taught in Holy Scripture, but was designed to remove misapprehensions as to the proper interpretation thereof." [6] The Presbyterian committee in its negotiations was also careful to say substantially the same thing.[7] Fears were further allayed by the fact that the proposed doctrinal basis of reunion was the standards of the Presbyterian Church as revised in 1903.

The plan of union included Concurrent Declaration Number 1, which stated: "It is mutually recognized that such agreement now exists between the systems of doctrine contained in the Confessions of Faith of the two Churches as to warrant this union." This Concurrent Declaration also emphasized the passage in the Presbyterian Confession of Faith as revised which states that "the ordination vow of ministers, ruling elders and deacons, as set forth in the Form of Government, requires the reception and adoption of the Confession of Faith only as containing the system of doctrine taught in the Holy Scriptures." [8]

For a day and a half the Assembly debated the plan of reunion.[9] Dr. Francis L. Patton, who had recently become president of Princeton Seminary, was pronounced in his hostility. "This," he said, "is the greatest question that has confronted the Church since the days of reunion [in 1869]. It is more important than revision, far more important, for it is, in effect, not necessarily in intention, an indirect way of revising the Confession of Faith on radical grounds." [10] But opposition was unsuccessful. The union movement was ably led on the floor of the Assembly and sentiment in its favor mounted steadily. The committee's report was finally adopted "by an overwhelming majority," followed by "prolonged applause." [11]

The General Assembly of 1905 found that 194 of the Church's 241 presbyteries, more than the necessary two-thirds majority, had declared their approval of the plan of union. The Assembly therefore instructed its committee to work out details for accomplishing the merger and report the next year.[12] The next year the reunion was duly consummated.[13] A large minority of the Cumberland Church declined to enter the union, with resulting lawsuits which were ultimately won by the recently united Church.[14]

The union with the Cumberland Church had unmistakable theological implications. The Presbyterian General Assembly had officially declared that there was sufficient theological agreement to warrant union with a Church which some had previously regarded as non-Calvinistic. This declaration had been endorsed by more than two thirds of the presbyteries of the Church. The action involved an official broadening of the Church's attitude toward certain doctrines. In coming years, too, many of the former Cumberland men supported the party favoring broader theological policies.

Acceptance of a church which had previously been considered non-Calvanistic indicated a broadening in Church policy.

One of the most important theological issues during the years 1904 to 1922 was the series of disputes over licensing candidates for the ministry in New York Presbytery. Though Union Seminary had withdrawn from the Presbyterian Church as a result of the General Assembly's veto of Dr. Briggs, the seminary was still attended by many Presbyterian students for the ministry. Some members of New York Presbytery, feeling that their presbytery was licensing candidates of insufficient orthodoxy, carried to the higher courts of the Church licensure cases which became objects of widespread interest. It was of course the Church's future theological character which was at stake. Was the liberal minority to be allowed to grow or would it be ecclesiastically sterilized and forbidden to reproduce its kind in a younger generation of liberal ministers? The liberals resisted this effort uncompromisingly, not only because it was damaging to their professional interests, but also because they were convinced that if successful it would alienate from the Church the intellectual classes, particularly of the rising generation. These were years, too, when the Church was deeply concerned about the insufficient number of its ministerial candidates,[15] a fact which increased the difficulty of enforcing exclusive policies against ministerial candidates. It is interesting that in spite of disputes over licensures and other theological issues which continued intermittently in New York Presbytery throughout the first quarter of the century, Presbyterians were the fastest growing of the five largest Protestant bodies in New York City.[16]

Was it proper to ordain liberal students from Union?

In 1910 the General Assembly received a complaint against New York Presbytery's licensing of three candidates. The complainants averred that the candidates had "refused to affirm their faith . . . in the Virgin birth of our Lord." The respondents, on the other hand, declared that the three candidates in question "do not deny the Virgin birth of our Lord, but were not prepared to affirm it with the same positiveness as for some other doctrine." Other doctrines were involved, but interest centered on this particular one. The Assembly's decision commended the anxiety of the complainants, declared that the alleged disbelief, if proved, would certainly constitute a barrier to licensure or ordination. "But it has not been proven that the candidates named in the complaint have in fact denied or seriously questioned these doctrines." The Assembly therefore dismissed the complaint for lack of evidence, but instructed its Committee on Bills and Overtures to prepare a deliverance regarding future licensures by the presbyteries.[17]

G. A-1910 dismissed questioning of some students doubts of the Virgin birth on the basis of a lack of evidence.

With a view to meeting this problem, the General Assembly of 1910 adopted a five-point doctrinal deliverance. Declaring that the Adopting Act of 1729 called upon the church judicatory to decide what articles of Presbyterian faith are "essential and necessary," the Assembly proceeded to name five doctrines as "essential": (1) the Holy Spirit so inspired the writers of Scripture "as to keep them from error"; (2) "our Lord Jesus Christ was born of the Virgin Mary"; (3) Christ offered up himself as "a sacrifice to satisfy divine justice"; (4) "he arose from the dead, with the same body in which he suffered"; (5) Christ "showed his power and love by working mighty miracles." The Assembly declared: "These five articles of faith are essential and necessary." Then, to avoid any danger of seeming to reduce the essential faith of the Church to this brief compass, it at once added: "Others are equally so." The Assembly then enjoined its presbyteries always to take care "not to admit any candidate for the ministry into the exercise of the sacred function, unless he declares his agreement in opinion with all the essential and necessary articles of the Confession." It was ordered that the deliverance be "read aloud in our churches and judicatories." [18]

There was precedent for these "five points" in the Portland Deliverance of 1892[19] and in other General Assembly pronouncements during the 1880's and 1890's which had emphasized Biblical literalism. But the "five points" of 1910 extended the battle line beyond Biblical inerrancy to additional theological areas under attack. Though not mentioning premillennialism, the "five points" noticeably resembled the points of the Niagara Bible Conference of 1895.[20] The large significance which this pronouncement by the General Assembly was soon to acquire was not fully realized at the time, and it was adopted in the closing session of the Assembly after many of the members had gone home.[21]

The readiness of twentieth-century "fundamentalism" to set forth the "fundamentals" of the Christian gospel in a few brief theological propositions is in itself an interesting phenomenon. The Protestant reformers—and especially Calvin—conceived of Christian truth as a systematic whole, having divine authority as a whole. It is true, Calvin recognized some parts of Christian truth as more central and important than others, but willingness to see truth dismembered and reduced to "essentials" was more congenial to the eighteenth century—to rationalism, seeking the lightest load of faith that reason must bear; and to pietism, satisfied with just enough theology to provide for conversion and holiness. The Presbyterian "Adopting Act" of 1729, a compromise measure[22] in the true spirit of that time, had reflected something of this selective, hierarchical conception of truth, when it had allowed subscribers to the Westminster Confession and Catechisms to reject articles not deemed "essential and necessary." Following the far-reaching cultural and theological changes of the nineteenth century, many—like Adolf Harnack at one extreme,[23] and the American fundamentalists, at the other—were trying to define what, after all, was the "essence" of Christianity, the irreducible minimum which can be retained or must be defended. The answers given at such opposite poles were different enough, but there were strange resemblances both in the formulation of the problem and in the method of treating it. The Presbyterian Church in formulating the "five points" in 1910 was not ostensibly drafting an abridged creed—the Assembly expressly stated that there were other doctrines which the Church considered "essential"—but for nearly three decades these "five points" were treated by the conservative party almost as the Church's real, working creed. But Dr. Machen and many of the extreme conservative Presbyterians, while heavily borrowing both support and strategy from the contemporary "fundamentalist" movement, never really accepted the name or the program of the "fundamentalists," at the double price of accepting premillennialism and of surrendering Calvinism as a distinctive and integrated system.

The attempt, for a decade and a half, to impose the five-point doctrinal deliverance of the General Assembly of 1910 as a minimum theological requirement in the licensing of ministerial candidates was repeatedly challenged, and became an increasingly sore point of discussion in Assembly meetings, in church newspapers, and in certain presbyteries.[24] Reënaction of the deliverance by the General Assemblies of 1916 and 1923[25] accomplished little toward settling the issue. Equilibrium between the two opposing theological parties in the Church was not to come until the whole matter of officially declaring certain doctrines "essential and necessary" was carefully restudied.

It was during these years that the General Assembly clarified the official attitude of the Church with reference to Union Theological Seminary. When a committee appointed in 1911 brought in three conflicting reports, the Assembly of 1913 created a new committee "to make a thorough investigation of all the legal, ecclesiastical and doctrinal questions involved." [26] The crux of the new committee's final report, presented to the Assembly of 1915, was its opinion that "the compact of 1870 is legally unenforceable, and the action of the Directors of the Union Theological Seminary in returning to the Charter method of selection of professors was," in the opinion of the committee, "in conformity with their legal duty." [27] This was the conclusion reached by the Subcommittee on Legal Questions, composed of three distinguished corporation lawyers, Messrs. Rush Taggart, George V. Massey, and Frank L. Loesch. The Subcommittee on Doctrinal and Theological Questions reported that "in brief, Union Seminary, in teaching, spirit, and by direct and formal act, has ceased to be theologically in any sense a Presbyterian institution as distinguished from any other denomination." [28] The third subcommittee, that on the Ecclesiastical Relations between Union Theological Seminary and the General Assembly, declared that the coöperative relation existing from the seminary's earliest days "was practically destroyed by the action of 1904-5, changing the terms of subscription for both Directors and professors." [29] The adoption of the report by the Assembly closed a chapter. The *Presbyterian Banner* commented with a sigh of relief: "This is final on this point, and should remove this subject from the field of discussion and as a matter of irritation in the Presbyterian Church." [30] But the *Presbyterian* later denounced what it considered the release of the seminary from the Compact of 1870.[31]

What was to prove to be an important influence on theological developments within the Presbyterian Church was the attempt, born of postwar confidence and optimism, to create an organic union of American evangelical churches. Tendencies toward church coöperation and union had increased greatly in America after the Civil War, and particularly toward the close of the nineteenth century, and the Presbyterian Church, in spite of its rather noisy internal theological differences, had been in the van of the growing union tendencies. Among Presbyterians, church union had been a conspicuous argument in favor of revising the Westminster Confession, and had achieved tangible expression in the Presbyterian-Cumberland merger. Presbyterians, too, had contributed an important share of the leadership and support in forming the Federal Council of the Churches of Christ in America. But it was World War I which gave unprecedented stimulus to church unity sentiment, almost forcing the American Churches to coöperate in spiritual and social emergency services. During the closing year of the war this growing ideal of church union found conspicuous expression in the Presbyterian Church when thirty-five presbyteries overtured the General Assembly of 1918 to propose to other ecclesiastical bodies an organic union of "all Evangelical Churches in the United States." [32] The Assembly "unanimously adopted by a rising vote" the resolutions offered by its Committee on Bills and Overtures, of which the evangelist, Dr. J. Wilbur Chapman, was chairman. The Assembly resolved, "That we, the Commissioners to the One Hundred and Thirtieth General Assembly now in session at Columbus, Ohio, do declare and place on record our profound conviction that the time has come for Organic Church Union of the Evangelical Churches of America." The Assembly authorized its Committee on Church Coöperation and Union to arrange for a convention, send invitations to the other American Churches, and prepare a tentative plan of organic union.[33]

G. A of 1918: organic union with all Evangelical churches in the U.S. proposed.

Seventeen church bodies sent 134 delegates to the organizing meeting in Philadelphia, December 4 and 5, 1918. The delegates adopted resolutions approving the effort to bring together the various church bodies, and planning for the formation of an Interim Committee to be followed as soon as possible by the creation of a Church Council.[34]

A Council on Organic Union met in Philadelphia in February 1920, at the call of the Ad Interim Committee, with eighteen denominations represented. The Ad Interim Committee presented a Plan of Union with a brief and very general doctrinal preamble followed by an administrative plan. Though starting modestly in the form of federation, the plan contemplated increasing centralization. "The United Churches of Christ in America" were to function through a Council meeting semiannually and through such executive and judicial commissions and administrative boards as the Council might appoint. The constituent denominations were to retain all powers not delegated. At least two alternative plans were submitted, and some expressed disappointment that the Plan of Union did not contemplate outright merger rather than a federated union, but the plan was adopted almost unanimously by the Philadelphia meeting.[35]

The case for union was weakened in the Presbyterian Church by the fact that the report to the General Assembly of 1920 was divided, President J. Ross Stevenson of Princeton Seminary presenting the majority report in favor of adoption, while President William McKibbin of Lane Seminary presented a minority report.[36] A much more serious blow to the proposals lay in overtures from 109 of the Church's 288 presbyteries which were alarmed over the substitution, in the preamble, of the more general phrase "the Christian Church" in place of the phrase "the Evangelical Churches" and asked the Assembly "not to give its assent or in any way commit the Church to any plan or union, or any united Council, membership in which is not limited definitely to evangelical Churches." [37]

The Plan of Union, sent down to the presbyteries by the Assembly of 1920,[38] was badly defeated, with 151 of the Church's 302 presbyteries rejecting it and only 100 endorsing it.[39] Nor did other American Churches respond with much enthusiasm to the plan.[40] There had been some confusion in the manner of submitting the plan to the presbyteries, but many Presbyterians felt that the doctrinal foundation was too meager, while others felt that the proposed organization was too weak to accomplish any real purpose, while still others regarded it as overlapping unduly the recently organized Federal Council of the Churches of Christ in America.

The chief significance of the negotiations for the present study is that the discussion of the proposal for organic union foreshadowed the heightened theological controversy of 1922 to 1936 which had long been pending. Some of the conservative leaders, looking back later on these proposals for organic union, considered them an immediate cause of the controversies that followed.[41]

But if, during the two decades under view, forces of ecclesiastical inclusiveness were developing within the Presbyterian Church, as illustrated in such events as the reunion with the Cumberland Church, efforts of a few to license and ordain ministerial candidates in defiance of the "five-point" doctrinal formula, and attempts to merge American Protestant denominations; there were also unmistakable signs that those who opposed change and cherished historic theological particularities were coming to a

Solidification of Fundamentalist position.

new group-consciousness in the face of the growing challenge to their traditional position. Feeling now less certain that they could retain sufficient control of the ecclesiastical machinery to perpetuate the old theological exclusiveness, the more pronounced Presbyterian conservatives were, during the years between 1904 and 1922, quietly developing a new *esprit de corps* which closely paralleled the rise of the nondenominational fundamentalist movement.

Thus, for example, Professor William Brenton Greene, Jr., of Princeton Seminary, took occasion at a religious conference in the autumn of 1905 to warn against ecclesiastical inclusiveness. "Broad Churchism," he said, "is the tendency to regard Church union as more important than Church distinctions. . . . It is ecclesiastical utilitarianism." [42] As early as 1909 the editor of the *Presbyterian* applied to Protestant liberalism the term "Modernism," [43] a designation already widely used of Roman Catholic liberalism and later to become familiar in Protestant circles during the "modernist-fundamentalist" controversy in the years following World War I. Voicing conservative views, two presbyteries overtured the General Assembly of 1911 concerning the theology of two Presbyterian members of Union Seminary faculty, but the matter was put to rest by friendly negotiation.[44]

An important event in stimulating a more aggressive conservatism in the Church was the coming of Dr. David S. Kennedy in 1911 to the editorship of the *Presbyterian*. He felt that growing liberalism constituted a deadly peril to the Church and must be fought to the death. The *Herald and Presbyter* of Cincinnati likewise spoke in behalf of aggressive conservatism. Dr. Kennedy's first editorial for the *Presbyterian*, which appeared in the issue of May 10, 1911, bore the martial title, "The Present Conflict." The editorial interpreted current theological differences within the Church as "the renewal of the old primitive conflict between cultured heathenism and historic Christianity." But Dr. Kennedy still felt very optimistic about the overwhelming conservatism in theology of the Presbyterian Church as a whole.[45]

Machen

The Rev. J. Gresham Machen, a brilliant young instructor in New Testament in Princeton Seminary, in an article on "Christianity and Culture," published in the *Princeton Theological Review* early in 1913, foreshadowed the role he was later to assume in the Church as a leader of the extreme conservatives. The Christian Church, he wrote, is in dire peril from a hostile contemporary culture. "She [the Christian Church] may simply allow the mighty stream of modern thought to flow by unheeded and do her work merely in the back-eddies of the current. . . . But her winnings will be but temporary. The great current of modern culture will sooner or later engulf her puny eddy." The only proper course for Christians to pursue, Mr. Machen insisted, is to master contemporary culture and consecrate it to the cause of Christ. Instead of continuing to retreat steadily before secular thought, Christian leaders should take the offensive and seek to create in the modern world an intellectual background congenial to Christian faith and conducive to conversion. Some of modern thought must be refuted, the rest made subservient to Christian purposes, "but nothing in it can be ignored." But unfortunately, Mr. Machen continued, "the Church has turned to easier tasks. And now she is reaping the fruits of her indolence. Now she must battle for her life. The situation is desperate. . . . The Church is perishing to-day through the lack of thinking." Controversy and struggle with the *Zeitgeist* lie before the Church as a sacred duty. If, however, the Church would seek an answer "not merely to the questions of the hour, but, first of all, to the eternal problems of the spiritual world, then perhaps, by God's grace . . . she might issue forth once more with power, and an age of doubt might be followed by the dawn of an era of faith." [46]

This was vigorous, realistic thinking, especially when viewed in the light of the effort to recover absolute values which was to appear in Europe after World War I and in America in the 1930's. The basic elements of Mr. Machen's later thought are already here. True Christianity, he says, is everywhere surrounded by intensely hostile forces. Even now the Church is losing ground badly and is in a desperate situation. Humanly speaking, her only hope lies in an all-out offensive against her powerful intellectual adversary. When, a few years later, it became clear that the Presbyterian Church was not going to form a solid front in attacking contemporary secularism and naturalistic theology outside of the Church in the way in which Mr. Machen thought necessary, he then directed his energies to waging a war against the more moderate form of liberalism found within the Church. Then, when conservatives refused to join forces with him in this intra-ecclesiastical struggle, he attacked them. These tactics, together with his regarding as "essential" views which an increasing number considered not essential, steadily reduced the number of Mr. Machen's potential allies and increased the number of his actual opponents. But much of his basic objective—though quite differently defined and pursued—is the avowed objective of the more "realistic" theological forces of the mid-twentieth century.

During World War I the editor of the *Presbyterian*, seeking to ally current patriotism with theological conservatism, spoke derisively of theological liberalism as a German product—"Germanism"—which should be repudiated as emphatically as the Kaiser's imperialism. Professor Robert Dick Wilson of Princeton Seminary went so far as to say that because the current controversy centered around the nature of the Christian Scriptures it dealt with the most important theological problem in all of Christian history, not excepting even the Arian controversy or the Protestant Reformation.[47]

Anxieties of extreme conservatives were also reflected in an attack on aspects of the Presbyterian foreign missionary program. Some have dated

The turning point in the Church's relation to its cultural environment came shortly after World War I.

the beginning of the most recent period of theological controversy in the Presbyterian Church from the discussion of the proposed merger of the evangelical Churches in the United States, 1918 to 1920. Others would date it from the discussion of foreign missions starting in 1921, or from a sermon by Dr. Harry Emerson Fosdick in May 1922. There is common agreement that a group of various issues, all soon after World War I, marked a new stage in the problem of the Church's relation to the changed cultural environment.

In 1921 there occurred what a committee of the Presbyterian Board of Foreign Missions later called "one of the most vigorous attacks on the trustworthiness of Presbyterian foreign mission work which the Board has ever known." [48] The Rev. William Henry Griffith Thomas, D.D., an Episcopal clergyman, addressing the Presbyterian Social Union of Philadelphia on January 24, 1921, startled the Presbyterian Church by saying that many missionaries to China, including some Presbyterians, were much affected by "higher criticism and modernism." His address, as condensed for publication, declared: "There are two distinct parties among the missionaries [in China]. . . . The fundamental question at issue in China is the same as it is here at home, the trustworthiness and divine authority of the Word of God." He considered the two chief causes of liberalism on the foreign field to be too great a desire to show points of agreement between Christianity and the Oriental religions, and the coming to the foreign field of graduates of liberal theological seminaries in America.[49]

Dr. Thomas worried because he found Liberals in China.

According to Mr. Charles G. Trumbull, who accompanied Dr. Thomas on a visit to China in the summer of 1920 and who was in agreement with his views, the "Bible Union of China"—an importation of American fundamentalism into that land—had been organized just after Dr. Thomas' visit.[50] Within three years the Union was claiming some 2200 members.[51]

A secretary of the Presbyterian Board of Foreign Missions, Dr. Arthur J. Brown, hastened to defend the board against the attack of Dr. Thomas. In a letter to Dr. Thomas he wrote: "Will you kindly furnish me at once with the names of the Presbyterian missionaries connected with our Board who in your judgment have departed from the evangelical faith." In reply to Dr. Brown, Dr. Thomas refused to assume the responsibility of preferring specific charges, and contented himself with a repetition of generalities: "I did not single out any individuals, nor do I intend to do so. It is *not* a case for making examples of any particular persons, because the matter is far too general and undisputed for this." Dr. Thomas' letter described his strategy: "I impressed on my hearers the other evening [i.e., at the January meeting of the Social Union] the importance of bringing influence to bear on the Boards to limit themselves to the sending forth of the right sort of men." Further letters were exchanged, but Dr. Thomas maintained his refusal to give names and specifications.[52] Instead of undertaking heresy prosecutions in the face of a sentiment increasingly adverse to such a procedure, conservatives sought to create vigorous sentiment, particularly among the laity, against inclusive ideas of the Church. The result was that their tactics sometimes exposed them to their opponents' countercharges of slander and false witness.

Throughout this and much of the debate of the next decade and a half, absence of definition of terms on both sides was conspicuous. Thus, critics of the more inclusive theological policies quietly assumed that deviation from the General Assembly's five-point doctrinal deliverance—even from its Biblical inerrancy clause—was apostasy, whereas defenders of the broader policies had a quite different conception of what would constitute departure from the Christian faith. The debate thus often presented the perplexing spectacle of apparent contradictions in statements of "facts," which were actually agreements as to facts, but disagreements as to their theological significance. Harmony was not to be restored until the Church, under the leadership of the Special Commission of 1925, would go beyond the seemingly contradictory statements of fact to reëxamine its formulation of "essential and necessary" doctrines.

Meanwhile the Presbytery of Philadelphia, within two weeks of Dr. Thomas' address to the Social Union, requested him to submit to the Presbyterian Board of Foreign Missions a brief of the address and asked that a representative of the board be invited "to make known, through the Presbyterian Social Union of Philadelphia, the facts about Foreign Missions in China."[53] Dr. Robert E. Speer, secretary of the Presbyterian Board of Foreign Missions, addressed the March meeting of the Social Union. According to the Philadelphia correspondent of the *Continent,* he "said Dr. Thomas was mistaken in his facts, guilty of misrepresentation and uncharitable in his judgment of the brethren."[54]

Dr. Speer, who was at this juncture thrust into the controversy, was, in the coming decade and a half, to do more in forming the theological policy of the Presbyterian Church than perhaps any other individual. After a career as football hero and near head of his class at the College of New Jersey, he had been snatched from his course at Princeton Seminary to be secretary of the Presbyterian Board of Foreign Missions. Almost immediately he had become one of the three or four principal leaders of a great forward thrust made by American Protestant foreign missions. In recruiting missionary volunteers, in formulating and directing missionary strategy, in moving popular audiences, he was unsurpassed. He had contributed to *The Fundamentals* and many of his deepest religious beliefs were very conservative, but as one who had been a broad reader and a leader in large practical affairs since early manhood, he could not accept any view of Christian "essentials" which would commit the Church to a detached and irrelevant existence. His theory, like his life, was intensely dynamic. "I wish," he told a correspondent in China at this time, "we could get up such a glow and fervor and onrush of evangelical and evangelistic conviction and action that we would be swept clear past issues like the present ones so that men who want to dispute over these things could stay behind and do so while the rest of us could march ahead, more than making up by new conquests for all the defections and losses of those who stay behind." [55] Dr. Speer considered the theological problems of ministerial subscription and of coöperation with other denominations the same on the foreign field as at home, and took the view that both at home and abroad the lines of fellowship should be neither narrower nor broader than the lines of true discipleship to Christ.

An administrative question in Presbyterian foreign missions which was discussed at this time and for a decade and a half was the question as to who was responsible for the orthodoxy of an ordained missionary—the board under which he served, or the presbytery of which he was a member. Here again the phenomenal development of the Presbyterian Church's administrative machinery during the nineteenth and twentieth centuries had never been completely integrated into the sixteenth- and seventeenth-century pattern of government by four ascending judicatories. The foreign board, as the official agency of the highest judicatory, the General Assembly, had the responsibility of developing a unified denominational program for the foreign field. But the Church's constitution gave the board no direct control over the ordination or discipline of ordained missionaries, which was reserved to their presbyteries. Some favored developing or interpreting the constitution in the direction of giving the board responsibility for the theological views of its missionaries. This would make for monolithic theological centralization and would mean that service as ordained missionaries under the Presbyterian Board would be in danger of being restricted to those who were in agreement with the theological position prevailing in the General Assembly at any particular moment. But with truer statesmanship Dr. Speer saw that all elements considered sufficiently orthodox for the Church's ministry at home must be allowed a place in missionary service. That is, the theological problem of the limits of fellowship and the meaning of creedal subscription was the same abroad as at home, and must be decided by the Church at home and not by the board staff. Dr. Speer therefore cast his powerful influence on the side of theological decentralization and pluralism—in constitutional terms, on the side of leaving full theological jurisdiction over the missionary in the hands of his presbytery. The responsibility of the board in this connection, he felt, was to inform a missionary's home presbytery of any alleged theological aberrations, and let the presbytery decide the case. This was the policy which had been endorsed by the General Assembly of 1905, and which led to a recommendation by the Assembly of 1932 that all foreign missionaries retain or resume membership in an American presbytery.[56] The foreign boards of American Congregationalists and Baptists, who were

Dr Speer realized that if the Board had the right to ordain and discipline its ministers, there was too much danger of having only men whose theological views matched those of the board.

historically more decentralized, had similarly left ordination and tests of orthodoxy in the hands of the constitutional ordaining bodies.[57] It is notable that during the intermittent theological discussions of the 1920's and 1930's coöperation between the Presbyterian Foreign Board and its missions in China continued on a high level.[58]

The Presbyterian Church at large was not indifferent to the issue that had been raised by Dr. Griffith Thomas' address in Philadelphia.[59] The General Assembly of 1921, receiving overtures from five presbyteries relating to foreign missions, decided that there was "nothing to disturb the confidence of the General Assembly in the Board of Foreign Missions and in the great body of its loyal Christian Missionaries," and took the additional action: "But for their own sakes, as well as for the benefit of the Missionary enterprise of our Church, be it resolved that the Board of Foreign Missions be instructed to examine further into these reports, and, if necessary, to take such action as, according to the Form of Government of the Presbyterian Church, the conditions may demand." The Assembly also declared that the primary responsibility in the selection of missionary personnel rested with the sessions and presbyteries which sponsored the candidates for the foreign field.[60] The *Presbyterian* regretted that the investigation had been committed to the board itself, rather than to a mixed body.[61]

The board issued its findings in the form of a circular letter to the denomination declaring that no indictments were presented, nor was any evidence received from any source verifying in the case of any individual the suspicions which had been cast in a general way. The *Continent* added the editorial comment: "Surely this finding—really a 'finding' of nothing—is enough to put a quietus on agitation derogatory to Presbyterian missionaries." [62]

Professor Charles R. Erdman of Princeton Seminary, a member of the Foreign Board since 1906, in measured but definite terms defended the Church's entire missionary force: "These reports [of doctrinal unsoundness] are too serious to be disregarded and are evidently made in too good faith to be treated lightly. . . .

"The Presbyterian Church is too intelligent to be thrown into a panic by charges which specify no offenders, and too fair-minded to condemn its messengers until their lack of fidelity has been determined beyond a doubt." He referred with approval to a reply received by the Presbyterian Board from the China Council: "The Council expresses the opinion that our body of missionaries is as loyal to the gospel of redemption as are the ministers and Christian workers of our Church in America, and that no member of our China force denies the deity of our Lord Jesus Christ." [63]

The next year the General Assembly made further efforts to allay the fears concerning Presbyterian missionaries which Dr. Thomas' address in Philadelphia had aroused among some in the Church,[64] as did also the

Assembly of 1924, which was under extremely conservative leadership.[65] With this, discussion of missionary affairs gradually subsided, and was not renewed for almost a decade. Meanwhile, the attention of the Church was directed to other matters.

12.

a new york pulpit

It was in 1922 that doctrinal discussions in the Presbyterian Church entered upon their most widely publicized phase. For a time the so-called "fundamentalist-modernist controversy" in the Presbyterian and other Churches became front-page copy in leading metropolitan dailies. The person upon whom the chief attention of Presbyterians for a time focused was the Rev. Dr. Harry Emerson Fosdick.

In 1918 three Presbyterian Churches in New York—the First, the Madison Square, and the University Place—united under the name First Church. Early the next year Dr. Fosdick, with presbytery's approval, was secured as associate minister and stated preacher without transferring his membership from the Baptist to the Presbyterian ministry. The congregation felt encouraged to make such an experiment in interdenominationalism by the unanimous resolution of the General Assembly, a few months before, favoring the organic union of evangelical Churches.[1] The same month in which Dr. Fosdick was invited to the First Church an article of his in the *Atlantic Monthly* put into the lips of the soldiers returning from France a demand for a more liberal type of Christianity in the home churches. The article drew the passing criticism of a number of Presbyterian conservatives.[2]

In the First Church pulpit in May 1922 Dr. Fosdick in a sermon entitled "Shall the Fundamentalists Win?" made a ringing plea that liberal theological views be tolerated by the Christian Churches. He had recently been in China, and had observed the opposition of the newly formed Bible Union of China to liberalism on the foreign field.[3] As a Baptist minister he had viewed with disfavor fundamentalist activities in that body. His plea for toleration was an eloquent expression, too, of what many Presbyterian liberals had long been desiring. Given a new title, the sermon was widely circulated among Protestant clergymen of the United States by an interested layman, with the consent but not on the initiative of Dr. Fosdick.[4]

Dr. Fosdick's basic contention was that liberals also were Christians and therefore could not rightfully be excluded from the Christian Churches. Mentioning three currently contested doctrines—the virgin birth, Biblical inerrancy, and the physical return of Christ—he insisted that these were not basic to the Christian faith and that therefore those who rejected them should be tolerated within the Churches. The implication throughout was that no Church should make theological requirements of its officers which extended beyond the most basic elements of Christian faith. This was of course in direct conflict with the dominant tradition of the Presbyterian Church. No one, for example, ever formally charged Dr. Briggs or Dr. Henry Preserved Smith with having denied the deity of Christ, or with having abandoned the Christian faith. They were suspended from the ministry by an overwhelming vote for having repudiated doctrines far less basic than the deity of Christ. Presbyterianism had been accustomed to hold its ministry to much more extensive theological requirements than those implied in Dr. Fosdick's sermon. But by this time opinion in the Presbyterian Church was noticeably changing. By the year 1922 many Presbyterians whose own theological views were conservative were implying that if a minister believed in the deity of Christ, his theology was above serious reproach. The decades between revision and the Fosdick incident, though comparatively quiet theologically, had brought decided changes of emphasis and viewpoint.

What particularly aroused conservatives against Dr. Fosdick's sermon were the wide publicity given it; the fact that it was delivered by a non-Presbyterian guest in a Presbyterian pulpit; and the challenging form in which it stated the issue. "Fundamentalists are out on a campaign to shut against them [liberals] doors of the Christian fellowship. Shall they be allowed to succeed?" "The Fundamentalists are giving us one of the worst exhibitions of bitter intolerance that the Churches of this country have ever seen." The fact that Dr. Fosdick made it quite clear that he did not hold the doctrines discussed removed the matter from the realm of mere theoretical discussion, and gave his opponents occasion for ecclesiastical action.[5]

Reactions to Dr. Fosdick's widely circulated sermon were not long in appearing in the Presbyterian Church.[6] The Presbytery of Philadelphia, historically a stronghold of conservative theology in the Church, took the lead, and on October 16, 1922, adopted an overture to the General Assembly. The overture declared that there had recently been in the pulpit of the First Presbyterian Church of New York City "a public proclamation of the Word which appears to be in denial of the essential doctrines of the Presbyterian Church in the U.S.A." Since Dr. Fosdick was a Baptist minister and not personally subject to Presbyterian jurisdiction, presbytery's overture throughout dealt with the "pulpit" rather than the man. After quoting in detail what Dr. Fosdick had said from this pulpit on May 21 regarding the virgin birth, the overture declared that "such a view of the incarnation of God in Jesus Christ is not in harmony with the standards of the Presbyterian Church." "The Presbytery of Philadelphia hereby respectfully overtures the General Assembly to direct the Presbytery of New York to take such action as will require the preaching and teaching in the First Presbyterian Church of New York City to conform to the system of doctrine taught in the Confession of Faith."

The overture closed with a veiled threat. It reminded the Assembly that in 1916 during the discussion of questions of licensure one presbytery had requested that New York Presbytery be exscinded from the Church. Matters had then been settled amicably after fraternal conference and the reaffirmation by the Assembly of the five-point deliverance. The overture left no doubt that Philadelphia Presbytery considered the matter extremely serious.[7]

Opinion in the Church over the Philadelphia overture was very mixed. As the controversy increased, the *Presbyterian* openly expressed its hope that the Presbyterian Church might be divided, with, of course, the conservatives remaining and the liberals withdrawing. The more liberal *Continent* vigorously combatted any such suggestion.[8] In January and February, 1923, letters were sent to individual conservatives in various parts of the Church urging their support of the Philadelphia overture. Opponents also circulated literature. The West, it was reported, showed little interest in the matter.[9] After all the publicity which had been given the Fosdick case, only 12 of the 461 overtures received by the General Assembly of 1923 related to it. Six presbyteries sent up overtures similar to that from Philadelphia, while another wrote "deprecating the assumption of the Presbytery of Philadelphia," and still another sent word expressly "not concurring" in the Philadelphia overture.[10]

In Pittsburgh Presbytery, one of the chief heirs in America of Scotch-Irish Presbyterianism, the proposal to endorse the Philadelphia overture and to instruct Pittsburgh's commissioners in the Assembly to support the Philadelphia program was defeated by an overwhelming majority.[11] This vote reflected the gradual change of theological tone that had been taking place in the Pittsburgh area of the Church, which had been—at least till the turn of the century—a principal stronghold, along with Philadelphia, of the stricter, more rigorous, type of Presbyterianism. The new, more moderate tone, which by the 1920's was becoming dominant in the Pittsburgh area, was seen also in the more conciliatory theological attitude being assumed by Western Seminary and by the *Presbyterian Banner*.[12]

This was a serious loss, which might prove disastrous, to the Church's more extreme right wing.

The contest for the moderatorship of the General Assembly of 1923 was unusually colorful, with the Hon. William Jennings Bryan as the candidate of the extreme conservatives, and with pressing issues confronting the Church. The candidate of the moderates, Dr. Charles F. Wishart, president of Wooster College, was elected by a slight majority. Mr. Bryan's known views on evolution and perhaps even his lifelong Democratic politics contributed something to his defeat. But the desire for tolerance and unity was the major factor in electing his opponent. Dr. Wishart had been nominated as one in whom theological conservatism and tolerance were combined. He sought to confirm this when he announced: "I look upon my election as a victory for tolerance rather than for liberalism." [13]

Having lost the contest to elect a moderator, some of the most extreme conservatives failed in the attempt to secure a categorical condemnation of evolution by the Assembly. The day before the Assembly voted on the Fosdick case, the Hon. William Jennings Bryan offered the following resolution:

"Resolved—That no part of the educational fund of the Presbyterian Church in the U.S.A. shall be paid to any school, college, university or theological seminary that teaches or permits to be taught as a proved fact, either Darwinism or any other evolutionary hypothesis that links man in blood relationship with any other form of life." [14] Mr. Bryan, with characteristic eloquence, argued for the motion before the Assembly "at length, arousing great enthusiasm and applause from all sections of the house." [15] After extensive debate, the Assembly, by a majority of two thirds or three fourths, adopted a substitute motion instructing synods and presbyteries in a general way to withhold official approval from any institution "where any teaching or instruction is given which seeks to establish a materialistic evolutionary philosophy of life, or which disregards or attempts to discredit the Christian faith." [16] For some time Presbyterians had been watching with interest the contemporary uproar over evolution which Mr. Bryan and others had been causing in the country,[17] but even the extreme conservatives—with rare exceptions—had not made opposition to evolution a major objective in their ecclesiastical program. A moderate paper like the *Presbyterian Banner* felt deeply relieved that Mr. Bryan's categorical condemnation of evolution had been defeated.[18]

Prospects for the success of the Philadelphia overture seemed dampened by the Assembly's refusal to elect Mr. Bryan or to endorse his resolution on evolution. For nearly five hours the Assembly debated majority and minority recommendations on the overture. Mr. Bryan and Dr. Macartney gave notable support to the minority report. "If you answer the overture in the negative," said Dr. Macartney, "you disappoint thousands of praying men and women, you discourage them in their battle for Christ and his kingdom." On motion of Mr. Bryan, the vote was taken by roll call and resulted in the adoption of the minority report by the wide margin of 439 to 359.[19]

Assuming the correctness of the accusations against the New York preacher, the Assembly in this action "expresses its profound sorrow that doctrines contrary to the standards of the Presbyterian Church, proclaimed in said Pulpit have been the cause of controversy and division in our Church and therefore would direct the Presbytery of New York to take such action, (either through its present Committee or by the appointment of a special commission) as will require the preaching and teaching in the First Presbyterian Church of New York to conform to the system of doctrines taught in the Confession of Faith; and that said Presbytery report its action in a full transcript of its records to the 136th General Assembly of 1924." The Assembly then reaffirmed the five-point doctrinal deliverance of 1910.[20] Eighty-five members of the Assembly signed a protest against this action, alleging, among other things, that it "condemns without proper hearing," and "seeks to impose upon the office bearers of our Church, doctrinal tests other than, or in addition to those solemnly agreed upon in the Constitution of our Church." [21]

An analysis of the Assembly's vote shows that it was the elders who carried the motion over the opposition of the ministers, for the ministers voted against it by a majority of two, while the elders supported it by a three to two majority. As the party of toleration noted with satisfaction, and extreme conservatives observed with alarm, almost everyone connected with any of the boards or offices of the Church opposed the action taken.[22]

A geographical analysis of the vote shows that Dr. Fosdick's chief support lay in New York and New Jersey, with the east central states running third. The greatest strength of the opposition to Dr. Fosdick lay in Pennsylvania, where those who voted were almost four to one in favor of the action taken. Interestingly enough, New England Presbyterianism, in contrast with the surrounding Congregationalism of the area, showed itself to be noticeably conservative. The vote is indicated in the adjoining table.[23]

By this time the larger public was taking an active interest in the contest. Presbyterian students at Mount Holyoke College who were strongly in sympathy with Dr. Fosdick drew up resolutions commending Christian unity and tolerance which were signed by some 425 of their fellow students and 62 faculty members. "Several hundred" students and professors of Cornell University addressed Dr. Fosdick, "pledging our unqualified loyalty to you as the leading American interpreter of the Christian religion for men and women of scientific training." [24]

Those in the Church favoring policies of toleration and peace were open in their criticism of the Assembly's action. President Hibben of Princeton University, a Presbyterian minister, gave his opinion that "a part of the

GEOGRAPHICAL ANALYSIS OF VOTE ON "PHILADELPHIA OVERTURE" IN GENERAL ASSEMBLY OF 1923

AREA	Number of Commissioners Voting in Affirmative	Number of Commissioners Voting in Negative	Number of Commissioners Not Voting	Percentage of Voting Commissioners of Area Voting in Affirmative
NEW ENGLAND	5	2	1	71%
NEW YORK (including "New York and Vermont, Welsh")	31	65	11	32%
NEW JERSEY	16	26	7	38%
PENNSYLVANIA	80	23	11	78%
SOUTH (entire Southeast and also Delaware, Maryland, Kentucky, Missouri, Oklahoma, Texas)	86	68	30	56%
EAST CENTRAL (West Virginia, Ohio, Indiana, Illinois, Michigan, Wisconsin)	78	78	28	50%
WEST CENTRAL (Minnesota, Iowa, North Dakota, South Dakota, Nebraska, Kansas)	71	38	20	65%
ROCKY MOUNTAIN	27	20	9	57%
PACIFIC COAST	45	37	24	55%
TOTALS	439	357	141	

Christian church has recently been stampeded through fear of a great teacher and prophet of righteousness in New York City, because the group which would call him to account does not speak his language or understand his thought." [25] Criticism of that part of the recent Assembly's action which reaffirmed the five-point doctrinal deliverance of 1910 was particularly emphatic. Dr. John Kelman, who had come from Scotland to accept the call of the Fifth Avenue Church in New York, told his congregation: "If it had been necessary for me to profess my agreement [i.e., with the five-point deliverance of 1910], I could not have accepted a call to any church in America." [26] Dr. Henry van Dyke of Princeton University said that, of the five doctrines, one was nonessential and four were non-Scriptural.[27]

Conservatives begin to consolidate their position Ralleys, etc.

The victory of the conservatives in the Assembly of 1923 was too close to leave them room for complacency. If the rest of their program for the Church was to be put into effect, their forces would have to be increased and disciplined for the task. A series of rallies in certain strategic cities was therefore planned.

Nearly three hundred attended a complimentary dinner in New York in October 1923. Dr. Macartney and Dr. J. Gresham Machen, assistant professor at Princeton Seminary, were among the speakers. Dr. Machen, who was now beginning to come to the fore as a conservative leader, though not yet occupying the central position that he later held in the movement, saw in united efforts by conservatives possibilities of a reformation "as great as that of the sixteenth century." As some five hundred had applied too late for accommodations at the dinner it was planned to meet again later in this strategic New York area.[28]

Meanwhile the conservatives held a rally in the Arch Street Church, Philadelphia, in December, attended by about a thousand ministers and laymen. The committee in charge had written to the fifteen living ex-moderators of the General Assembly, enclosing a call for the meeting and asking them to send a greeting if in hearty accord with the meeting. The response was hardly reassuring. Only nine replied, and of these four were cold or hostile.[29] The address of Dr. Maitland Alexander of Pittsburgh at this Philadelphia rally contained an interesting reference to the strategy of extreme conservatives at this time. He thought that there would be no "split" in the Church, nor any exodus of "orthodox" Presbyterians. His hope was that conservative lay sentiment could be so aroused that liberal ministers would be literally frozen out, and would peaceably withdraw from the Presbyterian Church. Other leaders shared this expectation.[30] Rather than undertake ecclesiastical prosecutions, they hoped to create a ground swell in the Church—especially among the laity—which would sweep all before it. The rallies were part of this program.

Rallies were held in New York in December and January. It was reported that "fundamentalist" Presbyterian elders of the New York area organized at about this time.[31] A similar rally in Pittsburgh in February adopted the following resolution: "We reaffirm our belief in our historic Confession of Faith, together with the historical interpretation of it made by our church courts, claiming no right of private judgment contrary to such interpretation." [32] It is strange indeed that this declaration is not qualified by any such phrase as "while remaining in the Church," or the like. The *Presbyterian Banner* pointed out the declaration in the Church's Constitution, "God alone is Lord of the conscience," and added, "To deny the right of private judgment is to surrender the very citadel of Historic Presbyterianism and turn our backs upon the Protestant Reformation." [33] Extreme conservatives later took a quite opposite view of the relation between the authority of the Church and the conscience of the individual.

A very noticeable fact about the various conservative rallies was that they centered in the East, at least two of them being held in the Synod of Pennsylvania, which the conservatives already dominated, and several in the Synod of New York, which they could never reasonably hope to win over. If the conservative program was to take deep root and secure permanent hold of the Church it must find secure lodgment in the vast regions west of Pittsburgh which held the balance of power in the Church and would eventually determine policies. The great east central group of states —West Virginia, Ohio, Indiana, Illinois, Michigan, and Wisconsin—whose commissioners to the General Assembly of 1923 had divided equally on the Fosdick vote, were crucial. If these should join New York in opposition to the extreme conservatives the west central and far western regions would be more likely to follow them in an inclusive churchmanship than to follow Pennsylvania and the South in the direction of exclusiveness. It was in the West that the program of extreme conservatism was to be wrecked. The Church west of the seaboard before long came to regard the whole controversy as a meaningless local squabble, and rose in its wrath to restore order. Philadelphia and New York and their respective allies no longer dominated the whole Church as they had in an earlier century.

Another fact about the conservative rallies of 1923 and 1924 worthy of remark is that inside control of them seems to have been held by an extremely small group of men. Several of these leaders were among the ablest men in the Church from every point of view, but it is noteworthy that a movement which hoped to exert lasting influence on a Church numbering nearly two million communicants did not have a larger number of leaders. Significant in the same connection was the fact that of the fifteen former moderators of the General Assembly who were solicited only five sent a favorable reply to the Philadelphia rally, and even of these five the majority were soon alienated. The centralization of conservative leadership which was apparent from the outset was destined to increase rapidly, as followers fell away and as more concentrated authority became necessary to direct publicity and to guide quickly and efficiently the votes of followers in presbyteries and Assemblies.

The General Assembly took its first action regarding Dr. Fosdick in 1923. That year and the first month of the next year witnessed the appearance of the two most important statements of opposing presuppositions underlying, respectively, the ecclesiastical policies of the two extreme parties. At the crucial theological point they directly contradicted each other. The two documents were Professor J. Gresham Machen's *Christianity and Liberalism*, and *An Affirmation*, the latter soon popularly spoken of as the "Auburn Affirmation."

Dr. Machen's book, published in 1923,[34] was based on the thesis that contemporary theological liberalism was not a harmless variation of historic Christianity, but that, on the contrary, Christianity and liberalism were two distinct and wholly different religions. Dr. Machen wrote: "We shall be interested in showing that despite the liberal use of traditional phraseology modern liberalism not only is a different religion from Christianity but belongs in a totally different class of religions." [35] Having laid down this general proposition, the author sought to show in detail how "Christianity" and "liberalism" differed fundamentally in their attitude toward doctrine in general, and, specifically, in their basic conceptions of God, man, the Bible, Christ, salvation, and the Church.

In his last chapter, on "The Church," Dr. Machen applied his thesis to the contemporary ecclesiastical situation with inexorable logic. If Christianity and liberalism are two entirely different and mutually exclusive religions, he declared, they cannot dwell together within the same Christian Church. It is unthinkable, he argued, that Christians should remain associated in the same ecclesiastical organization with anti-Christians, and that part of their contributions should go to the support of a message that contradicts all their deepest religious convictions.[36] No, one or the other of these religions must leave the shelter of the Church. By every historical right, he insisted, the Church belongs to those who have belonged to it through the centuries and who today accept its historical doctrines, that is, to the conservatives—or, in his terminology, to the "Christians," and not to the "liberals." If, however, liberalism should finally gain control of the Church and its machinery, he declared that conservatives would have no choice but to withdraw at whatever sacrifice and found a new and true Church.[37]

The argument of Dr. Machen's book was partly vitiated by the fallacy of the "undistributed middle." This book, as well as many of his public utterances and other writings, described "liberalism" in terms of its most radical naturalistic implications,[38] and then, by implication at least, included in this classification all those who differed from traditional orthodoxy even on subordinate points. It is no wonder that avowed liberals regarded his picture of "liberalism" as a gross caricature.[39] But, somewhat inconsistently, there were passages which frankly acknowledged that some who agreed with "liberalism" in rejecting Biblical inerrancy and in other points must nonetheless be recognized as true evangelical Christians.[40] If, then, there could be a moderate evangelical liberalism which had to be recognized as true Christianity, his whole extremist position stood self-condemned. Dr. Machen was echoing, in exaggerated form, an ambivalence which had been in the Princeton Theology from the beginning. The Princeton Theology had all along acknowledged that only saving faith in Christ was essential for true Christianity, but then had built its theology on the assumption of Biblical inerrancy in such a way that, to save itself, the Princeton Theology had to defend Biblical inerrancy as though such inerrancy were after all an "essential." Though Dr. Machen had become much more extreme and exclusive in his definitions than the earlier Princeton Seminary men, he still retained—more inconsistently than they—vestiges of a much broader theological foundation and a more inclusive ecclesiastical policy than he avowed.

Striking also was Dr. Machen's doctrine of the Church, taught in this book and in numerous other writings, implied in his ecclesiastical policy, and illustrated in the church divisions that later attended his movement. For him the Church was, in essence, a voluntary society, created *de novo* by contract by people who find themselves in theological agreement. "An evangelical church," he wrote, "is composed of a number of persons who have come to agreement in a certain message about Christ and who desire to unite in the propagation of that message, as it is set forth in their creed on the basis of the Bible." In constitution, though of course not in purpose, he likened the Church to a political club.[41] This was good Anabaptist doctrine and might even pass for Congregationalism, but it certainly was not Presbyterianism. The Presbyterian conception of the Church is organic. Presbyterian doctrine is that normally people are born into the Church.[42] At this important point Dr. Machen's battle for orthodoxy had led him to serious unorthodoxy as judged by the very standards he was so ardently seeking to defend. The consequences in repeated ecclesiastical divisions were direct and not long delayed.

The other notable statement, which in its theological presuppositions should be contrasted directly with Dr. Machen's book, was *An Affirmation*, here designated by its popular name "Auburn Affirmation." First published in January 1924 with the signatures of 150 Presbyterian ministers, it was republished in May 1924 with 1274 clerical signatures. It set forth, among other things, the theological basis on which some were advocating toleration. The Auburn Affirmation wisely avoided such vague and ambiguous terms as "liberals" and "liberalism." Instead, it addressed itself specifically to the five-point doctrinal deliverance of the Assembly of 1910, repeated in 1916 and 1923, which had declared that the inerrancy of the Bible, Christ's virgin birth, his offering up of himself as a sacrifice to satisfy divine justice, his physical resurrection, and his showing of his power and love by working miracles were each "an essential doctrine of the Word of God."

In what was theologically its crucial paragraph, the Auburn Affirmation challenged the Assembly's deliverance as follows: "Furthermore, this opinion of the General Assembly [i.e., the five-point deliverance] attempts to commit our church to certain theories concerning the inspiration of the Bible, and the Incarnation, the Atonement, the Resurrection, and the Continuing Life and Supernatural Power of our Lord Jesus Christ. We all hold most earnestly to these great facts and doctrines; we all believe from our hearts that the writers of the Bible were inspired of God; that Jesus Christ was God manifest in the flesh; that God was in Christ, reconciling the world unto Himself, and through Him we have our redemption; that having died for our sins He rose from the dead and is our ever-living Saviour; that in His earthly ministry He wrought many mighty works, and by His vicarious death and unfailing presence He is able to save to the uttermost. Some of us regard the particular theories contained in the deliverance of the General Assembly of 1923 as satisfactory explanations of these facts and doctrines. But we are united in believing that these are not the only theories allowed by the Scriptures and our standards as explanations of these facts and doctrines of our religion, and that all who hold to these facts and doctrines, whatever theories they may employ to explain them, are worthy of all confidence and fellowship." [43]

In contrast to Machen's position, the Auburn Affirmation claimed that the difference between the two factions occurred only on non-essential matters of belief.

It is thus apparent that the two extreme parties in the Church based their ecclesiastical policies on mutually contradictory theological presuppositions. Dr. Machen and many other conservatives said that conservative Christianity and liberalism were so different as to constitute two separate religions. The Auburn affirmation said that differences between conservatism and a moderate liberalism of the type attacked in the five-point doctrinal deliverance were so slight as to involve only nonessentials, the two agreeing in all their basic "facts" and differing only in explanatory "theories." Dr. Machen and the Auburn Affirmation each followed presuppositions to conclusions in thoroughly logical fashion. Dr. Machen argued that two distinct religions could not continue within the same Church; the Auburn Affirmation argued that because they did not differ on essentials the two parties could dwell together happily in the same Church. Toleration followed quite logically from these premises.

The Auburn Affirmation was ably drawn up. Like Dr. Fosdick's sermon it pleaded for toleration, but, unlike that sermon, it declined to commit the subscribers personally to any particular theological position. It was reminiscent of *A Plea for Peace and Work*[44] of Briggs-case days, but its theoretical foundations were more fully elaborated. "Some of us regard the particular theories contained in the deliverance of the General Assembly of 1923 as satisfactory explanations of these facts and doctrines." By thus completely eliminating the question as to whether any particular signer believed or disbelieved one or all of the Assembly's "five points," the matter was kept in the purely academic sphere, where the paper desired that it should remain. The point under discussion was not the truth or falsity of the five doctrines but the appropriateness of the Assembly's declaring them "essential doctrines" and the propriety of making them tests of ministerial fellowship.

Many conservatives who at that time or later favored a degree of toleration never signed the Affirmation. It is thus necessary to distinguish three parties in the controversy. (1) There were the extreme conservatives, many of whom agreed with Dr. Machen that Christianity and liberalism were essentially two distinct religions, and who at least faced in the direction of an ultimate division of the Church, even if not actually desiring it. (2) There was an extreme party of toleration, represented by the signers of the Auburn Affirmation, who felt that the theological differences between conservatives and liberals pertained to nonessentials and therefore need be no barrier to toleration. A number whose own theological views were conservative signed the Affirmation. (3) There was a third group composed of conservatives who would not go so far as the signers of the Auburn Affirmation in disparaging the theological differences between conservatives and liberals, but who nonetheless favored a policy of toleration. The theoretical basis of this group was more complex and less easily stated than that of the more extreme positions of Dr. Machen and the Auburn Affirmation. But it was this mediating group—essentially conservative in theology and temperament—that held the balance of power and eventually decided the issue.

The Auburn Affirmation was briefer in compass but broader in scope than Dr. Machen's book. Like his book, it dealt with theological presuppositions underlying the discussion of toleration, but, unlike his book, it also discussed constitutional aspects of the matter. The Affirmation, in fact, devoted more space to constitutional than to theological phases of the question. It claimed, as various individuals in the Church had already been saying, that the General Assembly's deliverance of 1910, 1916, and 1923 was unconstitutional, because for the Assembly to declare authoritatively that certain doctrines in the Confession are "essential" is in effect to amend the Confession. The Confession, however, can be amended only by the joint action of the Assembly and two thirds of the presbyteries, and not by the Assembly alone.

One of the earliest answers to the Affirmation was published by President J. Ross Stevenson of Princeton Seminary in the *Princeton Theological Review* for January 1924. Arguing from the history of Irish Presbyterianism in the eighteenth century, Dr. Stevenson sought to show, as against the claims of the Affirmation, that a certain strictness of creedal subscription was theologically desirable. He also defended, as against the claims of the Affirmation, the constitutionality of the Assembly's five-point doctrinal deliverance.

Other contemporary adverse comment also greeted the appearance of the Auburn Affirmation, but it is surprising that extreme conservatives were not more concerned about it at the time. They inclined at first to disparage its significance.[45] At the Assembly of 1924, at which conservatives were strong enough to elect the moderator, an overture from Cincinnati Presbytery called attention to the Affirmation. But the Bills and Overtures Committee, of which Dr. Maitland Alexander was chairman, and of which William Jennings Bryan was a member, recommended "no action." There was no minority report, and the Assembly concurred unanimously.[46] Years later, after the real significance of the Affirmation had become apparent, extreme conservatives had much to say about it, for the Auburn Affirmation, with its list of 1274 Presbyterian ministerial subscribers, soon proved to be a powerful influence in the Assembly and in denominational life.

The so-called "fundamentalist-modernist" controversy which had suddenly become widely publicized and greatly aggravated in the Presbyterian Church as a result of the Fosdick incident was not confined to that communion. A number of the major denominations were having similar struggles, as screaming headlines in many a leading metropolitan newspaper testified. So widespread had the matter become that Bishop William T. Manning of New York requested his Episcopal clergy to observe a Christmas truce. Ministers of many denominations followed the good advice.[47] The *Christian Century*, a leading liberal weekly, early in the new year declared almost in the tones of Dr. Machen, that "fundamentalism" and "modernism" were two distinct religions. "Two worlds have clashed, the world of tradition and the world of modernism. . . . There is a clash here as profound and as grim as that between Christianity and Confucianism. . . . The God of the fundamentalist is one God; the God of the modernist is another. . . . That the issue is clear and that the inherent incompatibility of the two worlds has passed the stage of mutual tolerance is a fact concerning which there hardly seems room for any one to doubt." [48]

But more moderate men refused to go to extremes on either the right or the left. "A working pastor" argued from the lessons of the recent World War that "war settles nothing." Claiming quite correctly that the great middle group to which he belonged was in a majority in the Church, he announced, "We will not be bludgeoned nor dragooned into a quarrel not of our seeking. If we are interested, it is only that we may use our precious energy to promote peace among those who ought to be brethren." [49] This spirit of postwar pacifism, already so widespread in the country and in the Church, operated strongly against any party—in this case the extreme conservatives—which sought to force a struggle over any issue. Against the background prevailing in postwar America, the vivid, even bloody, military figures of speech sometimes used by conservative speakers and writers were singularly unattractive to most Americans of the day.

The General Assembly of 1924, meeting in the midst of the widely publicized "modernist-fundamentalist" controversy, and having on its docket a report concerning the much-discussed Fosdick case, attracted national attention. Forty reporters from newspapers scattered throughout the United States from New York to Seattle, in addition to representatives of the press associations, were present.[50]

The preliminary contest for the election of moderator was of more than usual interest. The extreme conservatives supported their Philadelphia leader, Dr. Macartney, who was placed in nomination by William Jennings Bryan, while those who opposed the exclusive policies of churchmanship advocated by this group nominated Professor Charles R. Erdman of Princeton Seminary. Dr. Erdman was outstandingly conservative in his personal theological beliefs, as his sermons and numerous books had long made unmistakably clear. He had been a contributor to *The Fundamentals,* widely circulated in the preceding decade, and had latterly been a member of the committee supervising their publication. In 1915 he had signed the "Back to Fundamentals" statement published by the *Presbyterian.*[51] He had been a supporter of the attempt to unite the evangelical Churches of America, an effort launched by the unanimous action of the Assembly of 1918. In 1921 he had stoutly defended the Presbyterian Board of Foreign Missions against the unparticularized attacks of Dr. W. H. Griffith Thomas.[52] The fact that the opponents of a rigid and exclusive churchmanship were able to secure the support of Dr. Erdman and a growing number of others of the stanchest orthodoxy eventually doomed the program of theological exclusiveness. Unless the plan to enforce strict theological conformity could enlist the overwhelming majority of conservatives, it would be certain to meet defeat at the hands of a coalition of liberals and conservatives favoring more moderate policies.

When the votes were counted it was found that the extreme conservatives had elected Dr. Macartney moderator by the close vote of 464 to 446.[53] This majority of eighteen votes was far from enough to assure the victory of conservative policies in the coming sessions. Dr. Macartney's dignity and fairness as a presiding officer were praised by an editor who had not favored his election.[54]

The case of Dr. Fosdick was brought before the General Assembly of 1924 through a complaint of certain members of New York Presbytery against the way that presbytery had dealt with affairs in the First Church of New York. The General Assembly of the preceding year, it will be recalled, in answer to the Philadelphia overture, had directed New York Presbytery "to take such action . . . as will require the preaching and teaching in the First Presbyterian Church of New York to conform to the system of doctrines taught in the Confession of Faith." [55]

Pursuant to these instructions the New York Presbytery referred the Assembly's action to its special committee on the First Church which reported back to the presbytery early in 1924. The committee's report to New York Presbytery commented favorably on letters which it had received from the First Church session and from Dr. Fosdick, and recommended the adoption of four resolutions. (1) "The Presbytery states that it believes in the purpose and character of the preaching and teaching in the First Church of New York." (2) "The Presbytery expresses its confidence in the loyalty of the Session of the First Church." (3) The presbytery is ready to receive further reports and take further action as occasion may require. (4) "The Presbytery further declares that it sorrows deeply over controversy and strife." [56] While intended to be courteous and respectful toward the General Assembly and its authority, the whole temper of the report and the resolutions were warmly sympathetic to Dr. Fosdick and the First Church session, and obviously contemplated the maintenance of the *status quo*. The presbytery on February 4, 1924, adopted the report, including the recommendations, without debate by a vote of 111 to 28.[57] It was this action of the Presbytery of New York against which complaint was carried to the General Assembly of 1924.

The Assembly referred the New York complaint to its Permanent Judicial Commission. Reviewing the New York Presbytery's action in relation to the First Church, the Assembly's commission expressed the opinion that the presbytery had acted throughout in good faith. Referring to Dr. Fosdick's statement of beliefs in his letter to the presbytery's committee, the commission declared: "Unfortunately his statement is not as clear and unequivocal as in the judgment of the Commission it should have been in view of the agitation which has resulted because of the preaching of the sermon entitled—'Shall the Fundamentalists Win?'" The commission found the root of the difficulty in the anomalous situation of a non-Presbyterian minister permanently occupying a Presbyterian pulpit, and recommended the following solution: "If he [i.e., Dr. Fosdick] can accept the doctrinal standards of our Church, as contained in the Confession of Faith, there should be no difficulty in receiving him. If he cannot, he ought not to continue to occupy a Presbyterian pulpit. . . .

"We therefore recommend that the Presbytery of New York be instructed, through its committee or through the session of the First Presbyterian Church, to take up with Dr. Fosdick this question to the end that he may determine whether it is his pleasure to enter the Presbyterian Church and thus be in a regular relationship with the First Presbyterian Church of New York as one of its pastors." [58]

According to the Presbyterian constitution, the Assembly had the alternative of confirming the judgment of the commission as it stood or of reviewing it, and the Assembly by the decisive vote of 504 to 311 voted to confirm the judgment of the commission.[59] The decision was a deft stroke diplomatically. Outwardly it gave the conservatives what they had sought, the removal of the preacher; but it did this without reference to theological issues, so that no precedent was created regarding other preachers in Presbyterian pulpits who might hold similar views. The conservatives were given the form but not the substance of their desire. The action of the Assembly was quite properly regarded as a victory for those favoring moderation, rather than for the extreme conservatives. But it was of course widely regretted by admirers of Dr. Fosdick.[60]

In another case which came before the Assembly of 1924 extreme conservatives suffered an important reverse. The Assembly's action concerned an overture sent up by the Presbytery of Philadelphia, which requested that "all who represent the Church on the Boards, General Council, Theological Seminaries, and every other Agency of the Church be required to affirm or re-affirm their faith in the Standards of the Church, together with the historic interpretations as contained in the doctrinal deliverance of the General Assembly, notably that of 1910, which has been twice re-affirmed by the General Assembly." [61] It is obvious that the action proposed by the overture, if adopted by the Assembly, would permanently close the doors of official denominational leadership to all liberals. It would be a long step in the direction of creating a theologically exclusive Church.

The Assembly of 1924 referred the overture to its Permanent Judicial Commission which expressed the judgment: "The constitution of our Church clearly specifies the doctrinal requirements for ministers and elders, and any change in these must be by concurrent action of the Assembly and Presbyteries; the only method provided for amendment or modification." The commission's judgment that the overture was unconstitutional and that therefore no action on it should be taken was confirmed by the General Assembly.[62]

Extreme conservatives had thus failed at two vital points in the Assembly of 1924. Though they had previously won the formal five-point doctrinal deliverance of 1910, 1916, and 1923, and though they had succeeded in electing the moderator in 1924, they proved unable to get the Assembly to dismiss Dr. Fosdick on the alleged grounds that his teaching violated the five points; or to erect the five points into a requirement for specified types of officeholders. The five-point deliverance was gratifying to the conservatives as an abstract statement; but the effort to embody it concretely in the judicial decisions and administrative policy of the Church was still unsuccessful.

The Assembly's action regarding Dr. Fosdick and the pulpit of the First Church of New York laid upon the New York Presbytery the responsibility of settling the matter as directed. Presbytery's committee therefore

Dr. Fosdick said he'd quit before he'd accept an outworn creed

wrote to Dr. Fosdick interpreting the Assembly's action in the most generous sense possible, and urging him to accept the Assembly's invitation to become a Presbyterian minister. Dr. Fosdick, however, firmly declined, stating that his conscience forbade him to subscribe any ancient creed, nor could he endorse the sectarian spirit of the proposed settlement. Dr. Fosdick thereupon transmitted to the First Church his resignation as associate minister. With great regret the congregation accepted his resignation as associate minister, but expressed the hope that he might continue to make it his custom to preach for them. In reply Dr. Fosdick said that the Assembly's action clearly contemplated the termination of his preaching in the First Church in case he declined to enter the Presbyterian ministry. March 1 was fixed as the date when Dr. Fosdick's resignation as associate minister should become effective and his connection with the church should cease.[63]

Meanwhile, the "fundamentalist-modernist" controversy in various American church bodies continued to attract attention far beyond Presbyterian circles. President E. Y. Mullins of the Southern Baptist Theological Seminary, writing in 1924, found that young men were much concerned over the ecclesiastical differences of the hour.[64] Dr. Charles E. Jefferson, pastor of the Broadway Tabernacle, New York, and a noted liberal leader, was inclined to welcome theological struggle: "We have arrived at a season of religious controversy," he wrote. "This is a good sign. It proves that we are intellectually alive." Controversy, he thought, was as inevitable and as useful in religion as in politics and science.[65]

Echoes of the struggle in America were heard across the sea. The *British Weekly*, in the summer of 1924, ran a series of twelve articles on "Fundamentalism: False and True."[66] The same paper a little later published a letter from Dr. Machen and answered it in a leading article.[67] Having commented very favorably on Dr. Fosdick's visit to England earlier in the year, the *British Weekly* published with comment sympathetic to him the correspondence leading to the termination of his relations with the First Church.[68]

13.

the special commission of 1925

Theological matters at issue in the Presbyterian Church were far from settled by the spring of 1925. Extreme conservatives had succeeded in electing the moderator in 1924, but their victory in removing Dr. Fosdick was quite nominal and empty, because the Assembly had based its action on denominational rather than on theological grounds. The conservatives had failed completely in the effort to force men connected with seminaries and boards to subscribe the five-point deliverance. Nor did those favoring toleration have reason to feel satisfied, with agitation in the Church against them increasing, and with the Assembly already on record as declaring the disputed five doctrines to be "essential." Further action of some sort in the Church was therefore inevitable.

In the hope of ensuring a conservative victory at the Assembly of 1925, eight ministers sent a circular letter to fifteen hundred Presbyterian clergymen urging the election of "loyal" commissioners to the Assembly, and suggesting local "loyalty" rallies "for the purpose of instructing the people in the danger that threatens historic Presbyterianism." [1] An important presbytery even overtured the Assembly of 1925 "to exscind the said Presbytery of New York from the Presbyterian Church in the United States of America" because of that presbytery's alleged "long continued disloyalty to the doctrinal standards of the Presbyterian Church." [2]

If the conservatives were preparing for the Assembly of 1925, so too were those who favored policies of toleration. To counteract the circular letter sent by the eight extreme conservatives, thirty-one ministers addressed an appeal "For Peace and Liberty" to "the people and ministers of the Presbyterian Church, U.S.A." It was somewhat reminiscent of the "Plea for Peace and Work" of 1893.[3] This appeal of 1925 called attention to the fact that the Assembly of 1924 had declared unconstitutional the proposal to require certain church officers to subscribe the five-point doctrinal deliverance. "In spite of this decision of our highest court, efforts are still being made to impose these doctrinal interpretations upon ministers. . . . We appeal to our brethren in the presbyteries to stand firmly for the maintenance of our historic liberties." The same group also formed a subcommittee to circulate pamphlets to foster the unity, liberty, and peace of the Presbyterian Church.[4]

With opinion in the Church so sharply divided over theological and constitutional questions, each group turned with particular eagerness to the forthcoming election of a moderator. As in the previous year,[5] liberals and conservatives who were opposed to the purposes and methods of the extreme conservatives united in supporting Dr. Charles R. Erdman, a man whose theological conservatism was widely known. In view of current misunderstandings Dr. Erdman described his position: "I have always been a Fundamentalist in my beliefs. . . . If any men of more liberal theological views desire to vote for me, it is, of course, their privilege to do so. The platform on which I stand, however, is that of old-fashioned orthodoxy and Christian spirit and constitutional procedure."[6] Meeting in Columbus, Ohio, in an auditorium which was crowded to capacity for the exciting event, the General Assembly of 1925 elected Dr. Erdman. In less than an hour newsboys were shouting special editions containing the news.[7] The program of the extreme conservatives had suffered a defeat in the first trial of strength.

The theological issue was brought to a head in this Assembly of 1925 by the old question of licensure in New York Presbytery, which came before the Assembly through a memorial and a complaint. In a formal memorial New York Presbytery asked the Assembly "to determine by its Judicial Commission, the proper status of a Presbytery in its Constitutional powers in the matter of the licensing of candidates." The memorial then argued from the history of the Church in favor of the theory on which New York Presbytery had been operating, viz., that "a Presbytery is the only judge as to the qualifications of its candidates seeking licensure."[8]

A complaint made to the Assembly of 1925 by minority members of New York Presbytery declared that the presbytery had licensed two candidates each of whom had stated that "he could neither affirm nor deny the Virgin Birth." The Assembly's Permanent Judicial Commission in its judgment in the case declared that "this [i.e., the virgin birth] is the sole question of doctrine at issue." The commission saw in the case two important constitutional questions: "the right of the General Assembly to review the action of a Presbytery in licensing candidates for the ministry; and the necessary requirements for licensure."

As to the first question, representatives of the presbytery argued before the commission that "the jurisdiction of a Presbytery in the matter of licensure is exclusive, that its action therein is not subject to review," and therefore moved that the complaint be dismissed for want of jurisdiction. The commission admitted that the power of licensure was original in the presbyteries, but declared that the higher judicatories by their inherent powers of review and control had the right to decide whether a presbytery exercised its powers of licensure in accord with the Church's constitution. "The Church is not a mere confederation of Presbyteries—it is a united Church." The commission therefore overruled the motion to dismiss the case for lack of jurisdiction.[9]

The commission then dealt with the second question, "the necessary requirements for licensure." The issue here was clear-cut: in order to be licensed in the Presbyterian Church must a candidate be able to affirm faith in the virgin birth? The commission quoted the General Assembly of 1910 as declaring that "no one who is in serious doubt concerning this doctrine should be licensed or ordained as a minister." The commission added: "The General Assembly has repeatedly passed upon the importance of clear and positive views regarding this doctrine. It is the established law of the Church." The judgment of the commission therefore sustained the complaint and remanded the case to New York Presbytery "for appropriate action, in conformity with the decision herein rendered." The Assembly confirmed the commission's judgment.[10] The case was a severe blow to the proponents of inclusive churchmanship.

Extreme conservatives, of course, were delighted with the verdict,[11] while those in the Assembly who were of more liberal theological views were filled with dismay.[12] The liberal group had prepared alternative protests suited, respectively, to various possible decisions of the judicial case; so when the decision was announced they were ready immediately with their response. Dr. Henry Sloane Coffin, who was a commissioner from New York Presbytery, hurried to the platform and read the following protest:

"The sixteen commissioners of the Presbytery of New York, on behalf of the said Presbytery, respectfully declare that the Presbytery of New York will stand firmly upon the constitution of the Church, reaffirmed in the reunions of 1870 and 1906, which forbids the Assembly to change or add to the conditions for entrance upon or continuance in the holy ministry, without submitting such amendment to the Presbyteries for concurrent action."[13] A little later, interviewed by reporters, "Dr. Coffin was asked whether the Presbytery and the Synod of New York would 'bolt the decision.' 'Not until the last door is closed to us,' he replied."[14] Thirty-one of the Assembly's commissioners signed another protest against the decision.[15] The next day the *New York Times* announced developments in the Assembly with front-page headlines, "Assembly Censures New York Liberals; Split Threatens," and reported that "the protest threw the Assembly into a fever of excitement."

As soon as the case had been decided and the Assembly had ceased to sit as a court, Dr. Erdman yielded the moderator's chair to the vice-moderator, Elder John M. T. Finney, M.D., and from the floor of the Assembly moved the adoption of the following resolution: "That a Commission of Fifteen members be appointed to study the present spiritual condition of

Special Commission of 1925 to study the spiritual condition of the Church and the causes for unrest.

our Church and the causes making for unrest, and to report to the next General Assembly, to the end that the purity, peace, unity and progress of the Church may be assured." The Assembly adopted the resolution unanimously.[16] The creation of this Special Commission of 1925 was widely approved, and the appointment of its members, with Dr. Henry C. Swearingen, of St. Paul, as chairman,[17] met with general satisfaction. Except for one liberal and three or four ministers and elders who were extreme conservatives, the commission was composed of moderate conservatives, the group which held the balance of power in the Church. The members individually were well known and highly respected.

Many of the liberal men were deeply disturbed by the Assembly's decision which had declared affirmation of the virgin birth to be an absolute requirement for licensure and ordination, and more than a hundred of them met the evening after the decision to consider what could be done. Some even spoke of withdrawing from the Presbyterian Church.[18] The moderator, Dr. Erdman, whom all of them knew to be a strong conservative in his own theological views, visited the meeting. He told them that if they insisted on going out from the Church on the theological issue, they of course had the right to do so, but, he added, there was no need for them to leave the Church on the constitutional issue, because their interpretation of the constitutional question was the correct one. Instead of withdrawing at once, the liberals waited to see what direction church policies would take, and especially what the new Special Commission would do.

Dr. Erdman, after the adjournment of the Assembly, discussing the new Special Commission, saw in the enthusiasm with which the Assembly voted to create it "a determination to avoid disunion." "The Commission," he continued, "evidently has no inquisitorial purposes or powers; it is 'a friendly commission,' appointed to study conditions and to advise constructive measures." Referring to constitutional problems confronting the commission, he said: "Among these questions which have arisen is that of the relative powers of the Presbytery and of the General Assembly in the matter of licensing candidates for the ministry. Then again, there is the question as to the nature of a decision on the part of the Assembly; is it merely 'kindly advice,' or does it form a powerful precedent, or does it constitute law and establish a binding rule?" But he hastened to add that the powers of the commission were not limited to an analysis of constitutional problems.[19]

After the new commission had held its first meeting in September and had organized five committees,[20] new developments were not long in coming to its attention. The Presbytery of New York, for example, the next month voted not to license or ordain any more candidates until after the Assembly's commission had presented its final report.[21] In this same autumn of 1925 a "Committee on Protestant Liberties in the Presbyterian

Church" was formed to resist encroachment by the General Assembly on liberty of thought claimed for the Presbyterian ministry. Through ten of its members the committee presented its views to the Assembly's commission.[22] Very similar in purpose was a letter written to the commission by ninety-seven "younger ministers of the Presbyterian Church." They felt that a chief cause of existing unrest was "the wide difference of opinion in the church regarding the exact meaning of subscription to the Confession of Faith," and complained that the confusion had been greatly accentuated by the Assembly's inconsistent deliverances, the five-point deliverance issued in 1910, 1916, and 1923 being at variance with the bases of the reunions of 1870 and 1906 and with the Declaratory Statement of 1903. The writers desired "such immediate coördination and revision of the terms of subscription to the Westminster Confession as will make unmistakably explicit that it is not a final and perfect test of orthodoxy, but may be interpreted by each generation under the guidance of the spirit of Christ."[23] The *Presbyterian*, analyzing the seminary backgrounds of the signers of the letter, stated that of the ninety-seven, forty-five were from Union Seminary, while only two were graduates of Princeton Seminary.[24] The Assembly's commission heard individuals, too, as diverging in viewpoint as Drs. Machen, Coffin, William Adams Brown, and Macartney.[25]

A highly important factor operating against the extreme conservatives was the prevailing sentiment in the country—particularly strong amid the pacifism of postwar years—that ecclesiastical controversy was something essentially reprehensible. President Angell, for example, in his baccalaureate address at Yale University in the spring of 1926 when theological controversies within the Presbyterian and other denominations were being widely publicized, was quoted as having said: "All this [contemporary American] indifference to religion and contempt for Christianity is projected against a background of strife inside the Christian Church—at least in American Protestantism—which is far from edifying, however inevitable." [26]

During the year between the General Assemblies of 1925 and 1926 the Assembly's Special Commission held four meetings.[27] There was discussion of the mooted "five points"; of the advisability of broadening the subscription formula, somewhat after Scottish example; of the powers of the General Assembly in theological matters, particularly of the constitutional right of the Assembly to declare certain doctrines "essential" or to overrule presbyteries in licensing and ordaining candidates.[28] In Scotland the General Assembly was recognized as having greater authority over questions of licensure and ordination.[29] Two lawyers on the Special Commission who were conservative in theological viewpoint thought the Assembly ultimately had absolute powers in relation to candidates, even to the point of nullifying an ordination. They argued from the civil analogies of the general welfare clause of the federal constitution, and from the right of a court to nullify the election of a civil officer. One of them, however, became convinced that civil analogies did not apply, but the other persevered and dissented at this point from the commission's final report. "I cannot conceive of an organic body," he wrote, "in which there is no organic authority to settle questions relating to the general welfare." [30]

The basic question before the Special Commission of 1925 was how the constitution could be interpreted so as to remove the binding force from the "five points".

Testimony presented to the commission made it clear that if the Church did not give relief from the judicial decision of 1925 it would be in danger of losing its left wing; but that if it altered the formula of subscription to the Confession or substituted for the Confession a brief modern creed it would be in danger of losing its right wing.[31] During the commission's deliberations it was never even considered that the Church should repudiate the controverted doctrines.[32] It also seemed quite inexpedient to suggest that the Assembly propose to the presbyteries amendment of the constitution. Instead of allaying controversy this would extend it to every corner of the Church. The practical problem, then, reduced itself to the question whether, without amending the constitution or the subscription formula, the constitution could be so interpreted as to remove binding force from the "five points" without repudiating them as doctrines of the Church. In other words, could it be shown that the Church's history and constitution, properly interpreted, pointed to a much broader toleration than extreme conservatives were willing to grant? It was felt, too, that the Church's boards and interdenominational relations would be greatly aided by broader policies, illustrating once again the deep influence of the Church's work on its theological policy. There were differences within the commission—on occasion, some sharp differences—but these were overcome partly through Dr. Speer's wisdom and leadership,[33] so that it was possible to draft a unanimous report to the Assembly of 1926.

At the Assembly of 1926 public interest was so great that representatives of the secular and religious press filled both sides of a row of tables stretching continuously across the front of the auditorium.[34] Dr. W. O. Thompson, former president of Ohio State University, as one "who will carry on Dr. Erdman's program," was elected moderator by the clear-cut majority of 535 to 382. It is evident that the cause of extreme conservatism was already beginning to slip seriously, though the results were variously interpreted at the moment. In nominating the opposing candidate, the speaker had "kept saying that there was no one who wanted to divide the Church." The *Presbyterian Banner*, shrewdly anticipating later developments, commented on this statement, "Have the fundamentalists faced about on this question, or is there division among them . . .?" [35]

The report of the Special Commission of 1925 was regarded as the most important event of the Assembly of 1926.[36] After a first main section of "Preliminary Statements" the second main section of the commission's report dealt with "Causes of Unrest" in the Church, important among which were "doctrinal and theological causes." Without naming Dr.

Machen, the commission categorically repudiated his view that there were within the Presbyterian Church two mutually exclusive religions, and added that the resolution of the preceding Assembly creating a commission to assure the Church's "purity, peace, unity and progress" proved "that the Assembly believed in its own evangelical unity and in the evangelical unity of our Church at large." [37]

The third main section of the commission's report dealt with the "Constitutional Principle of Unity with its Historical Background." In this section the report, on the basis of a review of four controversies in the Church's history, developed the idea that "the Christian principle of toleration" was embedded deeply in the Church's constitution.[38] Noting that "divisions and schisms have not cured theological controversy in the Presbyterian Church" in times past, the commission called attention to the fact "that the Presbyterian system admits diversity of view where the core of truth is identical." But lest this plea for toleration might seem to remove restraining standards, the commission hastened to make clear that the Church and not the individual must decide the limits of tolerated divergence, "either *generally*, by amendment of the Constitution, or *particularly*, by Presbyterial authority, subject to the constitutional right of appeal." The commission added that "toleration does not involve any lowering of the Standards. It does not weaken the testimony of the Church as to its assured convictions." [39]

This historical approach to the controversy, which had been developed by the commission's Committee on Historical Background, of which Dr. Hugh T. Kerr of Pittsburgh was chairman,[40] set the whole problem in larger and truer perspective. Extreme conservatives, who with a very few exceptions had shown little interest in the Church's history, had all along tacitly assumed that their theological position and theirs alone was simon-pure American Presbyterianism, and that their liberal opponents represented a sinister deviation from this straight line. As an earlier part of the present study has noted,[41] the American Presbyterian Church has been from the beginning a combination of diverging tendencies, maintained in fairly equal balance. The commission did not go so far, but a case could be made for the contention that the real innovators were those who almost since the reunion of 1869 had been seeking to force the Church into an unprecedented unanimity in repudiating theological change. The main stream of the Church's life—at least previous to reunion—had not been "left wing" or "right wing" but mediating; and this fact the commission's report made admirably clear.

The fourth main section of the commission's report dealt with the "Power of the General Assembly and Effect of Its Actions." Here the commission pointed out that the General Assembly was not the heir of the General Synod which it superseded, because the General Assembly is a delegated body and has a written constitution over it, whereas the General

Synod was composed of all the ministers and a representative of every congregation in the Church and was not under a written constitution. "The (General) Synod was the whole Church," whereas the Assembly is not. "To quote actions of The (General) Synod therefore, as though they constituted controlling precedents as to the methods by which similar actions may be taken by the General Assembly, is clearly inadmissible," for "the General Assembly has limited, defined, and delegated powers." [42]

The commission's report distinguished four powers exercised by the Assembly. In its legislative and executive functions—the two being here treated together by the commission—the Assembly has the right to make deliverances, "but they are subject to modification or repeal at any time by a majority vote of the General Assembly." A third function of the Assembly which the commission distinguished was the judicial. When the Assembly renders a decision in a judicial case "the judgment in that particular case is final," and the decision stands "as a powerful and persuasive precedent until altered or reversed." But the Assembly has full power in a similar or identical case in the future to render a contrary judgment.

Still a fourth function of the Assembly is its role in amending the constitution. This cannot be done by legislative or executive deliverance, or by judicial decision of the Assembly, but only by the joint action of Assembly and presbyteries. The report contented itself with this broad declaration of constitutional principles, leaving for the next year the detailed application of them to the existing situation in the Church. The implication, however, was obvious that the commission would oppose the extreme conservatives' claim that the Assembly's five-point deliverance was binding.[43]

The report closed with a brief fifth section entitled "Conclusions and Recommendations," which mentioned matters still remaining to be discussed. Needing more time for the study of these the commission asked to be continued for another year, at the same time urging patience and mutual forbearance.[44]

When the commission's report was read to the General Assembly of 1926, seats on the main floor were filled, and the atmosphere was tense.[45] Amendments proposed from the floor were almost unanimously defeated, and the report as a whole was enthusiastically adopted. The tide was rapidly running out from under the extreme conservative cause, which now, in the opinion of the *Presbyterian Banner*, seemed to be "left without much of a following." [46]

One is surprised to find that the commission's report did not meet with more widespread opposition from extreme conservatives in this Assembly of 1926. Dr. Machen seems to have been one of the few to perceive immediately the diametric opposition between it and the program for which he stood. While the Assembly of 1926 was still in session, he told a friend: "If the evangelical [i.e., extreme conservative] party votes for this report its witness bearing is gone and all the sacrifices of the past few years will go for nothing." [47]

Opinion in the Church as a whole acclaimed the commission's report enthusiastically. The prominent Presbyterian elder, Mr. Will H. Hays, was quoted as calling it "a new magna charta." [48] A writer in the country's leading nondenominational religious weekly commented on the commission's report, "If there has been produced in the last two decades an ecclesiastical document of greater worth and significance than this it does not now come to mind." [49] The extreme conservatives, who had won the moderator's chair in the Assembly of 1924 and had even hoped soon to control the Church's machinery as a whole, now, in spite of their continuing attacks on the policies of the Church, were destined to pass from the offensive to the defensive and to become in ecclesiastical voting a steadily dwindling minority.

When, a year later, the General Assembly of 1927 met, it chose its moderator in "the briefest and most harmonious election of the last six years. . . . Everyone felt that Robert E. Speer, were he nominated, would sweep all before him in a tidal wave and so no one cared to go against him." [50] Dr. Samuel G. Craig, who the year before had become editor of the *Presbyterian*, recorded that "when Dr. Speer's name was mentioned, seemingly the entire Assembly rose to its feet and joined enthusiastically in prolonged applause." [51] Dr. Speer, like both nominees of the preceding year, was a member of the Special Commission of 1925.

It was at this Assembly of 1927 that the Special Commission of 1925 presented its final report. Except for a brief concluding study of "The Church's Progress" the entire report was devoted to a consideration of "The Church's Polity." Rejecting both extreme centralization and extreme decentralization, the commission favored a mediating view of the constitution in which powers of session, presbytery, synod, and General Assembly were balanced. But in relation to licensure and ordination, the commission, in language that was reminiscent of controversies about the constitutional powers of the American federal government, said that "the powers of the General Assembly are specific, delegated, and limited, having been conferred upon it by the Presbyteries; whereas the powers of Presbyteries are general and inherent." [52] But "the Constitution seems to make it clear that the General Assembly is to have a voice regarding licensure and ordination in extraordinary cases." A licensure can be revoked by a presbytery without judicial process, but an ordination cannot be. In cases of ordination therefore, "the Presbytery may be disciplined [by the General Assembly] for erroneous action . . . but the individual whom the Presbytery has ordained constitutionally can not be reached by this process." [53]

The commission completed its comments on polity with a discussion of "Essential and Necessary Articles." The commission noted that by the terms of the Adopting Act of 1729 the church judicatory was to decide only in specific cases as to whether or not a candidate's taking exception to a particular part of the Westminster Confession constituted the rejection of any "essential and necessary" article of faith. The Adopting Act conferred no authority upon any judicatory to state in categorical terms what doctrines were "essential and necessary" to all candidates. Furthermore, this authority was to be exercised by the ordaining body, either a presbytery or the old General Synod, whereas the General Assembly is not an ordaining body and under the present constitution does not occupy the same position as did the General Synod.

The commission asserted the right of the Assembly to issue declaratory deliverances to witness to the Church's corporate faith,[54] but hastened to add a word of caution: "It is probable that . . . most of the ministers and members of our Church will agree that the risk of such action [i.e., the General Assembly's issuance of declaratory deliverances designating certain articles as "essential and necessary"] is great, and that the General Assembly may well refrain from taking such a course, especially as it may be misconstrued as a virtual amending of our organic law by another method than that prescribed by the Constitution." [55]

Judicial decisions as well as declaratory deliverances might involve the problem of "essential and necessary" articles of faith. The commission declared that "the General Assembly, when acting in its judicial capacity, has a right to decide questions of this kind only as they apply to the specific case under consideration. . . . This is quite different from deciding, as a general proposition, that certain articles, when considered abstractly and logically, are essential and necessary to the system of doctrine contained in the Holy Scriptures." [56] Such a decision, the commission added, "cannot be made to rest properly upon a merely declaratory deliverance of a former Assembly. A judicial decision is grounded in the Constitution itself." The commission qualified this conclusion by adding that the only constitutional method whereby an Assembly could declare any article of faith essential and necessary would be for it "to quote the exact language of the article as it appears in the Confession of Faith. It could not paraphrase the language nor use other terms than those employed within the Constitution, much less could it erect into essential and necessary articles doctrines which are only derived as inferences from the statements of the Confession." [57] The five-point deliverance of 1910, 1916, and 1923 therefore was rejected.

The commission's report was "unanimously adopted without debate" by the Assembly of 1927.[58] The editor of the *Presbyterian* declared that for him "the impression received from hearing it read was highly favorable." [59]

As between the contrasting positions represented by Dr. Machen's *Christianity and Liberalism* and the Auburn Affirmation, the commission, without naming either of these documents, steered a careful course. As against Dr. Machen's view, the commission explicitly denied any evidence of the existence of two distinct and incompatible religions within the Church. But the commission did not go so far as the Auburn Affirmation and say that existing theological differences were mere differences of theory to explain facts of the faith held in common. The commission's view, however, fully repudiated the theological basis for the plea that liberals be expelled from the Church. On the constitutional question of the "five points," the commission agreed completely with the position taken by the Auburn Affirmation, viz., that the General Assembly does not have the constitutional power to give binding definitions of the Church's essential faith. Thus, when the Assemblies of 1926 and 1927 adopted the reports of the Special Commission, an important part of the Auburn Affirmation's theological argument and all of its constitutional argument became the official position of the Church. Everything of practical ecclesiastical importance—though not everything of theological statement—for which the Auburn Affirmation had contended was granted.

The work of this Special Commission of 1925 was therefore a turning point in the theological history of the Church since the reunion of 1869. It meant that moderate theological liberalism would have what it had unsuccessfully sought almost since the reunion, an acknowledged and assured place in the Church's life and thought. By assuring to local presbyteries greater autonomy and theological liberty at a time when the administrative functions of the Church had long been becoming more centralized, the commission made important concessions to cultural pluralism and theological diversity, concessions which were necessary to preserve the Church's unity. By denying that the General Assembly has the right to define authoritatively the "essentials" of the Church's faith, the commission eliminated the "five points" as a source of controversy and gave the Church greatly desired peace.

But in sweeping away by a stroke of interpretation much of the previously exercised power of the General Assembly to define and thus to preserve the Church's doctrine, the commission established a principle which has much broader implications than the Church has yet had occasion to draw from it. If the Church now has no means of authoritatively defining its faith short of the amending process—which could hardly function in the midst of sharp controversy—ecclesiastical power is seriously hindered for the future from preventing more radical theological innovations than those discussed in the "five points." This fact, combined with the increasing odium against heresy prosecution, would suggest that the Presbyterian Church is now depending on its group mind rather than on traditional Presbyterian authoritarianism for the preservation of its theological heritage. Perhaps the new sanctions will accomplish the same results as the old. Certainly they promise to be more peaceful.

But before the Special Commission of 1925 had completed its reports, conflict over current ecclesiastical policies suddenly appeared within Princeton Seminary, a stronghold of theological conservatism. This soon attracted the attention of the entire Presbyterian Church.

14.

a seminary reorganized

Princeton Theological Seminary, founded in 1812 as the first of the Presbyterian Church's seminaries, had, under the leadership of Dr. Archibald Alexander, its first professor, adopted a highly rational apologetic in conjunction with a strict doctrine of verbal inspiration. In the early stages of the Old School-New School debates, the seminary maintained a moderate position, but presently cast its weight solidly behind the Old School partisans. Some of the seminary's leaders viewed the reunion of 1869 with apprehension. Amid the discussion of Biblical and theological questions after the reunion, the seminary led the successful struggle against the newer views, as well as against any extended revision of the Westminster Confession. Until about the turn of the century, the seminary and others of like mind in the Church were able to "hold the line," in the face, however, of increasing desire for greater theological liberty.

Princeton seemed dedicated to the preservation of the status quo.

During the first quarter of the twentieth century a situation of potential tension between the seminary and the Church was developing, as the forces of theological change became gradually stronger while the seminary set itself even more resolutely to defend the theological *status quo*. Dr. Benjamin B. Warfield, second to none in learning among American theologians, dominated the seminary from his coming to the faculty in 1887 until his death in 1921. He was perhaps the country's most scholarly—and most unyielding—opponent of the so-called liberal theology. Though acknowledging that belief in the trustworthiness of Scripture is a sufficient foundation for saving faith in Christ, he thought an airtight defense which preserved every detail of a closely reasoned system of theology intact to be a wiser strategy than a theological alliance with those who, though agreeing on the "essentials" of Christianity, differed as to many other beliefs.[1] In their adherence to Calvinism, the Princeton Seminary professors were in essential agreement, most of them having themselves been trained at Princeton. As the Church's attitude toward theological liberalism became somewhat more tolerant in the twentieth century, the "Princeton position" in theology became increasingly self-conscious, and the gulf between it and the prevailing temper of the Church became more noticeable, a situation that was frought with some danger to both Church and seminary.

But there had always been in the seminary's theology elements out of which broader theological policies could be fashioned. Even while emphasizing verbal inspiration and stressing detailed elaboration of the Calvinistic system, the strictest Princeton men had acknowledged that basic faith in Christ was sufficient for essential Christianity, and that this faith did not presuppose the infallibility, or even the inspiration of the Bible, but only its basic trustworthiness. Even before the contest of the 1920's there had been on the faculty men like Drs. John DeWitt and John D. Davis who, while not in controversy with the stricter viewpoint prevailing in the faculty, represented a noticeably broader theological and ecclesiastical attitude.[2]

Alongside Princeton Seminary's theological tradition was another tradition extending from the seminary's earliest days and even antedating its theological position. This was the seminary's ecclesiastical position, adherence to what might be called a "high church" Presbyterian polity. The founders of Princeton Seminary, holding extreme presbyterian, as distinguished from congregationalizing, views of church government, believed that the whole Church is wiser and more to be trusted than any smaller part of the Church. After thorough discussion, the projected seminary was, in 1811, placed under the complete control of the General Assembly.[3] During the middle years of the nineteenth century, the seminary was identified with "Old School" Presbyterianism, whose tenets included not only strict Calvinistic theology, but also a high view of the authority and prerogatives of the Church's judicatories. The Old School Presbyterian Church, in sharp contrast with the more decentralized government of the New School Presbyterian Church, placed all its seminaries and missionary undertakings squarely under the control of its General Assembly. With this centralized polity Princeton Seminary was in the heartiest accord. For a considerable time after the reunion of 1869, the seminary found itself thoroughly *en rapport* with the dominant theological trends in the Church, which were still extremely conservative. It was therefore not until the twentieth century, when the domination of the Princeton type of theology was being widely challenged in the Church, that the two basic elements of the Princeton tradition—subjection to denominational control and polemic adherence to the "Princeton Theology"—even appeared to come into conflict with each other.

The internal organization of Princeton Seminary was altered in an im-

As the Church became more tolerant, a gulf between the dominant attitude of the Church and that at Princeton became ominously apparent

portant respect when the General Assembly of 1902, on recommendation of the seminary's Board of Directors, amended the "Plan" of the seminary to provide for a new official, a "President of the Seminary." The amended Plan provided that among other duties "he shall be the representative of the Seminary before the Church." [4] The next year the directors reported that Dr. Francis L. Patton, former professor in the seminary, and more recently president of Princeton University and lecturer in the seminary, had been elected first president of the seminary and also professor of the philosophy of religion.[5] Dr. Patton after his election retained his position ex officio as a member of the seminary's Board of Directors and was soon afterwards elected a trustee as well. Before the creation of the president's office the senior professor had been accustomed to preside at faculty meetings. Dr. Patton, not construing the powers of the presidency as broadly as the seminary's revised Plan would warrant, did not stress the executive and policy-making functions of the new office. For practical purposes he was hardly more than senior professor with a new title.[6] In 1913 Dr. Patton, having attained the age of seventy, resigned.[7]

There were many among Princeton Seminary alumni and directors in 1913 who felt that in securing a new president the seminary should seek someone who would bring the seminary into closer touch with the life of the Presbyterian Church. There was a feeling in some quarters that Princeton's place in the Church and in the religious world as a whole was not quite what it once had been.[8] By the year 1913 the gradual divergence between the "historic Princeton position" and emerging attitudes in the Church were threatening the seminary with partial isolation. Finally, after much deliberation,[9] the Board of Directors elected to the presidency Dr. J. Ross Stevenson, distinguished pastor and active churchman with membership on numerous General Assembly and interdenominational boards and committees. The determining factor in his election was the desire that the seminary might, under his leadership, be brought into closer relationship with the Church as a whole. Certain allusions in the formal charge which Dr. Patton, the former president, delivered at Dr. Stevenson's inauguration perhaps reflect this same expectation.[10]

But unsolved problems of churchmanship which had been troubling the Presbyterian Church for several decades soon threatened to disturb harmony within the seminary. In the General Assembly of 1920 Dr. Stevenson, as vice-chairman of the General Assembly's Committee on Church Coöperation and Union, had advocated the adoption of the Plan of Organic Union of Evangelical Churches. Dr. Charles R. Erdman also favored its adoption, but six members of the faculty opposed it, largely on the grounds that they considered its Preamble theologically inadequate.[11] In relation to the controversy in the Church at large during the early 1920's, members of the seminary held different attitudes. The majority of the faculty were in wholehearted sympathy with the program of the extreme conservative party in the Church. The minority of the faculty, also conservative in their personal theological beliefs, disapproved of the aggressive denominational program of the extreme conservatives.

The viewpoint represented by the faculty minority was of particular importance, because presently it became dominant in the faculty and in the control of the seminary, and gradually ushered in a new era of the seminary's history. Dr. van Dyke, writing from the university in the middle of the 1920's, told a friend that "with the greatest part of his [Dr. Machen's] theology no doubt the Seminary agrees. But the best men there, like Stevenson, Erdman, and Loetscher, state it in much milder and more attractive language, and they do not think, as he does, that liberal believers in Christ as their divine Lord and Saviour should either go out or be driven out of the Presbyterian Church. This of course is the crux of the whole situation." [12] Four men constituted the faculty "minority" during these years: Drs. J. Ross Stevenson, Charles R. Erdman, Frederick W. Loetscher, and J. Ritchie Smith. President Stevenson, unlike the other three, was not an alumnus of the seminary, and under circumstances then existing this greatly increased the difficulty of his position. His utterances, with lifelong consistency, attested his earnest evangelicalism and basic conservatism. He had held prominent pastorates and had had wide ecclesiastical experience. In personal background Dr. Erdman was perhaps the most conservative of the four. He and his father had both been editors of *The Fundamentals*, and his writings manifested a very notably conservative tone. But long experience in the pastorate and in denominational affairs had saved him from a purely doctrinaire attitude. Dr. Loetscher had studied in Berlin under Harnack and in Strassburg. He was perhaps the closest of the four to the viewpoint of the faculty "majority," but a disinclination to dogmatism and to extreme views of every sort made him increasingly dissatisfied with the steadily sharpening policies then prevailing. A student and admirer of both Warfield and DeWitt, he was far more akin to the latter, by whom he was deeply influenced.[13] Dr. J. Ritchie Smith's father, Dr. Joseph T. Smith, had been a former Old School pastor in Baltimore, at first not too happy over the reunion. But the years had seen the father assume increasing leadership in denominational and interdenominational interests, with noticeable broadening of sympathies. The son, as a young man reviewing Dr. Briggs's *Whither?* had agreed with Dr. Briggs in rejecting Biblical inerrancy.[14] At the seminary his views were moderate and his spirit irenic. In connection with their wider conceptions of Christian fellowship and coöperation, it is interesting to note that all of the faculty "minority" had served in pastorates—all except Dr. Loetscher for long periods—whereas only one of the "majority" had ever been a pastor, and that more than thirty years before.

Differences between these two groups within the seminary faculty inevitably became strongly colored by personal issues.[15] Dr. Henry van Dyke surrendered his pew in the First Church of Princeton as a protest against the strongly polemic tone of the sermons preached there by Dr. Machen as stated supply, but returned a year later when Dr. Erdman was installed as pastor.[16] When an editorial in the *Presbyterian*, attacking Dr. Erdman[17] was answered,[18] Dr. Machen too became involved.[19] When Dr. Erdman was a candidate for moderator of the General Assembly in 1924 and 1925, the majority of the faculty was opposed to his election. Student activities also created incidents. In October 1924, Princeton student representatives withdrew from the Theological Seminary Conference of the Middle Atlantic Union at Madison, New Jersey, and Princeton students organized a conservative League of Evangelical Students, which was later extended to other campuses.[20] All the members of the faculty agreed that the league's theological tenets and announced purposes were laudable enough, but the minority of the faculty considered its spirit divisive and its net effects definitely harmful.[21] The majority of the faculty, however, heartily endorsed the league, Dr. Machen regarding its formation as evidence of a spiritual revival.[22] Tension was further increased when on account of his disapproval of the new students' league the faculty passed over Dr. Erdman, who had served as faculty adviser to the Students' Association for many years, and elected Dr. Robert Dick Wilson, who was in sympathy with the league.[23] While these various personal issues were secondary, they did serve to accentuate the division already existing within the faculty over questions of ecclesiastical policy in the denomination.

Tensions mount within the seminary.

In May 1925, in response to a request of President Stevenson, the Board of Directors appointed a committee of seven to adjust problems within the faculty.[24] The committee's report, as adopted by the Board in October, declared:

"1. Your Committee has found every member of the faculty entirely loyal to the standards of our Church and to the pledge required by the Seminary. There is no room for doubt or criticism as to the faith or teaching of any professor or instructor in the Seminary.

"2. Such differences as have arisen are not due to doctrinal discord in the faculty but to the different attitudes of the members of the faculty to the discussion of questions which are agitating the whole Christian world, and to temporary conditions involving the personal relations of members of the Seminary to the government of our Church. If in these matters there is not the same unity that there is in matters of faith and doctrine, the members of the faculty in their conduct and writing are entitled to exercise that liberty of action and of opinion which is fundamental to our faith and form of government and particularly to the historic attitude of this Seminary." [25] While the vindication of the orthodoxy of all members of the faculty contained in these resolutions did much to set forth the controversy in its true light as a difference concerning ecclesiastical policies, the action of the directors did not remove the differences themselves and discord within the faculty continued unabated.

Affairs in the seminary took a new turn in the General Assembly of 1926. Early in May of that year the seminary's Board of Directors had elected Dr. J. Gresham Machen to the chair of apologetics and ethics,[26] an action confirmed the next day by the seminary's Board of Trustees.[27] Both boards were sharply divided in this action, since the differences existing in the faculty were reflected in both controlling boards, the majority of the directors and a minority of the trustees agreeing in general with the majority of the faculty. Dissatisfied with the existing situation, a number of directors and trustees requested the General Assembly of 1926 to investigate conditions in the seminary "alleged by these Directors and Trustees and by others to be subversive of Christian fellowship and to be jeopardizing the usefulness of the Seminary." [28]

The General Assembly's Standing Committee on Theological Seminaries to which the request was referred recommended:

"That the Assembly appoint a Committee of three ministers and two elders to make a sympathetic study of conditions affecting the welfare of Princeton Seminary, and to coöperate responsively with Seminary leaders in striving to adjust and harmonize differences and to report to the next Assembly.

". . . That as a corollary to this action the Assembly reserve judgment and take no action, either in approval or disapproval of the election of a Professor in the Seminary of Princeton, until this Committee shall have reported." [29] The Assembly's committee was unanimous in recommending the investigating committee, but a minority report supplemented this recommendation by urging that Dr. Machen's election be confirmed at once.

President Stevenson, invited to take the floor by vote of the Assembly, warned the commissioners that a divisive spirit was manifesting itself within the seminary and related the question of confirmation to this: "It is because some of us stand for the spirit manifested in the report of the commission of fifteen[30] that there is difficulty.

"There are honored men on this platform who could not be invited to the Princeton Theological Seminary because of the line of demarcation drawn by those who believe the time has come to make the differences clear. . . . This election [of Dr. Machen], I say is involved in that situation. . . .

". . . We are the agency of the combined old school and new school, and my ambition as President of the seminary is to have it represent the whole Presbyterian Church and not any particular faction of it. What I want is to have the light thrown on me, on members of the faculty and the whole institution. If there is to be judgment, let it fall where it will, and let the seminary go forward in the traditions of its founders." [31] That the president here formulated the issue clearly is seen by the amount of discussion that soon revolved around the clause, "represent the whole Presbyterian Church."

By a large majority[32] the Assembly adopted the majority report, creating a Committee of Five to visit the seminary and postponing action on Dr. Machen's election until the committee should report. Many who favored the program which the extreme conservatives had been conducting in the Church of course strongly disapproved of the Assembly's action.[33] Dr. Patton, writing in October from his retirement in Bermuda to a seminary director, expressed the hope that existing differences within the faculty "may find an amicable settlement through a reasonable compromise." [34] The *Presbyterian Banner* at once hailed this statement of the distinguished former president: "There speaks the true representative of Princeton." [35] The same letter from Dr. Patton then proceeded to speak at length and in the highest terms of Dr. Machen's qualifications for the chair of apologetics.[36]

The General Assembly's Committee of Five, with all members present, was in Princeton November 22, 23, and 24, 1926, and again later, to interview interested parties. The committee's meeting with about 125 alumni revealed differing opinions as to the causes of disagreement within the seminary, but also a strong conviction that harmony must be restored.[37]

On the morning of November 23 the committee met with the faculty. This meeting and the committee's subsequent conference with the faculty, together with written statements, revealed not only personal differences, but also important differences of attitude toward current ecclesiastical questions and differing conceptions as to the relationship in which the seminary should stand to the thought and life of the Presbyterian Church.

The real point at issue within the faculty was whether orthodoxy and tolerance were compatible. The majority of the faculty, for example, in a prepared statement took sharp issue with President Stevenson's speech at the recent Assembly in which he had said that he desired to make Princeton Seminary representative of "the whole Presbyterian Church." They interpreted this as meaning that he desired the seminary to be "inclusive of the different doctrinal points of view which now exist in the Church," [38] an interpretation which he repudiated.[39] Similarly, the statement of the faculty majority quoting from the Plan of the seminary implied that the "defense" of doctrine there mentioned called for aggressive and polemic policies of ecclesiastical action in doctrinal matters and could not be fully performed by setting forth Christian truth through academic argumentation alone.[40] Individual members of the faculty majority gave repeated testimony that they considered a difference in attitude toward ecclesiastical policies to be the principal point at issue within the seminary. Should the seminary take an irenic or a polemic attitude toward liberalism within the Presbyterian Church?[41]

President Stevenson, in his statement to the committee, pointed to this difference of viewpoint in regard to ecclesiastical policies: "Most of this [i.e., division within the seminary] may be explained by a difference of attitude within the faculty towards the Presbyterian Church of today, towards General Assemblies and their leadership, the Assembly of 1924 excepted, and towards the boards, agencies and enterprises of the Presbyterian Church." [42] Dr. Stevenson's opponents thought that vigorous controversy was immediately necessary to save the Church from the supposed perils of liberalism. He, on the other hand, charged that the course which they advocated must inevitably isolate Princeton Seminary and remove it from the main stream of denominational life: "Shall Princeton Seminary now, fretted by the interference of the General Assembly, in rebellion against the Presbyterian Church as at present organized and controlled . . . be permitted to swing off to the extreme right wing so as to become an interdenominational Seminary for Bible School-premillennial-secession fundamentalism?" [43]

Commenting before the committee on this same subject of the relation of the seminary to the Church, Professor J. Ritchie Smith, also a member of the minority of the faculty, said: "Historically and legally, there is no question that the seminary represents the whole Church. . . . It cannot be superior to the Church, nor separate from the Church, nor independent of the Church. It cannot be detached from the Church, and I should deprecate very cordially any policy of isolation from the Church." Dr. Loetscher regretted that amid what he called the current "theological panic" differences over church policy should have been so damaging to Christian charity.[44]

Existing policies of the faculty majority, however, were already tending to isolate the seminary.[45] The faculty declined for theological reasons to invite certain prominent Presbyterians to preach at the seminary and later changed the personnel of the faculty committee which had recommended inviting them.[46] A member of the faculty majority sometimes coached in advance guest speakers from the church boards addressing student meetings.[47] The attitude of Dr. Machen toward the church boards was openly hostile.[48] The committee itself called attention to the fact that during the previous year the seminary had given more financial aid to its non-Presbyterian than to its Presbyterian students,[49] a paragraph of the report to which the faculty by formal resolution later took exception.[50]

The *Presbyterian Banner* criticized what it regarded as Princeton's pronounced isolation. Commenting on a press report that the "majority group" at the seminary had told the Assembly's committee that it "holds for a theology as taught by the Presbyterian Church before 1870," the *Banner* remarked quite sharply: "What movement in the Presbyterian Church has Princeton supported since 1870? . . . Princeton may be standing where the Presbyterian Church stood in 1870, but not so the church itself. . . . If Princeton is standing where the church stood in 1870 it is time that it should move forward and stand where the church stands today. . . . This might be the solution and end of some of its troubles." [51] The same periodical continued the analysis of the Princeton situation the next week with the comment: "The majority of the faculty of Princeton Theological Seminary will not tolerate a difference, not of doctrine, but even of attitude towards doctrinal differences in others." [52]

The Assembly's Committee of Five after its study of the seminary situation was convinced that the tension caused by the pronounced differences of attitude toward ecclesiastical policy was revealing certain organizational weaknesses in the institution. It was felt that at various points the seminary's Plan and Charter failed to fix responsibility and define duties and prerogatives with sufficient clearness. There was, for example, within the faculty rather wide difference of opinion as to the exact nature of the president's office and powers.[53] Conversations with the Board of Directors and the Board of Trustees convinced the committee that the system of dual control, with the directors in charge of educational and the trustees in charge of financial matters, involved inevitable friction, especially when as at the moment the majority of one board sympathized with the faculty majority, while the majority of the other board favored their opponents.[54] In examining the structure of the seminary still further, the committee felt that the seminary's charter did not sufficiently ensure to the General Assembly ultimate control over the institution's property.

On the basis of its studies the Committee of Five prepared its report to the General Assembly of 1927,[55] which stated that "the root and source of the serious difficulties at Princeton . . . seem to be in the plan of government by two Boards." [56] To remedy the situation, the report recommended that the Assembly's Committee of Five be increased to nine and that the enlarged committee be instructed to take all necessary legal steps "to establish a single Board of Control for said Seminary, define the relationship and recognize the right of control of the General Assembly under the existing trusts, so as to assure the rights of the Presbyterian Church in the trust property and the instruction of the Seminary; and to co-operate in preparing a complete plan for the educational work of the Seminary under the administration of the new Board and under the direction and control of the Assembly." Pending the reorganization it was recommended that Dr. Machen's election and all other elections to the faculty be not approved and the consideration of them be deferred.[57]

In the General Assembly of 1927 a few minor amendments to the committee's report were adopted, most important of which was that the committee be increased to eleven instead of to nine, leaving the original five a minority in the new committee, and that the new committee, instead of being authorized to "complete the reorganization" was now instructed "to report to the next General Assembly for approval and adoption" whatever changes it might propose.[58] When the amended report was adopted by a vote of 503 to 323 the commissioners and spectators, according to a press account, rose and cheered.[59]

Because the Assembly had not attempted to make any final settlement of the Princeton question, some of the extreme conservatives still looked upon the situation hopefully.[60] The editor of the *Presbyterian*, for example, struck vigorous blows against the proposed reorganization: "All this talk about the alleged benefits of a one board control is but a 'smoke screen' to conceal the real objective of its advocates. . . . They want to get rid of the present Board of Directors because they know that as long as this Board directs the affairs of the Seminary, it will not become an inclusive institution. The ultimate objective of those advocating the reorganization of Princeton Seminary is an inclusive church, and their more immediate objective is the changing of Princeton Seminary into an inclusive institution because they see in it the chief obstacle in the way of making the Presbyterian Church, U.S.A. an inclusive church—a church in which so-called Fundamentalists and so-called Modernists shall have equal rights and privileges." [61] During this year between the Assemblies of 1927 and 1928, various groups within the seminary set forth their views and many presbyteries expressed themselves in one way or another on the matter.[62]

Meanwhile the Assembly's Committee of Eleven drafted its report, which was published shortly before the General Assembly of 1928 convened. The committee offered for the approval of the Assembly specific amendments to both Princeton Seminary's Charter and Plan. The proposed amendments to the Charter increased the Board of Trustees to thirty-three, eighteen ministers and fifteen elders, whose election must be approved by the General Assembly; who should hold the seminary property in trust for the Presbyterian Church in the U.S.A.; and who should be subject to the instructions of the General Assembly from time to time in the management of seminary affairs. The amendment to the Charter provided further that in the first election after the adoption of the amendment, one third of the new Board of Trustees should be elected from the existing Board of Directors, one third from the existing Board of Trustees, and one third from persons not members of either board, and all chosen "by a plan which the General Assembly shall provide." [63]

The proposed amendments to the seminary's "Plan" gave expression to the conviction of the Committee of Eleven that the remedy for existing difficulties lay in fixing responsibilities and in defining duties more definitely. The amended Plan, therefore, among other changes, reduced the two boards to one Board of Trustees; gave the trustees power, after a "full hearing and investigation," to remove president or professors without the approval of the Assembly, which had previously been required; and defined and enlarged the powers of the president of the seminary.[64]

A minority report signed by one member of the committee opposed the changes recommended, the chief ground of objection being that the Assembly, before voting on the reorganization, should be informed who were to comprise the new board.[65]

The General Assembly of 1928, after some discussion of the Princeton situation, substituted for both the majority and the minority reports of the committee a resolution offered by Dr. Mark A. Matthews, "that the further consideration of said Reports be postponed for one year, and that the Board of Directors of Princeton Seminary be and hereby is instructed to proceed immediately to compose the differences at the Seminary and to make a full report on these instructions to the next General Assembly." [66] The Assembly ordered the majority and minority reports placed on the docket of the next Assembly, continued the committee for another year, and requested a year's truce in discussion of seminary affairs in the Church at large.[67]

Pursuant to these instructions of the Assembly that the Board of Directors "compose the differences at the Seminary," the board created a "Group of Six" which sought to find a pacifying formula which all members of the faculty could sign, and which labored in other ways also.[68] But it was not found possible to "compose the differences," as was abundantly apparent from the fact that the Assembly of 1929 received six separate reports on the seminary. The majority and minority reports of the Committee of Eleven were carried over from the preceding year, and in addition there were majority and minority reports from both boards of the seminary.[69] Dr. Machen, who was a commissioner to this Assembly, entered into the debate, arguing that the proposed reorganization would remove Princeton from its historic evangelical foundations,[70] but, according to one account, "many listened to this contention with wondering incredulity." [71]

This Assembly of 1929 finally settled the Princeton issue by adopting the majority report of the Committee of Eleven, which provided for one board of control under an amended Charter and Plan.[72] The vote was not officially counted, but the action was taken by a decisive majority.[73] Hopes for an era of renewed good will were quickened when Dr. Macartney at the close of the vote, stepping forward, said to the moderator: "In behalf of the losing side I want to offer you thanks and gratitude for the eminent way in which you have presided over a most difficult Assembly." [74] "This gracious act was greeted with the greatest applause accorded any event in the Assembly." [75]

It should be noted that no provision of the Charter or Plan expressly relating to the seminary's theological position was weakened or even modified. The Assembly's election of the new board on the unanimous nomination of the Committee of Eleven[76] drew the comment, "The fairness and conservatism of this selection gave general gratification." [77] The Assembly directed that the new board, with Dr. Lewis S. Mudge as convener, should function provisionally as a Board of Directors until the charter amendments should be secured.[78] The Assembly formally declared the seminary's new Plan to be in force.[79]

With underlying issues definitively settled, the seminary rapidly returned to normalcy under the leadership of the new board. The board invited all members of the faculty, including the professors-elect,[80] to continue in the service of the seminary, and all but four did so. A number of existing vacancies in the faculty were filled before the next Assembly convened.[81] The Board of Trustees, serving as provisional Board of Directors, "unanimously" adopted the following declaration of policy: "In the one hundred and seventeen years of its history, Princeton Seminary has stood with firm steadfastness for the propagation at home and abroad, and for the scholarly defense of evangelical Christianity as formulated in the Standards of the Presbyterian Church. In taking up the duties assigned to it by the General Assembly, the temporary Board of Directors feels that it has a sacred mandate from the Assembly to continue unchanged the historic policy of the Seminary and to do nothing whatever to alter the distinctive traditional position which the Seminary has maintained throughout its entire history."[82] Early in the new year the board secured its charter amendments, which were duly approved by the Assembly.[83]

A statement by Dr. William Courtland Robinson, a former director and opponent of reorganization of Princeton Seminary,[84] made in May 1930, some two months after he succeeded Dr. Craig as editor of the *Presbyterian,* illustrates the widespread confidence which the new management of the seminary inspired: "That which many predicted and which some of us feared has not taken place. . . . We cannot find a single happening during this year now closing to which a conservative could take serious exception."[85]

Seen in the perspective of a quarter of a century the issue should perhaps be defined somewhat differently from the way it was by those who were in the midst of the struggle. The historic character of the differences between the "majority" and "minority" of the faculty did not come fully to view at the time. Actually each group represented a part and only a part of the seminary's theological heritage. The unfolding of events had finally made mutually incompatible two tendencies which had existed side by side in the Princeton Theology from the beginning—a broad and warm evangelicalism on the one hand and a highly rational orthodoxy and extreme literalism on the other. It was best for both parts of the seminary's tradition that open bifurcation came at last, and that each could develop more fully and consistently its inherent implications unhampered by a really alien tendency.

With Princeton Seminary's affairs removed from the area of ecclesiastical discussion by the Assembly of 1929 many felt that the controversies which had figured so prominently in the life of the Presbyterian Church throughout the 1920's were past, and that an era of theological peace and general good will was at hand.[86] But, as the event proved, such expectations were premature and were not fully to be realized in the Church for another seven years.

15.

protesters withdraw

The defeat of the extreme conservatives in the struggle over Princeton Seminary in 1929 did not mean that their program in the Presbyterian Church came to an end. In spite of injured prestige and diminishing numbers, some of them at once set up headquarters in Philadelphia, where there were created in rapid succession three independent organizations—Westminster Seminary, the Independent Board for Presbyterian Foreign Missions, and the Presbyterian Church of America.

The movement to drive all theological liberalism out of the Presbyterian Church and to enforce upon the entire ministry the strictest standards of orthodoxy, a movement which had dominated church councils in the 1880's and 1890's and which had for a brief period in the early 1920's made a serious bid to perpetuate its control, became, with the creation of Westminster Seminary in 1929, hardly more than a localized agitation in the Philadelphia area. This last phase of the struggle was characterized by the earnestness of despair.

It was quite understandable that the extreme conservatives who seceded from Princeton Seminary in 1929 chose Philadelphia as the site for their new seminary. Philadelphia Presbytery was historically a principal center of Presbyterian conservatism, and the conservative tone of much of Philadelphia's nondenominational life rendered that city highly congenial.[1]

A few weeks after the General Assembly had taken definitive action regarding Princeton Seminary, interested persons met to plan for a new seminary, and on September 25, 1929, in the Witherspoon Building, Philadelphia, Westminster Seminary was formally opened, with a faculty of eight and a student body of fifty-two.[2] During the early years of the seminary some prominent Presbyterians gave public evidence of their support; students came from a number of the leading Presbyterian churches with the encouragement of their pastors; and within a very few years Westminster graduates had become active members of a number of presbyteries. From the beginning Westminster professors and students spoke frequently at Presbyterian church services and other Presbyterian gatherings. Beginning in January 1935, the institution further extended its work by launching the "Westminster Seminary Hour," a series of weekly radio messages by Dr. Machen,[3] with a second series started the next fall.[4]

That Westminster Seminary during its first years exerted extensive influence among Presbyterians in the Philadelphia area was revealed in hearings before a Commission of Nine later appointed by the General Assembly of 1935 to visit the Philadelphia and Chester Presbyteries. Some who testified before the commission dated the period of serious controversy in and around Philadelphia from the founding of Westminster Seminary,[5] though others dated it half a dozen years earlier.[6] "There has been a definite and deliberate effort," one witness testified, "to seek to capture the Presbytery of Philadelphia . . . to use the Presbytery of Philadelphia as a platform from which to launch an attack upon the life of the Church itself." [7] By the autumn of 1935[8] the seminary had become a factor to be reckoned with in important regions of the Presbyterian Church.

A second institution founded in the Philadelphia area by Presbyterian extreme conservatives was "The Independent Board for Presbyterian Foreign Missions." Its organization in 1933 had been preceded by some discussion of missionary matters.

It will be recalled that Dr. W. H. Griffith Thomas' criticism of Presbyterian foreign missionary work in 1921[9] was followed by several years of critical consideration of the subject, which gradually subsided. The subject of foreign missions was, however, suddenly thrust into the limelight by the appearance of *Re-Thinking Missions*.

Rethinking Missions

In 1930 lay members of seven American Protestant denominations, of which the Presbyterian Church in the U.S.A. was one, acting independently of the denominational boards, engaged the Institute of Social and Religious Research to survey foreign missionary activity in India, Burma, China, and Japan. The data thus collected were submitted to a Commission of Appraisal of which Dr. William E. Hocking, professor of philosophy at Harvard University, was chairman, which on November 18, 1932, published its report under the title *Re-Thinking Missions: a Layman's Inquiry after One Hundred Years*. The theological presuppositions underlying *Re-Thinking Missions* were not those of traditional Christian orthodoxy. The Christian message was regarded as based on universal rational principles rather than on historical facts, with a very uncertain place left for the historical Jesus. There ran throughout, the implication that Christian truth is relative rather than absolute and that Christianity should coöperate with, rather than try to supplant, the non-Christian religions.[10]

The report at once had repercussions in the Presbyterian Church. Two days before the full text of the report was published, the Church's General Council rejected its theology, as did the Presbyterian Board of Foreign Missions five days later. Individual missionary leaders in the Church also soon expressed themselves adversely.[11] Dr. Speer, senior secretary of the Presbyterian board, was vigorous in his repudiation of the theology of the report.[12]

Controversy concerning Presbyterian foreign missions was stimulated during these days not only by the Laymen's Inquiry report, but also by articles from the pen of Mrs. Pearl S. Buck, distinguished author of *The Good Earth,* and a missionary under the Presbyterian board.[13]

Dr. Machen used the appearance of *Re-Thinking Missions* and of Mrs. Buck's articles as the occasion for renewed attack on the Presbyterian Board of Foreign Missions. He proposed that his Presbytery of New Brunswick send to the General Assembly an overture critical of the orthodoxy of the Presbyterian board, orthodoxy being defined substantially in terms of the much-discussed five-point doctrinal deliverance of 1910. After hearing an extended debate between Dr. Speer, whom the presbytery had invited to address it, and Dr. Machen, presbytery, by a majority estimated at two or three to one, rejected the proposed overture, and then adopted an overture to the Assembly, affirming its confidence in the board. All told, the Assembly of 1933 received overtures on foreign missions from seven presbyteries, three of them critical in tone, and four predominantly commendatory.[14]

In the General Assembly of 1933 it augured ill for the program of the extreme conservatives that their candidate for the moderatorship was defeated by a vote of 691 to 120. This same Assembly, by a vote variously estimated at three and a half or five to one, adopted a report heartily endorsing the Board of Foreign Missions and its work and proposing the reëlection of board members whose terms were expiring.[15]

Extreme conservatives were prepared for this action, and within a few moments of the adoption of the report one of them announced that "a new Board will be organized by Bible-believing Christians to promote truly Biblical and truly Presbyterian mission work." The organization of "The Independent Board for Presbyterian Foreign Missions" was tentatively effected in June and completed in October 1933. Dr. Machen was elected president of it, but some of the most prominent names connected with the Westminster Seminary movement were conspicuous by their absence, revealing the fact that extreme conservatives differed greatly as to the wisdom of organizing the board. Some, looking back a little later, thought that the creation of the board had seriously divided their forces and had weakened the influence of Westminster Seminary in Presbyterian circles.[16] Meanwhile the Presbyterian denominational board continued to emphasize its loyalty to the Church's standards, and sentiment in the Church rallied strongly behind it.[17]

There were advance signs that the General Assembly of 1934 might take vigorous action against the new Independent Board for Presbyterian Foreign Missions.[18] Before this Assembly convened the General Council sent to all commissioners-elect a forty-four-page document entitled "Studies of the Constitution of the Presbyterian Church in the U.S.A." drawn up by Dr. William B. Pugh. Citing numerous historical precedents, the paper asserted the broadest possible construction of General Assembly powers of control over its denominational agencies, and denied the right of Presbyterian ministers or members to form any sort of combination to resist or subvert this authority. A comparison of this document with the reports of the Special Commission of 1925 as adopted by the Assemblies of 1926 and 1927 graphically illustrates the way in which the Church was moving simultaneously toward administrative centralization and theological decentralization.[19]

In the General Assembly of 1934 it was evident that the strength of the extreme conservatives had suffered a further serious decline since the organization of the Independent Board, for this year their candidate for the moderatorship received only 87 votes out of a total of 905.[20] On recommendation of its General Council this Assembly, by an overwhelming vote, directed that the Independent Board desist from further functioning within the Presbyterian Church; that all Presbyterian ministers and laymen officially connected with that board terminate their relationship with it at once; and that all presbyteries having within their jurisdiction any who within ninety days failed to withdraw from the board should institute disciplinary action against such persons. A few of the Church's most influential nonfundamentalists were quietly out of sympathy with this action of the Assembly,[21] while friends of the Independent Board as well as some others vigorously denounced it, but presently it became evident that the great bulk of church opinion supported it.

An early result of this action of the Assembly was the ecclesiastical prosecution of Dr. Machen, the president and moving spirit of the Independent Board, by the Presbytery of New Brunswick in which his membership remained after the failure of his effort to transfer to Philadelphia Presbytery.[22] Receiving an open trial in response to his demands, the defendant regaled the newspaper public with criticisms of his judges and of the judicial proceedings. During February and March, 1935, the presbytery's judicial commission, acting as a court, conducted a number of hearings of the case, and on March 29 judgment was rendered in language reminiscent of the suspension of Dr. Briggs: "The Judicial Commission . . . does hereby judge and determine that the said Defendant, J. Gresham Machen, shall be suspended from the office of a minister in the

Presbyterian Church in the United States of America, until such time as he shall give satisfactory evidence of repentance." In a supplementary statement the commission recommended to the presbytery that the execution of the judgment be suspended until the case should finally be determined in the appellate courts of the Church.[23] Meanwhile critics of the denominational board continued active, as did its far more numerous supporters.[24]

By the time the General Assembly of 1935 convened none of the Independent Board cases had been completed, and most of them had not yet been initiated. There were some who hoped that this Assembly might pass on the constitutionality of the preceding Assembly's deliverance against the Independent Board, or even rescind it; but instead the Assembly reaffirmed it, voiced "hearty endorsement" of the denominational board and its staff, and assured Dr. Speer personally of "the full confidence of the Church and its heartfelt love."[25]

This Assembly of 1935 also took strong initiative to bring peace to remaining centers of controversy in the Church. In response to two memorials from ministers and elders of Philadelphia and Chester Presbyteries, the Assembly appointed a Special Commission of Nine, of which Dr. Henry Seymour Brown was chairman, "for the purpose of visiting, in a friendly and co-operative way, the said Presbyteries, in an endeavor to remedy such unfavorable or unconstitutional conditions as the Commission may find evident." [26]

Hearings which the Assembly's commission held in Philadelphia October 1 to 3 and November 19 to 21, 1935, at which more than a hundred individuals testified,[27] provided some interesting comments on the situation. One of the most mature presbyters traced the current controversy in the Presbyterian Church to the influence of the late Professor Benjamin B. Warfield of Princeton Seminary: "His pupils in the early years of this century are now carrying on his principles. . . . No modification of the Confession of Faith, and no union with any one Presbyterian denomination unless they would accept our particular interpretation of the Confession. . . . I would say that that position requires that the results of Biblical study and of discussion of one hundred years ago ought to be regulative of our attitude today." [28] Others, commenting further on theological aspects of the situation, noted that many of the extreme conservatives were premillennialists.[29]

It was evident that in the Philadelphia area, as previously elsewhere, the point at issue was not so much the personal orthodoxy of the disputants as it was whether or not liberalism should be tolerated within the Presbyterian Church.[30] The qualified way in which students from Westminster Seminary promised to support the denominational program was a frequent cause of controversy.[31] It was stated that the extreme conservative party which at the time controlled Philadelphia Presbytery was composed of only a minority of the pastors together with an overwhelming majority of the ministers without charge, including all the members of presbytery who were connected with Westminster Seminary, who supplied much of the leadership of the group.[32] Personal letters and the public press were extensively used to win laymen to the extreme conservative cause, and many pastors felt the indirect pressure thus put upon them.[33] To protect and further their interests, both parties in the Presbyteries of Philadelphia and Chester made use of party caucuses.[34] Of course personal relations in both presbyteries were often strained, and the controversy affected adversely local congregations and the standing of the Presbyterian Church in the community.[35]

On the basis of its findings, the Assembly's commission drafted a constructive twelve-point program, which the two presbyteries adopted.[36] The visit of the commission constituted an important contribution toward the restoration of peace in the area.

The most important factor, however, in restoring peace to the Presbyterian Church at this juncture was the settlement of ecclesiastical litigation. The action of the Assembly of 1935 in reaffirming the previous year's deliverance against the Independent Board and in appointing the Commission of Nine stimulated various hesitating presbyteries to enter upon judicial proceedings. The month after the Assembly, Philadelphia Presbytery voted to start judicial process against four members and an officer of the Independent Board, and the Synod of Pennsylvania, to which the cases were referred, acting through its Permanent Judicial Commission, found all five ministers guilty of the ecclesiastical offenses charged and sentenced them to suspension from the ministry.[37] Other presbyteries took similar action.

But the Presbytery of New York, on the other hand, held consistently to its long-standing spirit of tolerance and to its traditional New School disinclination to centralized authority, and respectfully declined to order prosecution of a church member who was connected with the Independent Board. The New York Presbytery declared: "Among our people there is widespread feeling against judicial processes." [38] Both before and after the meeting of the Assembly of 1935, the Independent Board suffered some loss through resignations.

In view of the close, even though informal, relations which existed between the Independent Board for Presbyterian Foreign Missions and Westminster Seminary, the storm which was gathering around the board inevitably descended upon the seminary also. Many of the original trustees of Westminster Seminary never approved of the Independent Board.[39] They regarded the seminary as a legitimate means of training up conservative ministers for the Presbyterian Church under independent and nondenominational auspices, but they looked upon the new board as divisive and as destined only to injure the seminary's influence.[40] As the board issue came to the fore, presbyteries became increasingly hostile toward the seminary and its graduates. Many early friends of the seminary were opposed also to the Constitutional Covenant Union, an organization supported by some of the seminary's leaders which was obviously preparing the way for a movement of withdrawal from the Presbyterian Church.[41]

Matters within the seminary came to a crisis when on October 22, 1935, the majority of the faculty, led by Dr. Machen, threatened to resign unless the trustees would formally endorse the aggressive type of ecclesiastical policy exemplified by the Independent Board and the Constitutional Covenant Union.[42] The majority of the trustees, who were unfavorably disposed toward these policies, faced the alternative of delivering the seminary to the faculty or of closing it. The result was that on January 7, 1936, one member of the faculty and thirteen members of the Board of Trustees, including some of its ablest and best-known leaders, resigned,[43] leaving the institution to identify itself more completely with the Independent Board and with the Constitutional Covenant Union under the leadership of the faculty majority.

To the General Assembly of 1936 four judicial cases involving members of the Independent Board came on appeal. In every one of these cases the Assembly confirmed the censures imposed by the lower judicatories.[44]

Within nine days of these judicial decisions, Dr. Machen and some of his followers organized an independent ecclesiastical body under the name of "The Presbyterian Church of America," a move which had been facilitated by the creation of the Presbyterian Constitutional Covenant Union the year before.[45] On June 11, 1936, the Constitutional Covenant Union, meeting in Philadelphia, formally declared itself dissolved. Then its former delegates and sympathetic visitors, to the number of thirty-four ministers, seventeen elders, and seventy-nine laymen, organized the Presbyterian Church of America. The ministers and elders constituted themselves a General Assembly and elected Dr. Machen moderator. By November the new denomination had 106 ministers on its roll.[46]

During the spring of 1937 differences over premillennialism, Christian liberty, and independency in church government led to a division within the new Church, some ministers and elders withdrawing from the Presbyterian Church of America to form a second separate denomination under the name of "The Bible Presbyterian Synod." The Presbyterian Church of America, which early in 1939 changed its name to "The Orthodox Presbyterian Church," experienced many difficulties.[47]

Though the withdrawal movement from the Presbyterian Church was inconsiderable numerically, it did raise some legal questions about property rights. The General Assembly of 1936, anticipating such problems, appointed a Special Committee on Legal Procedure which later reported that in a number of cases prompt action had made litigation unnecessary. Where litigation proved unavoidable, the Church was overwhelmingly successful in its contention that, in a "connectional" denomination like the Presbyterian with an integrated form of church government, local property rights, in the last analysis, are vested not in the local congregation, but in the denomination as a whole, and cannot be alienated from denominational control by congregational action.[48]

The termination of the judicial cases in 1936 marked the virtual cessation to date of theological controversy within the Church's judicatories. In spite of important internal diversities, the Church since 1936 has enjoyed the longest period of theological peace since the reunion of 1869.

conclusion

When Old School and New School Presbyterians reunited in 1869 on the basis of their common Westminster Standards "pure and simple," moderation triumphed over both extremes in the Church just as it had in the Old Side-New Side reunion of 1758.

The desire of the two theological traditions to maintain a moderate theology for the reunited Church was symbolized by their coöperation in conducting the *Presbyterian Review*. But new theological issues precipitated a half-century struggle to decide whether a moderate theological liberalism of the type proscribed by the "Portland Deliverance" of 1892 and by the "Five Points" of 1910 should be fully tolerated in the Church. By 1927 the more moderate, mediating policies which had always finally triumphed in the Church's crises, and which are to be regarded as manifesting the Church's truest theological character, once again prevailed. Thereafter those who still insisted on strict construction and expulsion of moderate liberalism were rapidly thrown on the defensive, and after 1936 ceased to exist as an institutionalized party within the Church.

The 1930's constituted a major turning point in the theological history of the Presbyterian Church. Just as the Church was opening its doors to a full recognition of moderate liberalism, new theological winds were blowing from the European Continent. On the basis of a quite different attitude toward metaphysics, "neo-orthodoxy" challenged theology to a new depth and realism, and theological interest was quickened in both Europe and America. A leading American theologian, not a Presbyterian, has rightly seen in the founding of *Theology Today* under the leadership of Dr. John A. Mackay and in the expansion of the Westminster Press signs of recently renewed theological vigor among Presbyterians.[1] And yet, memories and scars of the old fundamentalist-modernist controversy still largely inhibit among Presbyterians the frank and realistic discussion of theological questions which the times and the present opportunity call for. "The less theology the better" seems to be the lurking implication—at least so far as the Church's statistical growth is concerned.

But the contemporary social and cultural situation calls for fresh study of the inner meaning and practical application of Christian truth. Now that the Church, officially and institutionally at least, has left behind the inadequate and sterile formulations of the fundamentalist-modernist controversy, the way is open and the spirit of the age beckons to a more profound and constructive exploration of the Church's great evangelical heritage and the meaning of this for the present hour.

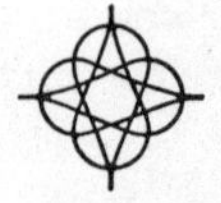

notes

abbreviations used in the notes

B.T.	The Dr. Charles A. Briggs Transcript, copied in longhand from his manuscripts by his daughter, Miss Grace Briggs. It is deposited in the Union Theological Seminary Library, New York. Comparison with originals in H.P. and W.P. and other copies in H.P. and W.P. attests the high trustworthiness of B.T.
G.A. *Mins.*	*Minutes* of the General Assembly of the Presbyterian Church in the U.S.A., designated by the year.
H.P.	The papers of the Hodge family, in Princeton University Library.
M.P.	The Dr. Clarence E. Macartney Papers, in the possession of Dr. Macartney, Beaver Falls, Pennsylvania.
Ml.P.	The Rev. John Miller Papers, in Princeton University Library.
Mn. P.	The President John Maclean Papers, in Princeton University Library.
S.P.	The Dr. Robert E. Speer Papers, in the possession of Mrs. Speer, Lakeville, Connecticut.
Sm.P.	The Dr. Joseph T. Smith Papers, in Presbyterian Historical Society, Philadelphia.
V.P.	The Dr. Henry J. Van Dyke, Sr., Papers, in Princeton University Library.
v.P.	The Dr. Henry van Dyke Papers, in Princeton University Library.
v.P.W.	The Dr. Henry van Dyke Papers *in re* the General Assembly's Committee on the Book of Common Worship, in Presbyterian Historical Society, Philadelphia.
W.P.	The Dr. Benjamin B. Warfield Papers, in the possession of the Rev. John E. Meeter, Christian Reformed minister, Englewood, New Jersey.

chapter 1—the wedding day

1 G. L. Prentiss to his wife, May 18, 19, 1870, in G. L. Prentiss, *The Bright Side of Life*, II (n.p., 1901), 238.
2 C. A. Briggs, *American Presbyterianism* (N. Y., 1885), p. 173, estimates that 15 of the Synod's 25 ministers were from Scotland or Ireland, and 10 from New England or Wales.
3 Cf. G.A. *Mins.*, 1926, p. 76.
4 *Records of the Presbyterian Church in the U.S.A.* (Phila., 1904), p. 94 (hereafter cited as *Records*).
5 Cf. G. Tennent, *The Danger of an Unconverted Ministry* (Phila., 1740).
6 *Records*, pp. 157-60.
7 *Ibid.*, pp. 285-88.
8 *The Constitution of the Presbyterian Church in the United States of America . . . Ratified . . . 1788* (Phila., 1789), p. 158.

4-18

9 L. J. Trinterud, *The Forming of an American Tradition* (Phila., 1949), pp. 261-64.

10 Text of the Plan of Union is in R. E. Thompson, *A History of the Presbyterian Churches in the U.S.* (N. Y., 1895), pp. 353-55.

11 I. W. Riley, *American Philosophy; The Early Schools* (N. Y., 1907), pp. 478-79; V. L. Parrington, *Main Currents in American Thought,* II (N. Y., 1927), pp. 61-82; C. Eaton, *Freedom of Thought in the Old South* (Durham, N. C., 1940), pp. vii-ix, 280-332.

12 G. H. Barnes, *The Antislavery Impulse 1830-1844* (N. Y., 1933), pp. 94-95; W. W. Sweet, *Religion on the American Frontier,* II, *The Presbyterians* (N. Y., 1936), 111-25.

13 Cf. W. Brown to H. J. Van Dyke, Jan. 15, 1868, V.P.; *Presbyterian,* Jan. 11, 1868, p. 4; May 8, 1869, p. 5; M. W. Jacobus, "The Union Question in Scotland," in *American Presbyterian Review,* I (1869), 58-76.

14 W. T. Hutchinson, *Cyrus Hall McCormick,* II (N. Y., 1935), 204-7; *The Biblical Repertory and Princeton Review,* XXXVII (1865), 271-313, 488-91, 652-56; H. A. Boardman to H. J. Van Dyke, April 21 [year not given], V.P.

15 J. H. Moore to C. Hodge, July 8, 1868, H.P.; cf. also A. A. Hodge to C. Hodge, June 15, 1869, H.P.; Hutchinson, *op. cit.*, pp. 206, 210, 229.

16 G.A. *Mins.*, 1865, pp. 553-54, 562-64; 1866, pp. 51-53, 60-62.

17 E. Erskine to C. H. McCormick, March 16, 1866, in Hutchinson, *op. cit.*, p. 210.

18 W. Brown to H. J. Van Dyke, April 11, 1865, V.P.

19 J. R. Wilson to H. J. Van Dyke, June 10, 1873, V.P.

20 C. Hodge, *The Reunion of the Old and New-School Presbyterian Churches* (N. Y., 1867), pp. 6, 18, 21; H. B. Smith, *The Reunion of the Presbyterian Churches . . .* (N. Y., 1867), pp. 13, 37, 42.

21 Cf. p. 1, above.

chapter 2 — shadows of coming events

1 Cf., e.g., R. H. Gabriel, *The Course of American Democratic Thought* (N. Y., 1940), pp. 37-38; R. B. Perry, *Puritanism and Democracy* (N. Y., 1944), pp. 624-26.

2 Cf. B. J. Loewenberg, "Darwinism Comes to America, 1859-1900," in *Mississippi Valley Historical Review,* XXVIII (1941-42), 341-58; A. M. Schlesinger, "A Critical Period in American Religion, 1875-1900," in Mass. Historical Society, *Proceedings,* Vol. 64, pp. 524-28.

3 C. Hodge, *What Is Darwinism?* (N. Y., 1874); J. McCosh, *The Development Hypothesis; Is It Sufficient?* (N. Y., 1876); *idem, The Religious Aspects of Evoluton* (N. Y., 1888); J. Bascom, in *American Presbyterian Review,* III (1871), 349-79; *Interior,* May 29, p. 6, Sept. 25, p. 4, Dec. 4, p. 4, 1873; *Presbyterian,* May 28, 1870, p. 5; Sept. 26, 1874, p. 8; Nov. 22, 1884, p. 10; Jan. 31, 1885, p. 3; Sept. 8, 1897, p. 28.

4 M. Curti, *The Growth of American Thought* (N. Y., 1943), pp. 242-43, 582-83.

5 C. A. Briggs to H. B. Smith, Jan. 24, 1867, and to his wife, June 22, 1874, B.T. 320, 698.

6 *Andover Review,* I-XIX (Jan. 1884-Dec. 1893); D. D. Williams, *The Andover Liberals, a Study in American Theology* (N. Y., 1941); W. Walker, "Changes in Theology Among American Congregationalists," in *American Journal of Theology,* X (1906), 204-18; *idem,* "Recent Tendencies in the Congregational Churches," in *American Journal of Theology,* XXIV (1920), 1-18.

4-18

7 Cf. H. A. Boardman to H. J. Van Dyke, n.d., V.P., J. C. Backus to J. Maclean, Mn.P.; A. A. Hodge to C. Hodge, June 15, 1869, and F. McFarland to C. Hodge, July 3, 1869, H.P.

8 *Interior*, March 13, p. 4, June 26, p. 4, July 3, p. 4, 1873; W. T. Hutchinson, *Cyrus Hall McCormick*, II (N. Y., 1935), 253.

9 F. L. Patton to H. J. Van Dyke, June 27, 1873, V.P.

10 *Interior*, Aug. 14, p. 4, Sept. 4, pp. 1, 4, Sept. 18, p. 1, Oct. 9, p. 1, Oct. 16, p. 4, 1873; Feb. 12, p. 4, Feb. 26, p. 4, March 5, p. 8, 1874.

11 A Committee of the Presbytery, ed., *The Trial of the Rev. David Swing before the Presbytery of Chicago* (Chicago, 1874), pp. 4, 8-14, 18.

12 *Ibid.*, p. 8.

13 *Ibid.*, pp. 278, 283-86.

14 A. C. Zenos, *Historical Sketch of Presbyterianism in the Chicago Area* (mimeographed, 1933. Copy in McCormick Seminary Library).

15 L. J. Halsey, *A History of the McCormick Theological Seminary* (Chicago, 1893), pp. 15-19, 83; J. G. K. McClure, *The Story of the Life and Work of the Presbyterian Seminary Chicago* (Chicago, 1929), pp. 1-34.

16 Hutchinson, *op. cit.*, pp. 18-21, 243-51.

17 H. A. Boardman to A. A. Hodge, July 23, 1874, H.P.; *Interior*, May 21, 1874, p. 4; *N. Y. Evangelist*, June 4, 1874, p. 1; April 19, 1888, p. 1.

18 F. L. Patton to H. J. Van Dyke, April 16, 1878, V.P.; *N. Y. Evangelist*, June 27, 1878, p. 1.

19 E. D. Morris, "Lane Memoranda, 1879-1886" (MS, in Lane Papers, McCormick Seminary Library); B.T. 1415; E. D. Morris, *Thirty Years in Lane and Other Lane Papers* (n.p., n.d.), pp. ix, 6-7, 12-13, 25-26, 189; H. P. Smith, *The Heretic's Defense* (N. Y., 1926), pp. 42-43.

20 *Biblical Repertory and Princeton Review*, XXXVII (1865), 272.

21 Committee Appointed by the Ministerial Association and also by the Presbytery, *Presbyterianism in Cincinnati: Its History, Position and Duty* (n.p., [1871]), pp. 3, 12.

22 *The Process, Testimony . . . Vote and Final Minute in the Judicial Trial of Rev. W. C. McCune* (Cincinnati, 1877), p. 125 (cited hereafter as *The Process*).

23 Z. M. H. [Zephaniah H. Humphrey of Cincinnati], "That 'Union Church' at Cincinnati, Ohio," in *Presbyterian*, Feb. 26, 1876, p. 7 (sympathetic to McCune); *The Process*, pp. 125-36; *Dr. Skinner's Answer to Dr. Morris* (n.p., [1876]), p. 2; T. H. Skinner, *Defense of Presbyterian Doctrine and Order* (Cincinnati, 1876), p. 14.

24 W. C. McCune, "Some Misapprehension," in *Presbyterian*, Feb. 12, 1876, p. 9; *The Process*, pp. 111, 128; T. H. Skinner, *Defense*, pp. 12, 25, 34; *Dr. Skinner's Answer to Dr. Morris*, p. 4.

25 Cf. T. H. Skinner, Jr., to John Maclean, July 2, 1867, Mn.P.

26 Text in *Reply of the Rev. Thomas H. Skinner to the Rev. J. G. Monfort, D.D.* (Cincinnati, 1876), pp. 8-10; E. D. Morris "To the Editor," *Cincinnati Gazette*, Jan. 21, 1876.

27 Skinner, *Defense*, pp. 3-4; *The Process*, pp. 51, 122-27, 165, 169, 172-79; *Dr. Skinner's Answer to Dr. Morris*, pp. 7-9; *The Complaint of the Rev. Thomas H. Skinner* (Cincinnati, 1876), pp. 4-5; G.A. *Mins.*, 1877, p. 576.

28 G.A. *Mins.*, 1877, p. 576.

29 Morris to Van Dyke, Sept. 14 [1877]; May 4 [1878]; Skinner to Van Dyke, Nov. 2, 1877; May 9, 1878; L. R. Smith to Van Dyke, May 9, 1878, V.P.

30 G.A. *Mins.*, 1878, p. 103.

31 A. Gosman to A. A. Hodge, April 9, 1877, H.P.

32 C. A. Briggs, "The Future of Presbyterianism in the United States," in *North American Review*, CCCCXL (July 1893), p. 5; cf. also L. J. Evans, *Preaching Christ: Sermons* (N. Y., 1893), p. 53.

20-29

chapter 3 — biblical criticism

1 "Formula Consensus Helvetica," in H. A. Niemeyer, ed., *Collectio Confessionum in Ecclesiis Reformatis Publicatarum* (Leipsic, 1840), p. 731.
2 F. Turretino, *Institutio Theologiae Elencticae,* I (Geneva, 1688), 7-10, 26-39, 49-53, 61-62, 70-71.
3 C. Hodge, in *Biblical Repertory and Princeton Review,* XXII (1850), 660-71; XXIX (1857), 692; *Systematic Theology,* III (N. Y., 1872), 84-85; A. A. Hodge, . . . *Inauguration of* . . . (Phila., 1877), p. 29; an engaging study is J. O. Nelson, "The Rise of the Princeton Theology" (MS, Ph.D. thesis, Yale University, 1935); Perry Miller, *The New England Mind; The Seventeenth Century* (N. Y., 1939), pp. 240-41; P. Miller, *Jonathan Edwards* (1949), pp. 177-78.
4 *The Plan of a Theological Seminary Adopted by the General Assembly . . . A.D. 1811* (Phila., 1811), p. 13.
5 Cf., e.g., J. W. Alexander, *The Life of Archibald Alexander* (N. Y., 1854), pp. 66-72; C. Hodge, *Princeton Theological Seminary. A Discourse* . . . (Phila., 1874), p. 21; A. A. Hodge, *The Life of Charles Hodge D.D. LL.D.* (N. Y., 1880), pp. 20-34.
6 Samuel Miller, *A Brief Retrospect of the Eighteenth Century,* II (N. Y., 1805), 195-202; C. Hodge, *Systematic Theology,* I, 343; III, 46, 261.
7 C. Hodge, *Princeton Theological Seminary. A Discourse* . . . , pp. 18-20.
8 A. Alexander, *A Brief Outline of the Evidences of the Christian Religion* (Princeton, 1825), pp. 54, 127, 190-95.
9 *Inauguration of the Rev. Archibald Alexander* (N. Y., 1812), p. 92.
10 A. Alexander, *Evidences* (1825), pp. 10, 12, 18.
11 A. Alexander, *The Canon of the Old and New Testaments Ascertained* (Princeton, 1826), p. 133.
12 *Inauguration,* pp. 62-63; *Canon,* pp. 29-35.
13 *Canon,* pp. 136, 141.
14 A. Alexander, *Evidences of the Authenticity, Inspiration, and Canonical Authority of the Holy Scriptures* (Phila., 1836), p. 222.
15 *Ibid.,* p. 241; *Inauguration,* pp. 68-72.
16 *Evidences,* pp. 225-27.
17 *Ibid.,* p. 228.
18 C. A. Salmond, *Princetoniana. Charles & A. A. Hodge* . . . (Edinburgh, 1888), p. 51; cf. also H. B. S[mith] in *Presbyterian Quarterly and Princeton Review,* N.S., I (1872), 395.
19 C. Hodge, *Systematic Theology,* I, 39-51; III, 81, 83.
20 *Ibid.,* I, 152-53, 155-57; *Biblical Repertory and Princeton Review,* XXIX (1857), 660-65, 672-77.
21 *Systematic Theology,* I, 163.
22 *Ibid.,* p. 169; "Inspiration," p. 687.
23 *Systematic Theology,* I, 10-11.
24 *Ibid.,* p. 15.
25 J. C. Backus to A. A. Hodge, April 25, 1877, H.P.; F. L. Patton, *A Discourse in Memory of Archibald Alexander Hodge* (Phila., 1887); Salmond, *Princetoniana,* pp. 104-10; *Addresses . . . in Memory of Archibald Alexander Hodge D.D. LL.D. . . . 1901.*
26 A. A. Hodge, *Addresses at the Inauguration of* . . . (Phila., 1877), pp. 28-29; *Popular Lectures on Theological Themes* (Phila., 1877), p. 77; *A Commentary on The Confession of Faith* (Phila., 1869), p. 51.
27 *Commentary,* pp. 54-55.
28 A. A. Hodge, *Outlines of Theology* (rev. ed., N. Y., 1879), p. 66.
29 *Popular Lectures,* p. 81.

30 *Inauguration*, pp. 25-26, 34-38.
31 *Inauguration of the Rev. Francis L. Patton, D.D., LL.D. . . . Seminary at Princeton* (Phila., 1881), pp. 24-27.
32 F. L. Patton, *The Inspiration of the Scriptures* (Phila., 1869), pp. 25-35, 112; *Induction of Rev. Francis Patton . . . Presbyterian Seminary of the North-West* (1873), pp. 45-49; *Inauguration* (1881), p. 29.
33 *Induction* (1873), pp. 52-55, 60; *Inauguration* (1881), pp. 29-30.
34 *Proceedings . . . Semi-centennial . . . of . . . Charles Hodge . . . 1872* (N. Y., n.d.), p. 52; cf. also A. A. Hodge, *The Life of Charles Hodge* (N. Y., 1880), pp. 430-31; *Biblical Repertory and Princeton Review Index Volume* (Phila., 1871), p. 11; C. Hodge, *Princeton Theological Seminary a Discourse . . .* (Princeton, 1874), pp. 17-18, these as cited by K. S. Gapp, "The Princeton Review Series" (MS, n.p., n.d., in Princeton Seminary Library), p. 82.
35 C. A. Briggs, *The Higher Criticism of the Hexateuch* (N. Y., 1893), p. 509; H. B. Smith and R. D. Hitchcock, *The Life Writings and Character of Edward Robinson* (N. Y., 1863), p. 85; cf. also pp. 6-7, 84-86, 97-99.
36 Mrs. H. B. Smith, *Henry Boynton Smith. His Life and Work* (N. Y., 1881), p. 74.
37 *Ibid.*, p. 59.
38 L. F. Stearns, *Henry Boynton Smith* (Boston and N. Y., 1892), pp. 147, 354; J. DeWitt, in *Presbyterian and Reformed Review,* VI (1895), 314.
39 Cf. H. B. Smith, *Introduction to Christian Theology*, ed. by W. S. Karr (N. Y., 1882), p. 39.
40 H. B. Smith, Address (1864) in *Faith and Philosophy*, ed. by G. L. Prentiss (N. Y., 1877), p. 274.
41 H. B. Smith, *Introduction to Christian Theology*, p. 191.
42 *Ibid.*, p. 194.
43 *Ibid.*, p. 200.
44 *Ibid.*, p. 204.
45 *Ibid.*, pp. 191-204; H. B. Smith, *The Inspiration of the Holy Scriptures A Sermon . . . 1855* (Cincinnati, 1891), pp. 4, 9-11.
46 *Inspiration*, pp. 5-8, 19; *Introduction to . . . Theology*, p. 204.
47 L. F. Stearns, *op. cit.*, p. 198; cf. also M. R. Vincent, in *N. Y. Evangelist*, July 21, 1892, p. 1.
48 B.T. 361; cf. also B.T. 174, 3082.
49 B.T. 320, 357a, 361, 366, 411.
50 In *American Presbyterian Theological Review*, N.S., II (1870), 105-33, 293-306.
51 C. A. Briggs, *Address by . . . on the Occasion of His Inauguration . . .* (N. Y., 1876), p. 15.
52 B.T. 773, 831.
53 P. C. Simpson, *The Life of Principal Rainy*, I (London, 1909), 306-403; J. S. Black and G. Chrystal, *The Life of William Robertson Smith* (London, 1912), pp. 179-451.
54 Cf., e.g., letters from J. S. Candlish, A. B. Bruce, B.T. 1127, 1344.
55 G.A. *Mins.*, 1878-79, pp. 125-26, 600.
56 *Ibid.*, 1880, p. 63; *Presbyterian Review*, I (1880), 567-68; B.T. 1220, 1223, 1301.
57 McCosh to C. H. McCormick, Jan. 18, March 11, 1881, in W. T. Hutchinson, *Cyrus Hall McCormick*, II (N. Y., 1935), 268-69.

chapter 4 — a theological journal

1 B.T. 1296; C. A. Briggs, in *North American Review*, CCCCXL (July 1893), 5; A. A. Hodge, *The Life of Charles Hodge D.D. LL.D.* (N. Y., 1880), p. 250.

29-42

2 F. L. Mott, *A History of American Magazines* (3 vols., Cambridge, Mass., 1930-38), I, 131-39; III, 66.
3 B.T. 888, 902, 931, 936, 957, 967, 972, 1005, 1018, 1022, 2617, 2845, 3356; and C. A. Briggs "Notebook," in B.T., Vol. III, pp. 76, 81-82.
4 C. A. Aiken to Briggs, Oct. 13, 1879, B.T. 1010; cf. also B.T. 1017, 1018, 1122.
5 B.T. 1002, 1019, 1027, 1031, 1037, 1047, 1652.
6 *Presbyterian Review,* I (1880), 3-7.
7 B.T. 1110.
8 B.T. 1037; cf. also B.T. 1661.
9 Cf. Briggs to A. A. Hodge, Nov. 29, 30, Dec. 3, 1880, H.P.
10 B.T. 1403, 1407, 1435; Briggs to Hodge, Jan. 15, 20, July 17, 1881, H.P.
11 Dr. Briggs's later statements to this effect seem quite warranted: Briggs, *The Higher Criticism of the Hexateuch* (N. Y., 1893), p. 130; Briggs, *General Introduction to the Study of Holy Scripture* (N. Y., 1899), pp. 286-87.
12 Briggs to Hodge, Dec. 8, 1880, H.P.
13 Cf. A. A. Hodge, *Outlines of Theology* (N. Y., 1879), pp. 66, 75.
14 *Presbyterian Review,* II (1881), 238, 242, 245.
15 B.T. 1390.
16 Warfield to Hodge, Jan. 6, 1881, H.P.; Briggs to Hodge, Jan. 24, 1881, H.P.; presumptively, the division between authors is at p. 238.
17 A. A. Hodge and B. B. Warfield, "Inspiration," *Presbyterian Review,* II (1881), 297.
18 *Ibid.*, p. 238.
19 *Ibid.*, p. 245.
20 A. A. Hodge, *Outlines of Theology* (N. Y., 1879), pp. 66, 75.
21 *Presbyterian Review,* II (1881), 225, 238.
22 *Ibid.*, pp. 242, 245.
23 *Ibid.*, pp. 236, 244.
24 G. F. Moore, *Independent,* March 30, 1893, p. 2; T. M. Lindsay, *Expositor,* I (1895), 278-93; R. E. Thompson, *A History of the Presbyterian Churches in the U.S.* (N. Y., 1895), pp. 262-63; cf. E. Brunner, *Revelation and Inspiration* (Eng. tr., Phila., 1946), p. 274, note 5.
25 *Presbyterian Review,* II (1881), 550-79.
26 C. W. Hodge to A. A. Hodge, July 6, 1881, H.P.; cf. also W. H. Green to Hodge, July 8, 1881, H.P.
27 B.T. 1602.
28 B.T. 1461; cf. also B.T. 1460, 1584, 1594, 1669; H. P. Smith, *The Heretic's Defense* (N. Y., 1926), p. 63.
29 Briggs to Hodge, July 30, 1881; Dec. 6, 1881; [Oct. (?), 1882], H.P.
30 *N. Y. Evangelist,* Jan. 12, 1882, p. 1; B.T. 1712; cf. also B.T. 1703, 1706, 1710.
31 *Presbyterian Review,* III (1882), 108-56; cf. B.T. 1536; Briggs to Hodge, Dec. 9, 1881, H.P.
32 H. P. Smith to Briggs, March 24, 1881, B.T. 1461.
33 Sept. 7, 1881, B.T. 1594.
34 *Presbyterian Review,* III (1882), 357-88.
35 B.T. 1833.
36 G.A. *Mins.*, 1882, p. 92; cf. also p. 116; B.T. 1833, 1838, 1864, 1899.
37 *Presbyterian,* April 1, p. 3, April 29, p. 4, Aug. 12, p. 4, Sept. 2, p. 7, Sept. 16, p. 6, Sept. 30, pp. 4, 10, 1882; B.T. 1785, 1793, 1901, 1954, 1973.
38 B.T. 1833, 1891, 1935.
39 B.T. 1856; similarly E. F. Hatfield, formerly New School, in B.T. 1917.
40 *Presbyterian,* Sept. 30, 1882, p. 10; B.T. 1958, 1991, 2015.
41 *Presbyterian,* May 26, 1883, p. 10.
42 S. I. Curtis, *Presbyterian Review,* III (1882), 553-88; W. J. Beecher, *ibid.*, pp. 701-31; cf. B.T. 1899, 1935, 1951.
43 *Presbyterian Review,* IV (1883), 99-130.
44 B.T. 2087, 2104, 2121; B. B. Warfield, in *Interior,* Feb. 15, 1883, p. 2.

45 F. L. Patton, "The Dogmatic Aspect of Pentateuchal Criticism," in *Presbyterian Review*, IV (1883), 341.
46 *Ibid.*, pp. 343-51.
47 *Ibid.*, pp. 363, 371.
48 Cf. below, p. 134.
49 B.T. 2153; cf. B.T. 2130a, 2150.
50 G.A. *Mins.*, 1883, pp. 631-32; cf. 1884, pp. 47-48; B.T. 2136, 2155, 2170.
51 *Presbyterian*, June 9, 1883, p. 11; cf. B.T. 2129, 2182, 3212.
52 Cf. B.T. 3052.
53 Pp. ix, 335-38.
54 Pp. 224-31.
55 Bruce to Briggs, B.T. 2345a, 2397.
56 B.T. 3121.
57 Pp. 337-38, 348, 409.
58 *Ibid.*, p. 412.
59 B.T. 2721, 3268b, 3274.
60 B.T. 3542, 3546.
61 Warfield to A. A. Hodge, Jan. 15, 1881, H.P.
62 Warfield to A. A. Hodge, *ibid.;* S. H. Kellogg to A. A. Hodge, Jan. 12, 1881, H.P.
63 Briggs to Warfield, Oct. 5, 1888; March 20, 1889, W.P.; B.T. 3559.
64 "Minutes of the Faculty," Princeton Theological Seminary (MS, in Princeton Seminary Library), June 4, p. 367, Oct. 8, p. 369, Oct. 11, p. 369, 1889; a full file of the Warfield-Briggs correspondence during their coeditorship is preserved in W.P.
65 B.T. 3730, 3740, 3745, 3752.

chapter 5 — revision attempted

1 Hodge to J. Johns, Nov. 13, 1874, H.P.; A. A. Hodge, *Life of Charles Hodge* (N. Y., 1880), p. 66; C. Hodge, *Systematic Theology* (3 vols., N. Y., 1871-72), I, 27; III, 880.
2 Cf. E. D. Morris to H. J. Van Dyke, March 14, 1890, V.P.
3 A. T. Innes, "The Creed Question in Scotland," in *Andover Review*, XII (July-Dec. 1889), 6; P. Schaff, *Creed Revision in the Presbyterian Churches* (N. Y., 1890), p. 12; Presbyterian Church of England, *Minutes of the Synod*, 1890, p. 433.
4 Alliance of Reformed Churches throughout the World Holding the Presbyterian System, *Proceedings*, 1877, p. 51; 1880, pp. 259-62, 498-99, 965-1123; 1884, pp. 31-48; cf. B.T. 1400, 1494, 1648, 2475, 2607.
5 Text in W. Walker, *The Creeds and Platforms of Congregationalism* (N. Y., 1893), pp. 577-82.
6 *The Trial of the Rev. David Swing . . .* (Chicago, 1874), p. 283; E. R. Craven to C. Hodge, Oct. 12, 1874, H.P.; *Presbyterian Quarterly and Princeton Review*, IV (1875), 539; L. J. Evans, *Preaching Christ; Sermons* (N. Y., 1893), p. 53.
7 For a list of more than 300 articles on revision, most of them after 1887, see W. S. Gilman to T. S. Hastings, Aug. 2, 1890, in "Hastings Scrapbook," Union Seminary Library, N. Y.; cf. also *Confession Revision; Being a Collection of 395 Articles . . . between Sept., 1887, and Oct., 1890.* Copy in Lane Papers, McCormick Seminary Library.
8 G.A. *Mins.*, 1888, pp. 115, 150.
9 *Ibid.*, 1889, p. 79; *N. Y. Evangelist*, May 30, p. 2, June 6, p. 2, 1889.
10 C. A. Briggs, *Whither? A Theological Question for the Times* (N. Y., 1889), pp. 1, 296-97, 22.
11 C. A. Briggs, in *How Shall We Revise the Westminster Confession of Faith?* (N. Y., 1890), pp. 1-2.

42-55

12 Schaff, *Creed Revision*, pp. v, 40, 42.
13 *N. Y. Evangelist*, Aug. 29, 1889, p. 6; W. J. Beecher, in *Homiletic Review*, XX (1890), 195.
14 F. L. Patton, *The Revision of the Confession of Faith. Read before the Presbyterian Social Union, N. Y., Dec. 2, 1889* (n.p., n.d.), pp. 13-15.
15 J. DeWitt and others, *Ought the Confession of Faith to Be Revised?* (N. Y., 1890), pp. 7, 10-13, 15-17.
16 Briggs to Warfield, June 26, 1889, W.P.; Briggs to Van Dyke, Oct. 2, 1889, V.P.; B.T. 3729; H. J. Van Dyke, in *N. Y. Evangelist*, March 13, 1890, p. 4.
17 Briggs, *Whither?* pp. ix-x, 27-28.
18 J. DeWitt and others, *op. cit.*, pp. 44-45, 49, 67.
19 *Ibid.*, p. 117.
20 *Presbyterian*, Oct. 12, p. 6, Nov. 16, p. 6, 1889.
21 J. T. Duffield, *The Revision of the Westminster Confession* (n.p., n.d.), pp. 1-8.
22 *Overture on Revision, Answers of the Presbyteries*, pp. 110-22.
23 *Ibid.*, pp. 6-7; G.A. *Mins.*, 1890, pp. 85-86.
24 G.A. *Mins.*, 1890, pp. 79, 85-86; *N. Y. Evangelist*, May 29, 1890, p. 8; T. A. Hoyt, *The Presbyterian General Assembly at Saratoga, May, 1890* (n.p., n.d.), pp. 6-7.
25 G.A. *Mins.*, 1890, p. 86; *Presbyterian Journal*, July 20, 1893, p. 2; *Presbyterian*, Aug. 29, 1900, p. 9.
26 *Andover Review*, XIV (1890), 69-74.
27 G.A. *Mins.*, 1890, pp. 87, 128; 1897, p. 18.
28 *Ibid.*, 1891, pp. 22-34.
29 *Ibid.*, 1892, pp. 128-38.
30 *Ibid.*, 1891, pp. 139-42; 1892, pp. 128, 202-5; *Presbyterian and Reformed Review*, III (1892), 532-42.
31 *Presbyterian and Reformed Review*, III (1892), 329.
32 G.A. *Mins.*, 1893, pp. 53, 177-98.

chapter 6 — the briggs case

1 C. A. Briggs, *General Introduction to the Study of Holy Scripture* (N. Y., 1899), p. 287.
2 B.T. 3651, 3652, 3662, 3667a; Briggs in *N. Y. Evangelist*, April 4, 1889, p. 1.
3 B.T., Vol. I, pp. 189, 191; Vol. II, p. 71.
4 B.T. 980, 3288; C. A. Briggs, *Whither? A Theological Question for the Times* (N. Y., 1889), p. vii.
5 B.T. 3717, 3725, 3740; J. DeWitt to B. B. Warfield, Oct. 5, 1889, W.P.; W. G. T. Shedd to Warfield, Dec. 20, 1889, W.P.; *N. Y. Evangelist*, Sept. 19, p. 4, Oct. 17, p. 1, Dec. 26, p. 2, 1889.
6 G. L. Prentiss, *The Bright Side of Life* (2 vols., n.p., 1901), II, 378; Briggs to Van Dyke, Oct. 23, 1889, V.P.; B.T., Vol. I, pp. 194-95, Vol. II, p. 71.
7 The W.P. prove that Dr. Warfield did not start preparations for this new venture until Oct. 28, after the Presbyterian Review Association had voted to discontinue.
8 B.T. 3826, 3856, 3881a, 4384, 5090, 5162, 5170, 5546.
9 B.T. 317a.
10 Dec. 20, 1890, B.T. 3957.
11 *N. Y. Evangelist*, Jan. 29, 1891, p. 4.
12 C. A. Briggs, "The Inaugural Address," in *The Edward Robinson Chair of Biblical Theology* (N. Y., 1891), p. 28.
13 *Ibid.*, p. 31.
14 *Ibid.*, pp. 32-33.
15 Cf. above, pp. 36-38; cf. also pp. 27-28, 32.
16 "The Inaugural Address," p. 35; cf. above, pp. 30-32.

17 "The Inaugural Address," p. 38.
18 *Ibid.*, p. 50.
19 *Ibid.*, p. 54.
20 Cf. I. A. Dorner, *Dorner on the Future State . . . a Translation* (N. Y., 1883), pp. 106-8.
21 B.T., Vol. I, p. 57.
22 B.T. 317a, 346a, 361.
23 "The Inaugural Address," pp. 55-56.
24 *Ibid.*, p. 56.
25 *Ibid.*, pp. 62, 67.
26 Dr. Briggs's statement in G. L. Prentiss, *The Union Theological Seminary . . . Another Decade of Its History* (Asbury Park, N. J., 1899), p. 332.
27 B.T. 4020b; *N. Y. Evangelist*, March 19, p. 4, April 2, p. 1, April 23, p. 8, May 21, p. 1, May 28, p. 4, 1891; *Andover Review*, XV (Jan.-June 1891), 304-9; XIX (Jan.-Dec. 1893), 99-113; P. Schaff, in *Forum* (Jan. 1892), p. 626; Prentiss, *Another Decade*, p. 317.
28 *N. Y. Evangelist*, April 30, 1891, p. 4.
29 B.T. 3425.
30 Cf. *N. Y. Evangelist*, April 30, 1891, p. 4.
31 Cf. F. Brown, in *Memorial Service . . . Charles Augustus Briggs . . . 1913* (n.p., n.d.), p. 32.
32 *N. Y. Evangelist*, March 19, 1891, p. 4.
33 B.T. 4001.
34 *N. Y. Evangelist*, Feb. 19, 1891, p. 6.
35 *Ibid.*, April 23, p. 8, May 21, p. 4, 1891.
36 *Ibid.*, May 14, 1891, p. 1.
37 B.T. 4020a; cf. B.T. 4337.
38 G.A. *Mins.*, 1883, pp. 706, 724; 1890, p. 209.
39 B.T. 3911, 4062, 4071, 4080, 4141, 4198; cf. also W.P. and V.P.
40 C. A. Briggs, in "In Memoriam Rev. William Adams D.D. LL.D." (N. Y., 1906, MS, in Union Seminary Library); B.T. 3494 (Dec. 24, 1887).
41 W. A. Brown, in *The Dedication of the New Buildings . . . 1910* (N. Y., n.d.), p. 57; cf. also B.T. 4165, 4166.
42 B.T. 4063.
43 *Ibid.*; M. R. Vincent, in *Memorial Service in Honor of . . . Thomas Samuel Hastings* (n.p., n.d.), p. 12; F. Brown, *op. cit.*, pp. 22-28; W. A. Brown, *op. cit.*, p. 58.
44 B.T. 4055, 4079, 4092, 4111; Briggs, *The Authority of Holy Scripture . . . Second Edition with Preface and Appendix* (N. Y., 1891); Prentiss, *Another Decade*, pp. 333, 549.
45 E. C. Smyth and Tucker, B.T. 4111.
46 May 15, 1891, B.T. 4098.
47 May 14, B.T. 4096.
48 May 19, text in Prentiss, *Another Decade*, pp. 544-45, and in B.T. 4104; cf. B.T. 4108, 4112.
49 May 22, B.T. 4114; text in Prentiss, *Another Decade*, pp. 545-50.
50 G.A. *Mins.*, 1891, pp. 45, 94.
51 Quoted by Prentiss, *Another Decade*, pp. 93-94; B.T. 4173; for an opposite viewpoint, cf. *N. Y. Evangelist*, June 18, 1891, p. 4; *N. Y. Observer*, July 9, 1891, p. 222.
52 *N. Y. Observer*, July 9, 1891, p. 222.
53 G.A. *Mins.*, 1891, pp. 94-105.
54 For varying impressions see *N. Y. Observer*, July 9, 1891, p. 222; *Andover Review*, XVI (July-Dec. 1891), 70-76; *N. Y. Mail and Express*, June 9, 1891; Prentiss, *Another Decade*, p. 278.

55-68

55 G.A. *Mins.*, 1892, pp. 53-67; Prentiss, *Another Decade*, pp. 158-82; cf. also B.T. 4166, 4174, 4211, 4392, 4398.
56 G.A. *Mins.*, 1892, pp. 67, 176; cf. also B.T. 4406a, 4411, 4445, 4464.
57 G.A. *Mins.*, 1893, p. 159; Prentiss, *Another Decade*, pp. 280-83.
58 Prentiss, *Another Decade*, p. 285.
59 G.A. *Mins.*, 1893, p. 161.
60 G.A. *Mins.*, 1892, pp. 232-33; *The Presbyterian Church in the U.S.A. against the Rev. Charles A. Briggs, D.D., Record of the Case* (n.p., n.d.), pp. 24, 31-39, 58, 68, 114 (hereafter cited as *Record of the Case*).
61 *Record of the Case*, pp. 147-49.
62 Briggs Diary, Jan. 8, 1893, in B.T., Vol. I, p. 227; Briggs, in Prentiss, *Another Decade*, p. 334.
63 G.A. *Mins.*, 1892, pp. 232-41.
64 W. G. T. Shedd, "The Appeal of the Prosecuting Committee . . . ," in *N. Y. Observer*, Jan. 21, 1892, p. 1.
65 G.A. *Mins.*, 1892, pp. 140-50, 152; cf. B.T. 4440, 4484, 4501.
66 G.A. *Mins.*, 1892, pp. 179-80.
67 Cf. above, pp. 30-32.
68 *N. Y. Evangelist*, June 23, p. 1, July 14, p. 1, 1892; *Andover Review*, XIX (1893), 108.
69 H. van Dyke, *The Bible As It Is; A Sermon . . . January 22, 1893* (N. Y., 1893), p. 18.
70 J. T. Duffield, "The Genesis and the Exodus of the Portland Deliverance," in *Independent*, Oct. 17, 1895, p. 5.
71 "The Inspired Word Deliverance," editorial in *Presbyterian Journal*, May 18, 1893, p. 312.
72 *The Case Against Professor Briggs*, Part II (N. Y., 1893), pp. 29-45.
73 *Ibid.*, pp. 47-77.
74 *Ibid.*, pp. 79-141.
75 *Ibid.*, pp. 158-60.
76 H. van Dyke, *op. cit.*, p. 16; H. S. Coffin, in *In Memory of The Rev. George Alexander, D.D.* (n.p., n.d.), p. 56.
77 *A Plea for Peace and Work* (n.p., Feb. 17, 1893), 4 pp.; T. van Dyke, *Henry van Dyke; A Biography* (N. Y., 1935), pp. 133-34.
78 W. B. Greene, Jr., "Broad Churchism and the Briggs Case," in *Presbyterian Journal*, May 18, 1893, p. 307.
79 *Presbyterian Journal*, Feb. 2, p. 65, March 16, p. 161, 1893.
80 W. A. Brown, *A Teacher and His Times* (N. Y., 1940), p. 157.
81 B.T. 4800.
82 *Presbyterian Journal*, June 1, 1893, pp. 1-2, 8.
83 G.A. *Mins.*, 1893, pp. 95-105.
84 *Ibid.*, pp. 132, 139; *Presbyterian Journal*, June 8, p. 5, June 15, p. 9, 1893.
85 *The Case Against Professor Briggs*, Part III, pp. 305-6.
86 G.A. *Mins.*, 1893, pp. 140-50, 165.
87 *Ibid.*, pp. 165-67, 172-73.
88 *Ibid.*, p. 163.
89 *Ibid.*, 1894, p. 45.
90 A. A. Hodge and B. B. Warfield, "Inspiration," in *Presbyterian Review*, II (1881), pp. 233, 237, 245; cf. above, pp. 30-32.
91 G.A. *Mins.*, 1893, pp. 167-68.
92 *Ibid.*, p. 169.
93 S. D. F. Salmond to Briggs, June 26, 1893, B.T. 4984.
94 *Independent*, Feb. 23, pp. 1-2, March 30, p. 8, 1893.
95 Letters, in Prentiss, *Another Decade*, pp. 323-28.
96 MI.P., June-Nov. 1893; also B.T. 4982, 4986, 4996, 5016, 5017, 5025.
97 B.T. 5018, 5674, 5712, 5747, 6125; B.T., Vol. I, pp. 352-54; G. Hodges, *Henry Cadman Potter, Seventh Bishop of New York* (N. Y., 1915), pp. 302-10.

chapter 7 — the smith case

1 Cf. above, p. 35; and below, p. 66; also B.T. 2338, 3343, 3662, 3922.
2 B.T. 3662, 4008, 4033; H. P. Smith, in *Biblical Scholarship and Inspiration* (3d ed., Cincinnati, 1892), pp. v-vii.
3 B.T. 4033, 4034, 4057.
4 Presbytery of Cincinnati, "Minutes," 1890-93 (MS, in Historical and Philosophical Society of Ohio), meeting of Dec. 21, 1891, p. 177; B.T. 4403.
5 McGiffert's letter to the *Herald and Presbyter,* under date of April 30, 1891.
6 June 6, 1891, B.T. 4144.
7 B.T. 2951, 3083, 3280, 3343, 3350, 3740, 4539, 4669, 4719, 4800, 5016; Morris in *N. Y. Evangelist,* Nov. 17, 1892, p. 1; Morris, *A Defense of Lane Seminary* (Cincinnati, 1893), pp. 24-28; H. P. Smith, *The Heretic's Defense* (N. Y., 1926), pp. 99-102, 118.
8 H. P. Smith to Briggs, Feb. 20, 1888, B.T. 3520.
9 *N. Y. Evangelist,* June 18, 1891, p. 4.
10 H. P. Smith, "How Much Is Implied in Ordination Vows?" in *N. Y. Evangelist,* March 17, 1892. Reprinted in *Biblical Scholarship and Inspiration* (3d ed.), pp. 126-30.
11 H. P. Smith, "The Sin of Schism" in *N. Y. Evangelist,* April 7, 1892. Reprinted in *Biblical Scholarship and Inspiration* (3d ed.), pp. 130-34.
12 Presbytery of Cincinnati, "Minutes," 1890-93, pp. 238-44.
13 G.A. *Mins.,* 1892, pp. 179-80.
14 Cf. above, pp. 56-57, 61-62.
15 Cf. above, pp. 15-16, 35, 63; cf. also below, p. 66.
16 B.T. 4542.
17 Presbytery of Cincinnati, "Minutes," 1890-93, pp. 250-396, *passim;* G.A. *Mins.,* 1894, p. 198; W. S. Plumer Bryan, *The Trial of Rev. Professor Henry Preserved Smith, D.D.* (Cincinnati, 1893), p. 7.
18 H. P. Smith, *Appeal and Argument . . . to the General Assembly . . . May, 1894* (N. Y., n.d.), p. 85.
19 H. P. Smith, *Appeal and Argument,* p. 10; G.A. *Mins.,* 1894, p. 199.
20 B.T. 4064, 4144, 4405, 4411.
21 G.A. *Mins.,* 1893, p. 156; B.T. 4426, 4427.
22 Morris to Briggs, March 29 [1893], B.T. 4792.
23 G.A. *Mins.,* 1893, p. 156; 1894, p. 230; text of protest in E. D. Morris, *A Defence of Lane Seminary* (Cincinnati, 1893), pp. 3-4; Morris to Joseph T. Smith, Aug. 28, 1893, Sm.P.
24 B.T. 4998b.
25 G.A. *Mins.,* 1894, pp. 109-11; B.T. 5182.
26 G.A. *Mins.,* 1895, p. 113.
27 *Ibid.,* 1897, p. 101.
28 *Ibid.,* 1932, p. 381.
29 H. P. Smith, *Appeal and Argument,* pp. 10-13; H. P. Smith, *The Heretic's Defense* (N. Y., 1926), pp. 111-12.
30 G.A. *Mins.,* 1894, p. 199.
31 H. P. Smith, *Appeal and Argument,* pp. 39, 42-45, 62, 70, 104-5, 122-23.
32 G.A. *Mins.,* 1893, p. 140; 1894, pp. 97-106.
33 B.T. 5156.
34 Mentioned, e.g., in *Presbyterian,* Oct. 3, 1894, p. 3.
35 B.T. 5889.

68-78

chapter 8—the aftermath

1 B.T. 4445, 4512, 4704, 4705, 4792, 4800; J. D. Wells to H. J. Van Dyke, May 14, 1891, V.P.; D. Schaff, *The Life of Philip Schaff* (N. Y., 1897), pp. 433-40.
2 B.T. 5015; C. A. Briggs, "The Future of Presbyterianism in the United States," in *North American Review*, CCCCXL (July 1893), p. 9.
3 B.T. 4994, 4995, 4999, 5036, 5043, 5055, 5056, 5064.
4 *Presbyterian Journal*, Nov. 16, p. 8, Nov. 23, p. 8, Dec. 7, p. 5, 1893; *Presbyterian*, April 11, 1894, p. 6.
5 B.T. 5167, 5183; *Presbyterian*, June 6, p. 9, June 13, pp. 4-5, 9, June 27, p. 4, July 18, p. 16, 1894; Feb. 20, 1895, p. 9.
6 B.T. 5088, 5158, 5162, 5229.
7 *Presbyterian*, May 22, p. 6, May 29, p. 4, June 5, p. 7, 1895; *Presbyterian and Reformed Review*, VI (1895), 730.
8 W. B. Pugh, *Summary of the Ecclesiastical Status of the Theological Seminaries of the Presbyterian Church in the U.S.A.* (mimeographed, Phila., n.d.), pp. 1-3.
9 S. M. Hopkins, *Auburn Theological Seminary and the General Assembly* (n.p., [1891]), pp. 5, 16; E. D. Morris, *A Defense of Lane Seminary* (Cincinnati, 1893), pp. 7-14.
10 G.A. *Mins.*, 1893, p. 25; 1894, pp. 48, 65-66; 1895, pp. 29, 33.
11 *Ibid.*, 1896, pp. 119-20.
12 *Ibid.*, 1893, p. 161.
13 *Ibid.*, 1895, pp. 55f.
14 *Ibid.*, 1896, pp. 123f.
15 Cf. below, pp. 99-100.
16 G.A. *Mins.*, 1893, p. 161.
17 *Ibid.*, 1895, pp. 77, 119.
18 *Ibid.*, 1897, pp. 57-59; cf. below, pp. 131-33.
19 Cf. also his somewhat more positive statements: A. C. McGiffert, *History and Theology; An Address . . . April 25th, 1898* (n.p., n.d.).
20 *George W. F. Birch vs. Rev. Arthur Cushman McGiffert, Ph.D., D.D., Appeal to the General Assembly* (n.p., n.d.), pp. 63-64.
21 *Presbyterian*, May 25, 1898, p. 25.
22 G.A. *Mins.*, 1898, p. 108; *Presbyterian*, June 1, 1898, pp. 4, 24; B.T. 5742.
23 *Presbyterian*, March 29, 1899, pp. 5-6.
24 F. Brown, "What Is Orthodoxy?" in *North American Review*, CLXVIII (1899), 409-17.
25 *Presbyterian*, May 10, 1899, p. 7.
26 G.A. *Mins.*, 1899, pp. 95-96; Birch vs. McGiffert, pp. 65-67; *Presbyterian*, May 24, 1899, p. 21.
27 G.A. *Mins.*, 1899, pp. 95-99.
28 *Birch vs. McGiffert*, pp. 73-75.
29 *Ibid.*, pp. 75-78.
30 *Birch vs. McGiffert*, pp. 1-52, 80-83.
31 Cf. B.T. 6118.
32 G.A. *Mins.*, 1900, pp. 82, 85; *Presbyterian*, April 11, p. 29, May 30, pp. 9-10, 1900.

chapter 9—the church's seminaries

1 C. W. Eliot, "On the Education of Ministers," *Princeton Review*, 59th Year (1883), pp. 353-54; R. L. Kelly, *Theological Education in America* (N. Y., 1924), pp. 84-90; W. A. Brown, *The Education of American Ministers*, I (N. Y., 1934), 81-82, 121.

2 G.A. *Mins.*, 1870, p. 80; 1873, p. 534; 1895, p. 116; 1900, pp. 53, 56-72; G. B. Stewart, in *Inauguration of . . . George Black Stewart, D.D. as President of . . . Auburn . . . 1899* (n.p., n.d.), pp. 53-54; Kelly, *op. cit.*, pp. 78-79, 91-94.

3 Kelly, *op. cit.*, pp. 28, 90; cf. during first two decades of the twentieth century pamphlets by Dr. Warfield and *Princeton Theological Review, passim.*

4 See above, pp. 54-55, 66, 70; and below, pp. 99-100.

5 W. J. Beecher, in *Presbyterian Review,* III (1882), 701-31.

6 W. J. Beecher, *The Old Tradition and the New* (n.p., n.d. [1903]), pp. 20-27; Beecher, *The Prophets and the Promise* (N. Y., 1905), p. 207; Beecher, *Reasonable Biblical Criticism* (Phila., 1911), pp. 14-20; B.T. 2076, 2104.

7 W. J. Hinke, Inaugural Address, in *The Auburn Seminary Record,* V (Jan. 10, 1910), 465-67; H. Creelman, *An Introduction to the Old Testament Chronologically Arranged* (N. Y., 1917), pp. 8-26.

8 *Addresses in Memory of Ransom Bethune Welch, D.D., LL.D. . . . 1890* (Auburn, 1891), pp. 10-13, 25, 38, 44.

9 T. G. Darling, in *Addresses at the Inauguration of the Rev. Timothy G. Darling D.D. . . . 1888* (n.p., 1889), p. 20; E. W. Miller, *An Address in Memory of the Rev. Timothy Grenville Darling, D.D. . . . 1906*, pp. 28-29; *Memorial Services . . . Auburn Theological Seminary . . . May 9, 1906* (n.p., n.d.), pp. 9, 16, 19, 31; H. A. Youtz, in *Harvard Theological Review,* IV (1911), 439-59; Youtz, *The Enlarging Conception of God* (N. Y., 1914).

10 H. M. Booth, in *Addresses at the Inauguration of the Rev. Timothy G. Darling, D.D. . . . 1888,* p. 4; Booth . . . *Inaugural Address . . . 1893* (n.p., n.d.), pp. 31, 36-38; *Addresses . . . Anniversary of the Reunion . . . 1895* (Phila., 1895), p. 57; Booth, *The Man and His Message; Addresses* (N. Y., 1899), p. 155.

11 G. B. Stewart, in *The Inauguration of . . . Harry Lathrop Reed, D.D. . . . 1926* (n.p., n.d.), pp. 10-14.

12 A. M. Dulles, *The Auburn Seminary Record,* I (Nov. 10, 1905), 303-21; Dulles, *What Is Necessary in the Christian Religion* (Auburn, 1919), pp. 7-8. Dr. Dulles was the father of John Foster Dulles and Allen W. Dulles.

13 Cf. above, p. 52.

14 B.T. 4039.

15 G.A. *Mins.*, 1939, pp. 253-57.

16 See above, pp. 12-15.

17 B.T. 1321, 1602; W. T. Hutchinson, *Cyrus Hall McCormick,* II (N. Y., 1935), 264.

18 B.T. 1393, 1398, 1418, 1420, 1489, 1515, 1602, 1630, 2056, 3693; F. L. Patton to A. A. Hodge, n.d., H.P.; cf. G.A. *Mins.*, 1881, p. 575; 1882, p. 88.

19 C. H. McCormick to D. Marquis, in Hutchinson, *op. cit.*, II, 267; B.T. 1707.

20 B.T. 1805, 1974, 4980.

21 E. L. Curtis, *Addresses at the Inauguration of Rev. Edward Lewis Curtis, Ph.D.* (Chicago, 1887), pp. 10-14; B.T. 2393, 2743, 3328, 4034, 4054, 4114, 4354.

22 See above, pp. 16-17; T. H. Skinner, *Questions in the Theological Course of the Seminary of the Northwest* (n.p., n.d.), 38 pp.; W. W. Harsha to B. B. Warfield, Nov. 13, 1889, W.P.

23 D. C. Marquis, in *Proceedings of the Alumni Association of the Theological Seminary of the Northwest* (1883); Marquis, in *Addresses . . . Inauguration of Rev. David C. Marquis, D.D. . . .* (Chicago, 1884), pp. 18-24; J. DeWitt to B. B. Warfield, Nov. 30, 1889, W.P.

24 B.T. 1974.

25 J. DeWitt to B. B. Warfield, May 17, 1890, in W.P.

26 W. G. Craig, in *McCormick Theological Seminary Inaugural Addresses . . .* (Chicago, 1892), pp. 7-24; cf. Craig to B. B. Warfield, Dec. 5, 1889, W.P.; J. G. K. McClure, *The Story of . . . the Presbyterian Theological Seminary, Chicago . . .* (Chicago, 1929), p. 124.

27 Cf. W. W. Harsha to B. B. Warfield, June 9, 18, 1890, W.P.

78-89

28 J. DeWitt to B. B. Warfield, Nov. 19, 24, 30, 1889, W.P.; J. G. K. McClure, *op. cit.*, pp. 71-85; A. C. Zenos, quoted in C. E. F. Howe, "Andrew C. Zenos, a Bibliography" (MS, 1943, in McCormick Seminary Library), pp. 179-80.

29 B.T. 1499; A. C. Zenos, "The Principles of the Higher Criticism, A Paper Read . . . 1884" (MS, in McCormick Seminary Library), pp. 5-14; Zenos, . . . *Inaugural Address . . . 1889 Hartford Theological Seminary* (Hartford Seminary Publications, No. 3), pp. 12-13; H. T. Kerr, in Presbyterian Theological Seminary, Chicago, *Alumni Review* (July 1942), pp. 3-9.

30 A. C. Zenos, . . . *Inaugural Address . . . 1889*, pp. 6-7; cf. also Zenos, in *McCormick Theological Seminary Inaugural Addresses* (Chicago, 1892), pp. 34-37; Zenos, *The Protestant Reformation and Its Influence 1517-1917* (Phila., 1917), p. 129; Zenos, *Presbyterianism in America; Past—Present and Prospective* (N. Y., 1937), pp. 180-81, 197, 200.

31 Cf. J. G. K. McClure, *op. cit.*, pp. 124-25.

32 A. C. Zenos, in *Inaugural Addresses* (1892), pp. 44-46; Zenos, *The History and Task of Biblical Theology* (n.p., 1895), pp. 30-34; Zenos, *The Elements of the Higher Criticism* (N. Y., 1895), pp. 143-50; Zenos, in *American Journal of Theology*, VIII (1904), 86-91.

33 J. G. K. McClure, *op. cit.; A. A. Hays, . . . Inaugural Address . . . 1915* (n.p., n.d.), pp. 9, 23-30.

34 W. C. Covert, in Presbyterian Theological Seminary, Chicago, *Alumni Review* (Jan. 1930), p. 172.

35 S. H. Kellogg, in *Presbyterian Review*, III (1882), 475-502.

36 *Bulletin of the Western Theological Seminary*, XVI (Oct. 1923), 1, 37-38, 41-42.

37 J. H. Snowden, *The Basal Beliefs of Christianity* (N. Y., 1911), pp. viii, 6, 64-76, 118-33; Snowden, *Making and Meaning of the New Testament* (N. Y., 1923), pp. 119-20, 230-33; Snowden, *Old Faith and New Knowledge* (N. Y., 1928), pp. 52, 91-101; Snowden, *What Do Present Day Christians Believe?* (N. Y., 1930), pp. 113-16, 225-29.

38 *N. Y. Evangelist*, May 24, 1888, p. 5.

39 R. D. Wilson to Briggs, Jan. 24, 1887, B.T. 3342.

40 *Bulletin of the Western Theological Seminary*, IX (Jan. 1917) *In Memoriam Matthew Brown Riddle.*

41 G.A. *Mins.*, 1872, p. 64; 1873, p. 533; W. A. Scott to H. J. Van Dyke, Sept. 23, 1870, V.P.; E. A. Wicher, *The Presbyterian Church in California, 1849-1927* (N. Y., 1927), pp. 269-83; C. M. Drury, *God Giveth the Increase* (mimeographed, n.p., n.d.).

42 W. Alexander to B. B. Warfield, Dec. 4, 19, 1889, W.P.; Alexander, *Is Revision of the Confession of Faith Desirable?* (n.p., 1890), pp. 1-19.

43 H. C. Minton, "Authority in Religion," in *Presbyterian and Reformed Review*, XI (1900), 201; cf. also Minton, *Christianity Supernatural; A Brief Essay on Christion Evidence* (Phila., 1900), pp. 15-21, 64.

44 *Synod of California at Long Beach vs. Prof. Day*, etc. (Oct. 1911) (n.p., n.d.); W. H. Oxtoby, *The New Covenant . . . Inaugural . . . 1914* (n.p., n.d.), pp. 28-29.

45 L. A. McAfee, in *Presbyterian*, Sept. 11, 1924, p. 12; M. G. Kyle, in J. E. Wishart, *The Fact of Prayer*, etc. (N. Y., 1927), p. 6.

46 G.A. *Mins.*, 1853, pp. 439-43; 1901, pp. 135-39, 222-28; 1928, p. 327.

47 *Ibid.*, 1870, pp. 68-70.

48 Cf. *Digest of the . . . Presbyterian Church . . .*, II (Phila., 1938), 431-639.

49 See above, pp. 21-28, 49-55, 63-66, 100; and cf. below, p. 100; see also the index of the present volume under names of various individual seminaries, and also under names of various individual professors.

chapter 10 — revision accomplished

1 Cf. above, pp. 39-41, for a brief discussion of factors in the background of the Presbyterian revision movement.
2 *Presbyterian*, May 16, 1900, p. 3.
3 G.A. *Mins.*, 1900, pp. 35, 46, 98.
4 *Ibid.*, p. 99; *Presbyterian and Reformed Review*, XI (1900), 672.
5 B. B. Warfield, *Revision or Reaffirmation* (Princeton, 1900), pp. 1-4.
6 C. A. Dickey to H. van Dyke, July 30, Aug. 3, 1900, v.P.
7 G.A. *Mins.*, 1901, p. 103.
8 J. T. Duffield, *The Confessional Crisis in the Presbyterian Church* (Princeton, 1900); Duffield, *Supplement to the Confessional Crisis* (Princeton, 1900); *Presbyterian*, Sept. 12, pp. 20, 28, Sept. 19, pp. 20-21, 1900.
9 *Presbyterian*, Sept. 5, 1900, pp. 9-10.
10 *Ibid.*, Oct. 17, p. 7, Nov. 28, p. 4, 1900.
11 Cf. also *Presbyterian*, March 20, p. 8, April 10, p. 3, April 17, p. 11, 1901.
12 *The Creed Revision; Addresses delivered before the Presbyterian Union of New York, March 4, 1901* (N. Y., 1901), pp. 1-6.
13 *Ibid.*, pp. 6-10.
14 *Ibid.*, pp. 10-15.
15 *N. Y. Observer*, March 7, 1901, p. 303.
16 G.A. *Mins.*, 1901, pp. 96, 102-6, 182; J. DeWitt, in *Presbyterian and Reformed Review*, XII (1901), 676-77.
17 G. Vos, in *Presbyterian and Reformed Review*, XIII (1902), 2-3, 36-37.
18 G.A. *Mins.*, 1902, pp. 87, 91.
19 Assembly's Committee of Revision 1901, *Two Brief Statements of Faith and Five Letters from Professors of Systematic Theology* (n.p., n.d.), pp. 1-23; cf. also B.T. 6412.
20 *Presbyterian*, Dec. 11, 1901, p. 28.
21 *Ibid.*, Feb. 12, 1902, pp. 20, 24.
22 G.A. *Mins.*, 1902, pp. 86-97.
23 J. DeWitt to H. van Dyke, April 3, 1902, v.P.W.
24 W. A. Brown, in *American Journal of Theology*, X (1906), 411; G.A. *Mins.*, 1905, p. 85.
25 G.A. *Mins.*, 1902, pp. 86, 150.
26 F. R. Beattie, "Confessional Revision in the Presbyterian Church, North," in *Union Seminary Magazine* (Oct.-Nov. 1902), pp. 10, 27.
27 *Presbyterian*, June 20, 1900, p. 4; June 4, 1902, p. 3.
28 *Ibid.*, March 25, 1903, p. 8.
29 *Presbyterian Journal*, March 26, 1903, p. 15.
30 G.A. *Mins.*, 1903, pp. 123-28.
31 *Ibid.*, p. 123.
32 *Presbyterian Journal*, May 3, 1903, p. 14.
33 As quoted in *Presbyterian Journal*, June 4, 1903, p. 9.
34 Cf. W. A. Brown, in *American Journal of Theology*, X (1906), 403-4; G. J. Slosser, in *Religion in Life*, IV (1935), 473; A. C. Zenos, *Presbyterianism in America* (N. Y., 1937), p. 103; R. H. Nichols, in *Church History*, XV (1946), 68.
35 E.g., A. M. Dulles, *The True Church (Historical and Scriptural)* (N. Y., 1907), p. 278.

91-109

chapter 11—the emerging issue

1 S. G. Cole, *The History of Fundamentalism* (N. Y., 1931), pp. 23-24, 34, 53-61; J. M. Mecklin, *The Survival Value of Christianity* (N. Y., 1936), p. 6.
2 G. Santayana, *Winds of Doctrine* (N. Y., 1926), p. 188.
3 G.A. *Mins.*, 1873, p. 485; 1874, p. 86; 1875, p. 480; [Joseph T. Smith] to C. A. Dickey [between 1903 and 1906], Sm.P.
4 *Presbyterian*, June 11, p. 4, Sept. 10, p. 28, 1902; cf. also G.A. *Mins.*, 1904, p. 129.
5 G.A. *Mins.*, 1903, pp. 122-23.
6 *Ibid.*, 1904, p. 119.
7 *Ibid.*, p. 129.
8 *Ibid.*, p. 137.
9 *Presbyterian*, June 22, 1904, p. 6.
10 *Ibid.*, June 1, 1904, p. 28.
11 *Ibid.*, p. 5; G.A. *Mins.*, 1904, pp. 148, 157-58.
12 G.A. *Mins.*, 1905, pp. 67-68.
13 *Ibid.*, 1906, pp. 124, 150, 152.
14 Cf. *Digest . . . of the Presbyterian Church* . . . (2 vols., Phila., 1938), I, 647-57; II, 45-91; for a sociological analysis of the Cumberland union of 1906 see H. M. Miller, "Institutional Behaviour of the Cumberland Presbyterian Church" (MS, Ph.D. thesis, New York University, 1940), pp. 76-79, 116-17, 173.
15 Cf. G.A. *Mins.*, 1901, pp. 39-40; 1904, p. 197; 1905, pp. 59, 142, 232-37; 1906, p. 53; 1907, pp. 109-10, 201; *Presbyterian*, Dec. 14, 1904, p. 7.
16 D. W. Dodson, "Protestant Church Trends of New York City, 1900-1936" (MS, Ph.D. thesis, New York University, 1940), pp. 56-58.
17 G.A. *Mins.*, 1910, pp. 192-93.
18 *Ibid.*, pp. 272-73; cf. the analogous but later and much more carefully framed articles of the Southern Presbyterians, in Presbyterian Church in the U.S., G.A. *Mins.*, 1939, p. 71; cf. also the less analogous "Brief Statement" of the Scottish United Free Church in 1921, text in J. R. Fleming, *History of the Church in Scotland, 1875-1929* (Edinburgh, 1933), pp. 313-16.
19 Cf. above, pp. 56-57, 61-62, 65.
20 S. G. Cole, *op. cit.*, pp. 34, 98.
21 Cf. G.A. *Mins.*, 1910, p. 277.
22 See above, p. 2.
23 A. Harnack, *Das Wesen des Christentums* (Leipzig, 1900), 189 pp.; *What Is Christianity?* (Eng. transl., London, 1901), 301 pp.
24 Cf., e.g., G.A. *Mins.*, 1911, pp. 183, 197; 1912, p. 192; 1916, p. 130.
25 *Ibid.*, 1916, pp. 131-32; 1923, p. 253.
26 *Ibid.*, 1911, pp. 206-7; 1913, pp. 104-5; *Presbyterian*, May 28, 1913, pp. 10f.
27 G.A. *Mins.*, 1915, p. 148.
28 *Ibid.*, p. 160.
29 *Ibid.*, p. 161.
30 *Presbyterian Banner*, June 3, 1915, p. 5.
31 *Presbyterian*, April 5, 1917, p. 3.
32 G.A. *Mins.*, 1918, p. 153.
33 *Ibid.*, p. 154.
34 *Ibid.*, 1919, pp. 117-29; Philadelphia *Public Ledger*, Dec. 4-6, 1918; *Presbyterian*, Dec. 12, 1918, p. 4.
35 G.A. *Mins.*, 1920, pp. 117-22; Philadelphia *Public Ledger*, Feb. 3-6, 1920; *Presbyterian*, Feb. 12, 1920, p. 4.
36 G.A. *Mins.*, 1920, p. 98.
37 *Ibid.*, pp. 27f, 98.
38 *Ibid.*, p. 98.
39 *Ibid.*, 1921, pp. 41-42.
40 *Ibid.*, pp. 82-83.

41 Cf., e.g., *Presbyterian*, Feb. 5, 1925, p. 20.
42 *Princeton Theological Review*, IV (1906), 306.
43 *Presbyterian*, Jan. 20, 1909, p. 4; cf. also May 12, 1909, p. 4.
44 G.A. *Mins.*, 1911, p. 140; W. A. Brown, *A Teacher and His Times* (N. Y., 1940), pp. 128-29; *Continent*, May 18, p. 703, June 1, pp. 806-7, 1911; *Presbyterian*, May 3, p. 3, May 17, pp. 2-3, May 31, p. 4, 1911.
45 *Presbyterian*, July 26, 1911, p. 5.
46 J. G. Machen, "Christianity and Culture," *Princeton Theological Review*, XI (1913), pp. 11-15.
47 *Presbyterian Banner*, May 16, 1918, p. 1478.
48 *Presbyterian*, March 22, 1934, p. 13.
49 *Ibid.*, Jan. 6, p. 24, Feb. 10, pp. 6, 8, 1921; *Continent*, Jan. 13, 1921, p. 53; *Presbyterian Banner*, April 7, 1921, p. 28.
50 Open letter of C. G. Trumbull to *Continent*, April 14, 1921, p. 438.
51 W. H. G. Thomas, "Modernism in China," *Princeton Theological Review*, XIX (1921), 637; J. W. Lowrie, in *Bulletin of the Bible Union of China*, No. 10 (Dec. 1922), p. 2; *Ibid.*, No. 14 (Oct. 1923), p. 1; cf. also P. Hutchinson, in *Journal of Religion*, II (1922), 207, 337-61.
52 *Presbyterian Banner*, April 7, 1921, p. 28.
53 Presbytery of Philadelphia, "Minutes" (MS, in Presbyterian Historical Society, Phila.), 1918-25, p. 191.
54 *Continent*, April 7, 1921, p. 415.
55 R. E. Speer to W. M. Hayes, July 8, 1921, File No. 1912, Presbyterian Board of Foreign Missions, N. Y.
56 G.A. *Mins.*, 1905, pp. 124-25; 1932, p. 124.
57 E. D. Burton, in *American Journal of Theology*, XXIV (1920), 321-38.
58 S. H. Moffett, "The Relation of the Board of Foreign Missions of the Presbyterian Church in the U.S.A. to the Missions and Church Connected with it in China" (MS, Ph.D. thesis, Yale University, 1945), pp. 98-103.
59 *Continent*, March 3, 1921, p. 240; *Presbyterian*, March 17, 1921, p. 6; *Presbyterian Banner*, April 14, p. 6, April 28, p. 30, 1921.
60 G.A. *Mins.*, 1921, pp. 20-21, 195f.
61 *Presbyterian*, June 16, 1921, p. 7.
62 *Statement of the Presbyterian Board of Foreign Missions*, Oct. 11, 1921; *Continent*, Nov. 17, 1921, p. 1309.
63 *Presbyterian*, Dec. 29, 1921, p. 10; also Jan. 4, 1923, p. 8; C. R. Erdman, *Within the Gateways of the Far East* (N. Y., c. 1922), pp. 41, 127.
64 G.A. *Mins.*, 1922, I, 238.
65 *Ibid.*, 1924, p. 187; cf. also *Presbyterian Banner*, Nov. 8, 1923, p. 3; June 5, 1924, pp. 3, 7; *Presbyterian*, Jan. 3, 1924, p. 23.

chapter 12—a new york pulpit

1 First Presbyterian Church of New York, *The First Presbyterian Church of New York and Dr. Fosdick* (n.p., n.d.), pp. 5, 12; cf. above, p. 100.
2 H. E. Fosdick, "The Trenches and the Church at Home," in *Atlantic Monthly*, CXXIII (1919), 22-33; *Presbyterian*, Feb. 20, p. 6, March 6, p. 10, March 20, pp. 26-27, 1919.
3 Cf. above, p. 104.
4 Letter from Dr. Fosdick, *Presbyterian*, Dec. 7, 1922, p. 6; Ivy L. Lee to C. E. Macartney, March 6, 1923; Jan. 22, Feb. 4, 1924, M.P.
5 H. E. Fosdick, *Shall the Fundamentalists Win?* (stenographically reported by Margaret Renton, n.p., n.d.), pp. 1-14.

109-129

6 *Presbyterian Banner*, July 13, pp. 8-10, July 20, pp. 8-10, Nov. 9, p. 7, 1922; *Continent*, Oct. 1922, p. 1240.
7 Presbytery of Philadelphia, "Minutes" (MS, in Presbyterian Historical Society, Phila.), 1918-25, pp. 287, 291-94.
8 *Presbyterian Banner*, Oct. 26, 1922, p. 7; *Presbyterian*, Oct. 26, p. 7, Nov. 2, p. 25, Nov. 23, p. 4, 1922; Feb. 15, 1923, pp. 8, 9, 26; *Continent*, Nov. 16, 1922, p. 1451.
9 J. R. Stevenson to C. E. Macartney, Feb. 2, 1923, M.P.; so also J. G. K. McClure to H. van Dyke, Jan. 28, 1924, v.P.
10 G.A. *Mins.*, 1923, p. 23.
11 *Presbyterian Banner*, May 17, 1923, p. 5.
12 Cf. above, pp. 80-81.
13 *Presbyterian Banner*, May 24, pp. 5, 26, June 28, p. 5, 1923.
14 *Ibid.*, May 31, 1923, p. 31.
15 *Ibid.*
16 G.A. *Mins.*, 1923, p. 212.
17 Cf. *Presbyterian Banner*, March 31, p. 5, April 7, p. 5, 1921; Feb. 9, p. 4, April 6, p. 5, Dec. 28, p. 8, 1922.
18 *Ibid.*, June 7, 1923, pp. 4, 14.
19 *Presbyterian*, May 31, p. 10, June 7, p. 9, June 14, p. 7, 1923; *Presbyterian Banner*, June 7, 1923, p. 30.
20 G.A. *Mins.*, 1923, p. 253.
21 *Ibid.*, p. 338.
22 *Presbyterian*, June 7, pp. 12-13, June 14, pp. 7, 26, 1923.
23 The table is based on the votes of synods in *Presbyterian*, June 28, 1923, p. 12. The total negative there given is "357" instead of "359." The complete roll call vote is printed *ibid.*, July 12, 1923, pp. 20-21.
24 *Mount Holyoke News*, June 11, 1923, pp. 2, 7; *Literary Digest*, June 16, 1923, p. 31.
25 *Presbyterian*, Sept. 20, 1923, p. 10.
26 *Ibid.*, June 7, 1923, p. 6.
27 *Ibid.*, Sept. 20, 1923, p. 10.
28 *Ibid.*, Nov. 8, 1923, pp. 9, 21.
29 Philadelphia *Public Ledger*, Dec. 11, 1923; *Presbyterian*, Dec. 20, 1923, pp. 6-7, 9.
30 *Presbyterian*, Dec. 27, 1923, pp. 7, 10; Jan. 17, 1924, pp. 9, 12.
31 *Ibid.*, Dec. 27, 1923, p. 20; Jan. 10, p. 21, Jan. 24, p. 20, 1924.
32 *Presbyterian*, Feb. 14, 1924, p. 12.
33 *Presbyterian Banner*, Feb. 28, 1924, p. 5.
34 J. G. Machen, *Christianity and Liberalism* (N. Y., 1923), Preface.
35 *Ibid.*, p. 7.
36 *Ibid.*, pp. 171-72.
37 *Ibid.*, p. 166.
38 Cf. *ibid.*, p. 173 and *passim.*
39 Cf. W. P. Merrill, *Liberal Christianity* (N. Y., 1925), pp. 11-14.
40 J. G. Machen, *op. cit.*, pp. 75, 172.
41 *Ibid.*, pp. 168-69, 175.
42 Westminster Confession of Faith, Chapter XXV, Section II.
43 *An Affirmation* (Auburn, N. Y., May 5, 1924), p. 6.
44 See above, pp. 58-59.
45 *Presbyterian*, March 5, p. 12, Dec. 10, p. 4, 1925.
46 G.A. *Mins.*, 1924, pp. 27, 202; *Presbyterian Advance*, June 5, 1924, p. 11; *Presbyterian*, Jan. 23, 1936, p. 22.
47 *Presbyterian*, Jan. 3, 1924, p. 21.
48 *Christian Century*, Jan. 3, 1924.
49 *Presbyterian Banner*, March 6, 1924, pp. 7-8.
50 *Ibid.*, June 5, 1924, p. 4.
51 *Presbyterian*, April 22, 1915, p. 18.
52 Cf. above, pp. 100-101, 107.

53 *Presbyterian Banner*, May 29, 1924, p. 26; *Presbyterian*, June 13, 1924, p. 10.
54 *Presbyterian Banner*, June 5, 1924, p. 4.
55 G.A. *Mins.*, 1923, p. 253.
56 *The First Presbyterian Church of New York and Dr. Fosdick*, pp. 5-29.
57 *Presbyterian*, Feb. 14, 1924, p. 5.
58 G.A. *Mins.*, 1924, pp. 195-96.
59 *Presbyterian Banner*, June 5, 1924, p. 4.
60 *Ibid.*; *Literary Digest*, June 21, 1924, p. 33; *Christian Century*, Oct. 2, 1924, pp. 1266-69.
61 Presbytery of Philadelphia, "Minutes," 1918-25, pp. 349-50, 354; cf. *Presbyterian Banner*, May 15, 1924, p. 3.
62 G.A. *Mins.*, 1924, pp. 196-99.
63 *First Presbyterian Church of New York and Dr. Fosdick*, pp. 33-61; *Presbyterian Banner*, Dec. 11, 1924, p. 24; G.A. *Mins.*, 1925, pp. 78-82.
64 E. Y. Mullins, *Christianity at the Cross Roads* (N. Y., c. 1924), p. v.
65 C. E. Jefferson, *Five Present-Day Controversies* (N. Y., c. 1924), pp. 9-10.
66 *British Weekly*, June 19-Sept. 4, 1924.
67 *Ibid.*, Sept. 11, 1924, pp. 501, 509.
68 *Ibid.*, May 1, p. 95, May 22, p. 168, Oct. 9, p. 27, Nov. 13, p. 153, 1924.

chapter 13—the special commission of 1925

1 *Presbyterian Banner*, Jan. 15, p. 3, March 12, p. 5, 1925.
2 G.A. *Mins.*, 1925, p. 20; cf. also *Presbyterian*, Dec. 18, 1924, p. 8.
3 Cf. above, pp. 58-59.
4 *Presbyterian*, March 5, p. 12, March 19, p. 4, 1925.
5 Cf. above, p. 121.
6 *Presbyterian Banner*, May 7, 1925, p. 5.
7 *Ibid.*, June 4, 1925, p. 5.
8 G.A. *Mins.*, 1925, pp. 28-29.
9 *Ibid.*, pp. 83-86.
10 *Ibid.*, pp. 83, 86-88.
11 *New York Times*, May 27, 1925; *Presbyterian*, June 25, p. 4, Sept. 10, p. 6, 1925; *Princeton Theological Review*, XXIII (1925), 379-80.
12 G.A. *Mins.*, 1927, p. 78.
13 *New York Times*, May 27, 1925.
14 *Ibid.*
15 G.A. *Mins.*, 1925, pp. 207-9.
16 *Ibid.*, p. 88; *Presbyterian Banner*, June 4, 1925, p. 9.
17 G.A. *Mins.*, 1925, p. 310.
18 *Christian Century*, June 16, 1927, p. 742; R. H. Nichols, in R. Niebuhr, ed., *This Ministry, the Contribution of Henry Sloane Coffin* (N. Y., 1946), p. 52.
19 C. R. Erdman, "The Special Commission of 1925," in *Presbyterian Magazine*, Aug. 1925, p. 405.
20 *Minutes of the Special Commission of 1925 of the General Assembly of the Presbyterian Church, U.S.A.* (mimeographed, in Presbyterian Historical Society, Phila.) (cited hereafter as *Commission Minutes*), Sept. 22-24, 1925, pp. 5-6.
21 *Presbyterian Banner*, Oct. 15, 1925, p. 5; *Presbyterian*, Nov. 5, 1925, p. 4.
22 *Commission Minutes*, Dec. 1-3, 1925, p. 2.
23 *Presbyterian Banner*, Dec. 31, 1925, p. 26.
24 *Presbyterian*, Jan. 7, p. 4, Feb. 18, p. 4, 1926.
25 *The Written and Verbal Statements . . . Presented to the Special Commission of 1925 . . . Dec. 2, 1925* (mimeographed, Phila., n.d.) (cited as *Statements . . . to the Commission*).

129-142

26 *Presbyterian*, July 15, 1926, p. 4.
27 G.A. *Mins.*, 1926, p. 62.
28 *Statements . . . to the Commission, passim.*
29 H. R. Mackintosh to R. E. Speer, Oct. 22, 1925, S.P.
30 N. G. Moore to H. C. Swearingen, May 13, 1927, S.P.; also miscellaneous correspondence in S.P.; G.A. *Mins.*, 1927, p. 86.
31 *Statements . . . to the Commission, passim.*
32 E. W. Work to C. R. Erdman, S.P.
33 *Commission Minutes*, March 11-12, 1926, pp.1-4; also Presbyterian Church, U.S.A., *Special Commission of Nine, Hearings . . . in . . . Phila. . . . 1935* (mimeographed, in Presbyterian Historical Society, Phila.), p. 485.
34 *Christian Century*, June 17, 1926, p. 785.
35 *Presbyterian*, May 27, 1926, p. 5; *Presbyterian Banner*, June 3, 1926, p. 7.
36 *Presbyterian Banner*, May 27, 1926, p. 7.
37 G.A. *Mins.*, 1926, pp. 70-71.
38 *Ibid.*, pp. 72-77.
39 *Ibid.*, pp. 77-80.
40 *Commission Minutes*, Sept. 22-24, 1925, p. 6; "Committee on Historical Background, Report to the Commission" (MS, in Presbyterian Historical Society, Phila.), Dec. 2, 1925.
41 Cf. above, pp. 1-8.
42 G.A. *Mins.*, 1926, pp. 80-81.
43 *Ibid.*, pp. 82-84.
44 *Ibid.*, pp. 84-87.
45 *Presbyterian Banner*, June 3, 1926, p. 10.
46 *Ibid.*, June 10, 1926, p. 11.
47 J. G. Machen telegram to C. E. Macartney, May 29, 1926, M.P.
48 *Presbyterian Banner*, June 3, 1926, p. 10.
49 *Christian Century*, June 17, 1926, p. 787.
50 *Presbyterian Banner*, June 2, 1927, p. 8.
51 *Presbyterian*, June 9, 1927, p. 8.
52 G.A. *Mins.*, 1927, pp. 58-62.
53 *Ibid.*, 65-69.
54 *Ibid.*, p. 80.
55 *Ibid.*, p. 81.
56 *Ibid.*
57 *Ibid.*
58 *Ibid.*, p. 58.
59 *Presbyterian*, June 9, 1927, p. 13; cf. also *Presbyterian Banner*, June 9, 1927, p. 7; A. C. Zenos, *Presbyterianism in America . . .* (N. Y., 1937), p. 102; R. H. Nichols, in R. Niebuhr, ed., *This Ministry; the Contribution of Henry Sloane Coffin*, pp. 52-53.

chapter 14—a seminary reorganized

1 Dr. Warfield's theology is suggestively discussed in W. D. Livingstone, "The Princeton Apologetic as Exemplified by the Work of Benjamin B. Warfield and J. Gresham Machen; a Study in American Theology 1880-1930" (MS, Ph.D. thesis, Yale University, 1948).
2 F. W. Loetscher, "John DeWitt," *Princeton Theological Review*, XXII (1924), 177-234; F. W. Loetscher, "John D. Davis," *ibid.*, XXIV (1926), 529-67.
3 *Presbyterian Digest*, 1930, II, 437.
4 G.A. *Mins.*, 1902, pp. 135, 140, 196-97.
5 *Ibid.*, 1903, pp. 152, 189.

129-142

6 W. C. Robinson, *Princeton Theological Seminary: Its Troubles As Viewed by Amicus* (n.p., n.d.), p. 8.
7 G.A. *Mins.*, 1913, p. 324.
8 Cf. letter of secretary of Board of Directors to President-elect Stevenson in 1915, *Presbyterian Banner*, May 17, 1928, pp. 2, 9.
9 Robinson, *op. cit.*, p. 9.
10 F. L. Patton, "A Theological Seminary," *Princeton Theological Review,* XIV (1916), 72, 80; cf. also statement by J. R. Stevenson to Board of Directors, p. 1, "Minutes of the Board of Directors" (MS, in Princeton Seminary Library), May 11, 1925, pp. 492-93.
11 Special Committee to Visit Princeton Theological Seminary, *Report to the General Assembly . . . 1927* (Phila., n.d.), p. 61 (hereafter cited as *Report 1927*).
12 H. van Dyke to D. S. Schaff, Jan. 23, 1924, v.P.
13 Cf. F. W. Loetscher, "John DeWitt," pp. 227-28.
14 J. R. Smith, in *N. Y. Evangelist*, Dec. 26, 1889, p. 2.
15 G.A. *Mins.*, 1927, pp. 96-99.
16 *Presbyterian*, Jan. 10, 1924, p. 12; Jan. 15, 1925, p. 12.
17 *Ibid.*, Jan. 15, 1925, p. 12.
18 *Presbyterian Advance*, Jan. 22, 1925, p. 24.
19 *Presbyterian*, Feb. 5, 1925, pp. 20-21.
20 G.A. *Mins.*, 1927, p. 90; "Minutes of the Faculty" (MS, in Princeton Seminary Library), 1903-26, pp. 530, 537, 540; *Presbyterian*, Nov. 6, 1924, p. 12.
21 *Report 1927*, pp. 153-55; J. R. Stevenson's Statement to Board of Directors, p. 12, in "Minutes of the Board of Directors," May 11, 1925, pp. 492-93.
22 J. G. Machen, *What Is Faith?* (N. Y., 1925), p. 42; Machen, *The Attack Upon Princeton Seminary: A Plea for Fair Play* (n.p., 1927), p. 14.
23 "Minutes of the Faculty," March 21, 1925, p. 538; *Report 1927*, pp. 63-65, 70; J. R. Stevenson's "Statement," pp. 15-16; Oswald T. Allis, "Princeton Seminary and Its Student Adviser," *Presbyterian*, April 23, 1925, p. 16; cf. also *Presbyterian of the South*, April 22, 1925, p. 2.
24 "Minutes of the Board of Directors," May 11, pp. 492-93, June 12, pp. 508-9, 1925; G.A. *Mins.*, 1927, p. 100.
25 "Minutes of the Board of Directors," Oct. 10, 1925, pp. 521-23; G.A. *Mins.*, 1928, p. 218.
26 G.A. *Mins.*, 1926, p. 266.
27 *Report 1927*, p. 87.
28 G.A. *Mins.*, 1926, p. 174.
29 *Ibid.*, pp. 174-75.
30 The report of the Commission of Fifteen (Special Commission of 1925) had been enthusiastically received by this same Assembly two days before; cf. above, pp. 130-32.
31 *N. Y. Times*, June 3, 1926; cf. "Minutes of the Faculty," Oct. 2, 1926, pp. 4-5; "Minutes of the Board of Directors," Oct. 12, 1926, pp. 559-60.
32 *Presbyterian Banner*, June 10, 1926, p. 28.
33 *N. Y. Times*, June 3, 1926; *Presbyterian*, June 10, 1926, p. 12.
34 *Presbyterian*, Dec. 2, 1926, p. 13.
35 *Presbyterian Banner*, Dec. 9, 1926, p. 8.
36 *Presbyterian*, Dec. 2, 1926, p. 13; so also "Minutes of the Board of Directors," Oct. 1, 1926, pp. 575-76.
37 G.A. *Mins.*, 1927, pp. 88-90.
38 "Minutes of the Faculty," Oct. 2, 1926, pp. 4-5; *Report 1927*, p. 68.
39 *Presbyterian*, July 8, 1926, p. 6.
40 *Report 1927*, p. 69.
41 E.g., *ibid.*, pp. 73, 75, 117-21, 133, 143.

143-152

42 *Ibid.*, p. 52.
43 *Ibid.*, pp. 57, 60.
44 *Ibid.*, pp. 151, 153-58.
45 *Ibid.*, p. 48.
46 *Ibid.*, p. 66.
47 *Ibid.*, p. 164.
48 *Ibid.*, pp. 15, 114, 177-81.
49 *Ibid.*, p. 11.
50 "Minutes of the Faculty," Oct. 1, 1927, p. 70; cf. also J. G. Machen, *The Attack Upon Princeton Seminary*, p. 47.
51 *Presbyterian Banner*, Dec. 2, 1926, pp. 8-9.
52 *Ibid.*, Dec. 9, 1926, p. 8.
53 *Report 1927*, pp. 9-10, 16, 162.
54 *Ibid.*, pp. 16-17, 40-47, 85-93, 101.
55 Contained in *Report 1927*, pp. 3-50; and, in the slightly amended form in which it was later adopted by the Assembly, in G.A. *Mins.*, 1927, pp. 87-134.
56 *Report 1927*, p. 47.
57 *Ibid.*, pp. 49-50.
58 For the amendments compare *Report 1927*, pp. 49-50 with G.A. *Mins.*, 1927, pp. 133-34.
59 *Presbyterian Banner*, June 2, 1927, p. 9.
60 *Presbyterian*, June 9, p. 13, Aug. 4, pp. 6-8, 1927.
61 *Ibid.*, July 21, 1927, p. 9.
62 G.A. *Mins.*, 1928, pp. 25-35; "Minutes of the Faculty," Oct. 1, 1927, p. 70; J. R. Stevenson, *The Historical Position of Princeton Seminary* (N. Y., 1928); *Presbyterian Banner*, Dec. 1, 1927, p. 4; Jan. 19, 1928, p. 6; *Presbyterian*, May 24, 1928, p. 12.
63 G.A. *Mins.*, 1928, pp. 225-26.
64 *Ibid.*, pp. 227-45.
65 *Ibid.*, pp. 247-50.
66 *Ibid.*, 1928, p. 59.
67 *Ibid.*, pp. 59-60, 149.
68 "Minutes of the Board of Directors," June 20, pp. 9-10, Oct. 9, pp. 6-9, Dec. 13, pp. 3, 6-7, 1928; Jan. 29, pp. 3-5, 11-13, March 15, p. 7, 1929; "Minutes of the Faculty," Oct. 6, 1928, pp. 120-22.
69 G.A. *Mins.*, 1929, p. 44.
70 *Presbyterian*, June 13, 1929, p. 13.
71 *Presbyterian Banner*, June 6, 1929, p. 10.
72 G.A. *Mins.*, 1929, pp. 80, 94-110.
73 *Presbyterian Banner*, June 6, 1929, p. 10.
74 *Ibid.*; cf. also G.A. *Mins.*, 1929, p. 110.
75 *Presbyterian Banner*, June 6, 1929, p. 10.
76 G.A. *Mins.*, 1929, p. 117.
77 *Presbyterian Banner*, June 6, 1929, p. 11.
78 G.A. *Mins.*, 1929, pp. 134-35.
79 *Ibid.*, p. 143.
80 *Ibid.*, 1930, p. 40; cf. also *ibid.*, 1929, p. 292.
81 *Ibid.*, 1930, p. 103.
82 *Presbyterian Banner*, Sept. 5, 1929, p. 4.
83 G.A. *Mins.*, 1930, p. 104.
84 Cf. Robinson, *Princeton Theological Seminary: Its Troubles As Viewed by Amicus.*
85 *Presbyterian*, May 15, 1930, p. 4.
86 Cf. *Presbyterian Banner*, June 6, 1929, p. 9; June 5, 1930, p. 8; June 11, 1931, p. 7.

chapter 15 — protesters withdraw

1 S. G. Cole, *History of Fundamentalism* (N. Y., 1931), p. 233; *Presbyterian*, May 7, p. 28, June 25, p. 32, Oct. 8, p. 20, 1931.
2 *Presbyterian*, Oct. 3, pp. 8, 20, Nov. 7, p. 13, 1929.
3 *Ibid.*, Jan. 10, p. 17, Feb. 28, p. 10, 1935. Later published in book form, J. G. Machen, *The Christian Faith in the Modern World* (N. Y., 1936).
4 *Presbyterian*, Oct. 17, 1935. Later published in book form, J. G. Machen, *The Christian View of Man* (N. Y., 1937).
5 Presbyterian Church U.S.A., *Special Commission of Nine, Hearings . . . in . . . Philadelphia . . . 1935* (mimeographed, in Presbyterian Historical Society, Phila.), pp. 15, 490, 615 (cited hereafter as *Commission Hearings*).
6 *Ibid.*, p. 527.
7 *Ibid.*, p. 146.
8 *Ibid.*, p. 581.
9 Cf. above, pp. 103-8.
10 *Re-Thinking Missions: a Laymen's Inquiry after One Hundred Years* (N. Y. and London, 1932), pp. 49, 55-58, 70.
11 *Christianity Today*, Dec. 1932, p. 19; Presbyterian Board of Foreign Missions, *Action . . . November 21, 1932* (pamphlet), and *A Statement . . . January 15, 1935* (pamphlet); *Presbyterian Banner*, Nov. 17, 1932, p. 9; *Presbyterian*, Nov. 24, 1932, p. 6.
12 R. E. Speer, in *Presbyterian Banner*, Nov. 24, 1932, pp. 9-11; Speer, *The Finality of Jesus Christ* (N. Y., 1933); Speer, in *Missionary Review of the World*, LVI (1933), 7-27.
13 P. S. Buck, in *Christian Century*, Nov. 23, 1932; in *Harper's Monthly Magazine*, Jan. 1933.
14 J. G. Machen, *Modernism and the Board of Foreign Missions of the Presbyterian Church in the U.S.A.* (n.p., n.d.), pp. 1, 3; *Christian Century*, May 3, 1933, p. 602; *Christianity Today*, Mid-April, 1933, pp. 19-22; G.A. *Mins.*, 1933, pp. 27-28.
15 G.A. *Mins.*, 1933, pp. 153, 158-60; *N. Y. Times*, May 26, 1933; *Christianity Today*, June 1933, p. 12; *Presbyterian Banner*, June 8, 1933, p. 3.
16 *Christianity Today*, June, pp. 1, 13, July, p. 1, Oct., p. 11, 1933; *Presbyterian*, May 16, 1935, p. 9; *Commission Hearings*, pp. 90, 317, 467, 785, 876.
17 Presbyterian Church U.S.A., Board of Foreign Missions, *A Statement . . . January 15, 1934* (pamphlet); *idem, The Reply . . . to a Friendly Statement from the Presbytery of Chester* (pamphlet); G.A. *Mins.*, 1934, pp. 28-40.
18 *Presbyterian Banner*, Nov. 9, p. 3, Dec. 7, p. 3, 1933; *Christianity Today*, May 1934, p. 22.
19 Cf. above, pp. 130-35.
20 *Christianity Today*, July 1934, p. 39.
21 G.A. *Mins.*, 1934, pp. 115-16; R. E. Speer to M. A. Matthews, Feb. 20, 1935, S.P.; H. S. Coffin, in *Religion in Life*, IV (1935), 194-203.
22 *Presbyterian*, March 22, 1934, p. 9.
23 J. G. Machen, *Statement to the Special Committee of the Presbytery of New Brunswick* (pamphlet, Phila., March 5, 1935); *Christianity Today*, Feb., pp. 222, 233, April, p. 265, 1935; *Presbyterian*, March 14, p. 4, April 4, p. 13, 1935.
24 Cf., e.g., *Sunday School Times*, March 16, 1935, p. 179; C. McIntire, *Dr. Robert E. Speer*, etc. (pamphlet, n.p., April 11, 1935); G.A. *Mins.*, 1935, pp. 27-38; *Presbyterian*, April 25, 1935, p. 17.
25 G.A. *Mins.*, 1935, pp. 27-29, 52, 109-10, 120, 127.
26 *Ibid.*, pp. 110-14, 356.
27 *Ibid.*, 1936, pp. 118-19.
28 *Commission Hearings*, pp. 642, 651.
29 *Ibid.*, pp. 233, 400.
30 *Ibid.*, p. 839.

152-156

31 *Ibid.*, pp. 52, 58, 247, 340, 374, 447, 454, 488, 496, 742, 1017.
32 *Ibid.*, pp. 8-13.
33 *Ibid.*, pp. 125, 127, 590, 596, 703, 705, 761.
34 *Ibid.*, pp. 40, 66, 477, 696, 750, 847, 885, 895, 905.
35 *Ibid.*, p. 18 and *passim.*
36 G.A. *Mins.*, 1936, pp. 117-27; 1937, pp. 153-54.
37 Presbytery of Philadelphia, "Minutes" (MS, in Presbyterian Historical Society, Phila.), 1935-41, pp. 10-15; Synod of Pennsylvania, *Minutes*, 1936, p. 12.
38 *Christianity Today*, Feb., 1936, p. 210.
39 E. H. Rian, *The Presbyterian Conflict* (Grand Rapids, 1940), p. 95.
40 *Christianity Today*, Aug. 1934, p. 60; Aug., p. 49, Nov., p. 122, 1935.
41 *Presbyterian*, Feb. 6, 1936, p. 13.
42 *Ibid.*; Rian, *The Presbyterian Conflict*, p. 98.
43 *Presbyterian Guardian*, Jan. 20, 1936, p. 132.
44 G.A. *Mins.*, 1936, pp. 83-101, 138-42.
45 *Presbyterian Guardian*, June 22, 1936, pp. 113-17; *Christianity Today*, Aug. 1935, p. 66.
46 Presbyterian Church of America, *Minutes of the First General Assembly . . . June 11-14, 1936*, pp. 3-15; *Minutes of the Second General Assembly . . . November 12-14, 1936*, pp. 30-32.
47 Orthodox Presbyterian Church, *Minutes of the Fifth General Assembly . . . February 9, 1939, and of the Sixth General Assembly . . . May 10-12, 1939*, p. 11; E. H. Rian, *The Presbyterian Conflict*, pp. 235-43; R. S. Marsden, *The First Ten Years; The Orthodox Presbyterian Church 1936-1946* (Phila., n.d.), 104 pp.
48 G.A. *Mins.*, 1936-42, see Index, *s.v.* "Legal Procedure, Special Committee on."

notes for the conclusion

1 W. M. Horton, in *Christendom*, XI (1946), 143.

bibliographical note

Valuable for orientation in the heritage of the Presbyterian and Reformed Churches, but too extensive for listing here, is primary source material of other Presbyterian and Reformed bodies; the literature of the Alliance of Reformed Churches throughout the World Holding the Presbyterian System; and discussions of the Presbyterian and Reformed heritage in the literature of the present-day Ecumenical Movement. The American environment since the Civil War must be studied in periodicals and monographs dealing with the political, social, cultural, and theological history of the period. These materials are too numerous and diversified to be included in an abbreviated bibliography on Presbyterian theological issues.

The student of recent American church history is embarrassed by the superabundance of materials available. To attempt anything like a complete listing of source materials for the most recent period even for a single major denomination would be as bulky as it would be unnecessary. While the writings cited in the notes of the present work constitute only a fraction of those used, they are representative of the whole, and places and dates of publication have been given in the first citation in each chapter.

The most important types of primary source materials dealing with theological issues in the Presbyterian Church since 1869 may be classified as follows:

I. Official Publications of the Presbyterian Church

The records of the highest Presbyterian judicatory from 1706 to 1788 are contained in a single volume, *Records of the Presbyterian Church in the United States of America* (Philadelphia, 1841; with index, 1904), and thereafter in the annual volume, *Minutes of the General Assembly of the Presbyterian Church in the U.S.A.* The minutes of most of the synods for the most recent decades have been printed. Presbytery minutes, with rare exceptions, are in manuscript, minutes of some presbyteries being deposited in the Presbyterian Historical Society, Philadelphia, but most of the post-Civil War presbyterial minutes in local depositories. Official records of the various seminaries and church boards and subdivisions of boards for the period are in the possession of the respective seminaries and boards.

The numerous revised editions of *The Constitution of the Presbyterian Church in the United States of America* are valuable in dating changes in the church's polity in response to changing forces. The *Digest of the Acts and Deliverances of the General Assembly of the Presbyterian Church in the United States of America* (2 vols., Philadelphia, 1938, and numerous earlier editions) contains in Volume I quotations from General Assembly actions illustrative of Presbyterian church law, and in Volume II numerous documents illustrative of the history of the Presbyterian Church.

Some of the material presented by committees or commissions to the General Assembly, and not found in the minutes of the General Assembly, has been preserved in printed, mimeographed, or manuscript form in the Presbyterian Historical Society. Statements published at critical times by the various church boards are of value. The great quantity of promotional leaflets, periodicals, and books published by the boards is not primarily concerned with theological issues and for that reason is omitted from this restricted bibliography.

II. Unofficial Presbyterian Periodicals

From before the middle of the nineteenth century until after World War I unofficial religious weeklies and quarterlies played an important role in the Presbyterian Church, but the second quarter of the twentieth century witnessed their almost complete disappearance. With low publication costs and wide lay interest, the Presbyterian Church once supported many of these weekly newspapers simultaneously. In some cases they were able to pay a yield on their investment and an editorial salary that compared favorably with that of the larger pastorates. Editors were usually unblushingly partisan, plunged with gusto into current controversies, and wielded important influence in church affairs. The weeklies contain also numerous signed articles by church leaders, and are extremely valuable for authentic atmosphere and contemporary opinion. Presbyterian progressives in the late nineteenth century often complained that only the *New York Evangelist* within the Church represented their views. The more important weeklies in the period after 1869 were the following:

Christianity Today. Philadelphia, 1930-51. A monthly, later a quarterly newspaper; later still only intermittently published.

Church Times, The. Utica, New York, 1940-46.

Continent, The. Chicago, 1870-1926. From 1870 to 1910 it was *The Interior.* In 1910 it merged into *The Presbyterian Advance* (*q.v.*).

Herald and Presbyter. Cincinnati, 1839-1925. From 1839 to 1868 it was *The Christian Herald.* In 1925 it merged into *The Presbyterian* (*q.v.*).

Interior, The. See *Continent, The.*

New York Evangelist, The. New York, 1830-1902.

New York Observer, The. New York, 1823-1912.

Presbyterian, The. Philadelphia, 1831-1948. In 1948 it merged with *Presbyterian Life*, an official publication.

Presbyterian Advance, The. See *Presbyterian Tribune, The.*
Presbyterian Banner, The. Pittsburgh, 1852-1937.
Presbyterian Journal, The. See *Westminster, The.*
Presbyterian Observer, The. Baltimore; Philadelphia, 1872-95.
Presbyterian Tribune, The. Nashville; New York; Utica, New York, 1910-. From 1910 to 1934 it was *The Presbyterian Advance.*
Westminster, The. Philadelphia; New York, 1875-1910. From 1875 to 1904 is was *The Presbyterian Journal.* In 1910 it merged into *The Interior,* later *The Continent* (*q.v.*).

Presbyterian quarterly journals dealt with current religious topics in solid articles sometimes running to fifty or more pages. Learned and often lengthy book reviews were also a feature of these journals. Their influence on the more intellectual few extended beyond the Church and at times beyond the national boundaries. The leading Presbyterian theological journals during the period were the following:

American Presbyterian Review, The. New York, 1859-71. From 1859 to 1862 it was *The American Theological Review,* and from 1863 to 1868 it was *The American Presbyterian and Theological Review.* In 1871 it merged with *The Biblical Repertory and Princeton Review* (*q.v.*).
Biblical Repertory and Princeton Review, The. See *Princeton Review, The.*
Presbyterian and Reformed Review, The. New York; Philadelphia, 1890-1902. It superseded *The Presbyterian Review* (*q.v.*) and was superseded by *The Princeton Theological Review* (*q.v.*).
Presbyterian Quarterly and Princeton Review, The. See *Princeton Review, The.*
Presbyterian Review, The. New York, 1880-89. It was superseded by *The Presbyterian and Reformed Review* (*q.v.*).
Princeton Review, The. New York, 1825-88. From 1825 to 1871 it was *The Biblical Repertory,* with varying subtitles; from 1872 to 1877 it was *The Presbyterian Quarterly and Princeton Review;* from 1878 to 1884 it was *The Princeton Review;* and from 1886 to 1888 it was *The New Princeton Review.*
Princeton Theological Review, The. Princeton, 1903-29. It superseded *The Presbyterian and Reformed Review* (*q.v.*).

III. Private Manuscript Collections

There is a wealth of private letters of value to the present study. This type of writing reveals inside knowledge of events and intimate opinions found nowhere else. Few if any of these collections have been used in previously published studies. These manuscript collections will be found listed under "Abbreviations Used in the Notes," immediately preceding the "Notes" of the present volume.

IV. Other Primary Source Materials

Pamphlets and books by theological seminary professors, church executives, pastors, and occasionally by laymen are available in great numbers. In general the writings by seminary professors are the most useful of these for the present study. Library catalogues of the theologians' own seminaries of course offer the fullest guide to their published writings.

The various controversies of the period each produced a spate of pamphlets, not to mention articles and stories which they inspired in the religious and secular press. Dr. Benjamin B. Warfield made extensive collections of pamphlets and newspaper clippings, preserved in the Princeton Seminary Library. So, too, did Dr. Charles A. Briggs, and these are preserved in the Union Seminary Library, New York. The Thomas S. Hastings Scrapbook in Union Seminary Library, New York, also contains informing newspaper clippings. Proceedings of the more important heresy trials of the period have been printed, some at great length.

Reminiscences, like Henry Preserved Smith's *The Heretic's Defense; A Footnote to History* (New York, 1926) and William Adams Brown's *A Teacher and His Times* (New York, 1940) and others are valuable for color and perspective, but like all literature of this type must be subordinated to the contemporary records.

biographical index

topical index